CW01500430

FOURTEENTH CENTURY ENGLAND

VIII

Drawing on a diverse range of documentary, literary and material evidence, the contributors to this volume examine several inter-related topics on political, social and cultural matters in late medieval England. Aspects of both arms production and armigerous society are explored, from the emergence of royal armourers in the early fourteenth century to the social implications of later armour and armorial bearings. Another major focus is the church and religion more broadly. The nature and significance of the ceremonial entry, the *adventus*, of bishops is explored, as well as the legal impact of provisions in shaping church–state relations in mid-century. Religious constructs of women are considered in a comparative analysis of orthodox and Lollard texts. Finally, a group of papers looks at aspects of politics at the centre, with an examination of the queenship of Isabella of France and the issue of the Mortimer inheritance in the early years of Richard II.

Fourteenth Century England

ISSN 1471–3020

The series aims to provide a forum for the most recent research into the political, social, economic, ecclesiastical and cultural history of the fourteenth century in England. Submissions are welcomed; please contact a member of the editorial board for further information.

FOURTEENTH CENTURY ENGLAND

VIII

Edited by J. S. Hamilton

THE BOYDELL PRESS

First published 2014
The Boydell Press, Woodbridge

ISBN 978–1–84383–917–0

The Boydell Press is an imprint of Boydell & Brewer Ltd
PO Box 9, Woodbridge, Suffolk IP12 3DF, UK
and of Boydell & Brewer Inc.
668 Mt Hope Avenue, Rochester, NY 14620–2731, USA
website: www.boydellandbrewer.com

A catalogue record for this book is available
from the British Library

CONTENTS

CONTRIBUTORS

Beth Allison Barr, Baylor University

Philip Caudrey, University of Tasmania

Katherine Harvey, University of London

Mark King, University of Cambridge

Malcolm Mercer, Royal Armouries, Tower of London

Shelagh Mitchell, University of Southampton

Lisa Benz St John, independent scholar

Charlotte Whatley, University of Houston

PREFACE

Now well into its second decade, *Fourteenth Century England* aims to bring to publication the findings of recent and current research projects in a wide range of topics relating to politics, government, society and culture of the fourteenth century in England.

Several of the papers in this collection have their genesis in papers given under the auspices of the Society for Fourteenth-Century Studies at the annual International Medieval Congress, Leeds, and in sessions of the Society of the White Hart at the annual International Congress on Medieval Studies, Kalamazoo. I should like to thank the other members of the editorial board of *Fourteenth Century England* – James Bothwell, Gwilym Dodd, Chris Given-Wilson and Nigel Saul – for their assistance in the organization of the sessions at Leeds as well as their careful reading of and comments on submissions for this volume. I should similarly like to thank Mark Arvanigian for his organization of the sessions of the Society of the White Hart at Kalamazoo. While this and other volumes of *Fourteenth Century England* are not limited to papers previously presented in these venues, both conferences continue to provide lively settings for thoughtful discussion, debate, and at times disagreement, all of which fosters new approaches to this field of study.

To Caroline Palmer and the staff of Boydell & Brewer I once again offer heartfelt thanks for their expertise and support, both material and personal. Their unstinting support of this series and Medieval Studies in general is deeply appreciated.

The next volume of *Fourteenth Century England* (IX, 2016) will be edited by James Bothwell and Gwilym Dodd. Potential contributors may contact Dr Bothwell at the School of History, University of Leicester, University Road, Leicester, LE1 7RH or jsb16@le.ac.uk; and Dr Dodd at the Department of History, University of Nottingham, University Park Nottingham, NG7 2RD or gwilym.dodd@nottingham.ac.uk.

J. S. Hamilton
October 2013

ABBREVIATIONS

AALT	Anglo-American Legal Tradition
BIHR	*Bulletin of the Institute of History Research*
BL	British Library
BPR	*Register of Edward the Black Prince*, 4 vols (London, 1930–33)
CChR	*Calendar of Charter Rolls*
CCR	*Calendar of Close Rolls*
CCW	*Calendar of Chancery Warrants*
CFR	*Calendar of Fine Rolls*
CIPM	*Calendar of Inquisitions Post Mortem*
CLBL	*Calendar of the Letter Books of the City of London*, ed. R. R. Sharpe, 11 vols (London, 1899–1912)
CP	G. Cockayne, *The Complete Peerage of England, Scotland, Ireland, Great Britain and the United Kingdom* etc., ed. V. Gibbs *et al.*, 12 vols in 13 (London, 1910–59)
CPR	*Calendar of Patent Rolls*
CW	*Calendar of Wills proved and enrolled in the Court of Hustings, London, 1258–1688*, ed. R. R. Sharpe, 2 vols (London, 1889–90)
CYS	Canterbury and York Society
EETS	Early English Text Society
EHR	*English Historical Review*
Foedera	*Foedera, conventions, litterae et cujuscunque generis acta publica*, ed. T. Rymer, 10 vols in 40 pts (The Hague, 1739–45)
HPC	*The History of Parliament. The House of Commons, 1386–1421*, ed. J. S. Roskell, L. Clark and C. Rawcliffe, 4 vols (Stroud, 1992)
JBS	*Journal of British Studies*
JMH	*Journal of Medieval History*
Liber Albus	Worcester Cathedral Library, *Liber Albus*
LMA	*London Metropolitan Archives*
ODNB	*The Oxford Dictionary of National Biography*, ed. H. C. G. Matthew and B. H. Harrison, 60 vols (Oxford, 2004)
PCM	London, College of Arms, *Processus in Curia Marescalli*, 2 vols
PROME	*The Parliament Rolls of Medieval England*, ed. P. Brand, A. Curry, C. Given-Wilson, R. Horrox, G. Martin, W. Ormrod and J. Phillips, 16 vols (Woodbridge, 2005)

Reg.   *The Register of John Grandisson, Bishop of Exeter, A.D.*
Grandisson   *1327–1369*, ed. F. C. Hingeston-Randolph, 3 vols (London,
                  1894–99)
RS   Rolls Series
Scrope v.   *The Controversy Between Sir Richard Scrope and Sir Robert*
Grosvenor   *Grosvenor in the Court of Chivalry c.1385–1390*, ed. N. H.
                  Nicolas, 2 vols (London, 1832)
SR   *Statutes of the Realm*, 11 vols (London, 1801–28)

Unless otherwise specified, all unpublished documents are in The National
Archives (TNA), Kew.

KING'S ARMOURERS AND THE GROWTH OF THE ARMOURER'S CRAFT IN EARLY FOURTEENTH-CENTURY LONDON

Malcolm Mercer

Introduction

Until the establishment of Henry VIII's workshops, the domestic manufacture of arms and armour has generally been written off as rather insignificant, the assumption being that there was a preference for purchasing both basic and fine-quality armour from Italy, Flanders or Germany.[1] The establishment of his own armour workshop at Greenwich by Henry VIII shortly after his accession in 1509 has been identified quite rightly as one of the new king's earliest ambitions. Emulating the court workshop of the Emperor Charles V established at Innsbruck in 1505, Henry VIII was able to create a domestic industry capable of producing fine-quality armour within a very short space of time. Armourers from Milan, the Low Countries and Germany were brought to England, where they set up the new workshop. Within fourteenth-century studies, however, the king's armour, its manufacture and custody have been investigated primarily within the context of massed quantities of armour stored at the Tower of London and elsewhere. There remains a limited understanding of the organization of the armourer's craft, those armourers who were active in London, their relationship with the crown, and how they sought to meet the needs of the monarch.[2]

Because the activities of armourers within England have been seen as insignificant in comparison to those of their European counterparts, little attention has been paid to those who did participate in the craft and trade. Consequently, any discussion of the office of king's armourer, or strictly speaking *armator regis*, has been ignored, and T. F. Tout's general observations that they had a permanent base in the Tower of London from the late thirteenth century, and that they were part of a group of craftsmen whose

---

[1]   T. Richardson, 'The Royal Armour Workshops at Greenwich', in *Henry VIII: Arms and the Man 1509–2009*, ed. G. Rimer, T. Richardson and J. P. D. Cooper (Leeds, 2009), pp. 148–9; P. Terjanian, 'The King and the Armourers of Flanders', in *Henry VIII: Arms and the Man*, pp. 155–9; T. Richardson, 'Armour in England, 1325–99', *JMH* 37 (2011), 304–20.

[2]   It is interesting to note that in 1992 Matthias Pfaffenbichler commented that literature on the medieval armourer was extensive, but rather patchy and scattered; moreover, researchers had tended to focus on armour rather than armourers: M. Pfaffenbichler, *Armourers* (London, 1992), p. 71.

primary attachment was to the king's household, have been widely accepted without further question or refinement.[3] However, during this same period there is evidence to suggest that king's armourers acted as an important link between the armourers' community and the crown, supplying and manufacturing armour for the king, his household, and the royal forces.

In this article I will seek to demonstrate that the domestic industry was more advanced than previously thought. The following discussion will begin by looking first at evidence of the organization and activities of armourers in London in the late thirteenth and early fourteenth centuries. It will then investigate arrangements for the maintenance and custody of the king's armour during the reigns of Edward I and Edward II, setting this against the developments taking place within the great and privy wardrobes. It will finish with an examination of the emergence of a group of linen and metal-working specialists following the accession of Edward III and the relative importance of each element during the first half of the fourteenth century.

The armourer's craft and trade in late thirteenth- and early
fourteenth-century London

An understanding of the nature and organization of many of the crafts and trades of London in the thirteenth and fourteenth centuries is restricted by the poor survival of documentary and physical evidence. However, there is sufficient evidence to argue that during this period there was no uniform or coherent armourer's craft or trade in the city. The term 'armourer' encompassed a broad range of individuals drawn from both cloth and metal-working specialists, who were engaged in the production, procurement and supply of arms and armour. The continuing importance of cloth-based defensive equipment in warfare ensured the prominence of those craftsmen during the first half of the fourteenth century. This was in fact the first element within the armourer's craft to organize itself. Tailors and linen armourers had already formed a fraternity in 1272 known as the 'The Fraternity of Tailors and Linen Armourers of St John the Baptist in the City of London' and had almost certainly developed structures for self-regulation by the end of the thirteenth century.[4]

It is likely that the prolonged period of military activity under Edward I and Edward II in Wales, Scotland and France generated a need for increased regu-

3   T. F. Tout, *Chapters in the Administrative History of England*, 6 vols (Manchester, 1920–33, repr. 1967), iv, 388–91, 445.
4   C. J. ffoulkes, *The Armourer and his Craft from the 11th to the 15th Century* (London, 1912), pp. 91, 94–5; M. Davies and A. Saunders, *The History of the Merchant Taylors Company* (Leeds, 2004), pp. 8, 12–13. Davies and Saunders quite correctly emphasize the increasingly close connections that existed between king's armourers and the tailors and linen armourers which developed out of the wars of Edward I and his successors with Scotland and France.

lation of arms and armour-related crafts during the early fourteenth century.[5] There is firm evidence that there was already some form of assessment to determine the quality of arms produced. In 1320, for example, Manekin le Heaumer, Gillot le Hauberger and Reginald le Hauberger were amongst those appraising spearheads in London. This was presumably because they possessed the knowledge of metal-working techniques.[6] However, towards the end of Edward II's reign, in 1322, a set of ordinances was generated by the armourers' community and presented to the mayor of London for approval. These were designed to ensure that the armour produced was of a sufficient standard: namely, that aketons[7] and gambesons[8] covered with sandal or silk cloth were filled with new cotton cloth rather than old cotton or linen. Moreover, it was declared illegal to repair and cover old bascinets[9] and to export them out of the city; and newly made helmets were not to be covered before sale and had to be approved by the mayor or designated citizens. The emphasis of the ordinances was on cloth-based armour and activities in which tailors and linen armourers were involved, namely the finishing off of metal items. The activities of specialist, metal-working armourers were not regulated until the second quarter of the reign of Edward III, when helmet makers presented their own set of ordinances to the mayor for approval in 1347.[10]

Armourers undoubtedly engaged to varying degrees in both the manufacture of and trade in defensive equipment. Armour and other defensive equipment could be made and supplied by cloth workers, such as tailors and linen armourers, or metal workers, such as helmet makers or hauberk makers; or even supplied, repaired and restored by furbishers. It would also appear that cofferers (makers of chests) might occasionally engage in the armourer's trade. In 1322, for example, Saloman le Cofferer was one of those directed

---

[5]   M. Prestwich, *War, Politics and Finance under Edward I* (London, 1972), pp. 105–6, 176; R. A. Kaner, 'The Management of the Mobilisation of English Armies: Edward I to Edward III', University of York PhD thesis (1999), pp. 226–8. The late thirteenth and early fourteenth centuries were of course a period when a number of crafts and trades actively sought formal recognition and protection of their activities through the enrolment of ordinances either through the mayor and alderman of London or by obtaining charters from the crown: G. Unwin, *Guilds and Companies* (London, 1904), p. 88; C. M. Barron, *London in the Later Middle Ages: Government and People 1200–1500* (Oxford, 2004), pp. 202–4, 207–8.

[6]   *CLBL* E, p. 132.

[7]   Quilted coat usually worn underneath armour.

[8]   Generally worn over armour, often richly decorated and embroidered, and in some instances designed to be worn as independent body defences.

[9]   A form of helmet that could be fitted with a visor that remained popular until the beginning of the fifteenth century.

[10]   *CLBL* F, pp. 167–78. Robert de Shirwode, Richard Bridde and Thomas Canoun were chosen as wardens. For Robert Shirwode see E. Ekwall, *Two Early London Subsidy Rolls* (Lund, 1951). A John de Shirwode, armourer, was resident in Fleet Street in the fourteenth century: BL, Additional MS 34,789 fol. 30.

to assess armour purchased by the sheriff of Surrey and Sussex from a group of London armourers.[11]

Certain armourers engaged in other business activities, including the importing and exporting of different types of commodity. Roger le Heaumer, for instance, imported wine, while John le Clerk and Bartholomew le Armurer both imported wool. In the 1320s John Priour (probably senior), alderman of Tower Ward, was described as an armourer and a vintner, although his main occupation was importing wool.[12] While particular armourers lent money or were prepared to extend credit to others, it is not known how widespread this practice was within the armourers' community. William de Wolde, resident in Bread Street Ward, for example, lent money to William de Southwick of Northamptonshire, Nicholas de Benesend of Berkshire, John Pykot of Heydon in Essex, and Robert Goodwin of Aylesbury in Buckinghamshire between *c*. 1307 and 1318. Very few seem to have lent money to the crown, though, apart from those who were already connected to it by service or commerce.[13]

Although there was no obvious centre for the production of armour in London in the late thirteenth and early fourteenth centuries, it is possible, by drawing upon a combination of sources based around the subsidy records of 1292, 1319, 1332 and 1338–39, along with evidence found in deeds and wills of the late thirteenth and early fourteenth centuries from amongst the collections of the Corporation of the City of London, to highlight the presence of concentrations of armourers in particular wards, primarily Bread Street, Cheap, Coleman Street, and Farringdon Extra. Of these, the highest numbers were found in Cheap and Farringdon Extra. William de Grantham, for example, was active in the parish of St Sepulchre (Farringdon Extra) from at least the mid-1270s, while William Cosin was active in the parish of St Mary Colechurch (Cheap Ward) from the early 1280s.[14] In some instances residence might also reflect a distinction in the type of armourer, whether from the tailoring or the metal-working branches of the craft. Fleet Street, in Farringdon Extra Ward, was the home to Hugh le Armurer and was also one of the principal centres for cutlers and furbishers. This more than likely indicates that Hugh was primarily involved in producing and supplying metal components for armour.[15]

---

[11] *CLBL* E, pp. 170–1; Ekwall, *London Subsidy Rolls*, p. 293.

[12] *CLBL*, F, p. 13; E 122/69/9 m. 1r, 70/1 m4r; Ekwall, *London Subsidy Rolls*, p. 344. Bartholomew le Armurer was probably the armourer from Bruges of the same name: *CPR 1324–27*, p. 326.

[13] C 241/53/200; 62/205, 211; 66/39; 84/97; 109/25, 28; R. L. Axworthy, 'The Financial Relationship of the London Merchant Community with Edward III, 1327 to 1377', University of London PhD thesis (2000), pp. 158, 179 n. 24, 180 n. 34.

[14] *LMA* CLA/023/DW/02/01, pp. 28v, 56r. During the 1280s Reginald le Hauberger is also mentioned as the former owner of a tenement in the parish of St Mary Colechurch: *Catalogue of Ancient Deeds*, v, no. A11943.

[15] Ekwall, *London Subsidy Rolls*, pp. 87, 305–14; C. Welch, *History of the Cutlers' Company of London*, 2 vols (London, 1916), i, 27.

It is likely that some of the properties named in business and private documents of armourers incorporated the workshops where they carried out the
manufacturing process. The sixteen-year lease taken by Simon le Heaumer
and his wife Matilda of a tenement in the parish of St Bride's in Fleet Street
in 1318 was probably a residence and workshop combined.[16] The seven-year
lease taken in 1349 by the armourer William Sparke, of a property on Birchin
Lane just off Cornhill, was very clearly stated to be just a shop.[17] William de
Wolde was probably a linen armourer, though, and would not have required
the same facilities as Simon le Heaumer. Unlike tailoring, a property adapted
for metal-working required particular equipment and specialized tools.[18]
Properties were clearly adapted for the manufacture of metal armour. Stephen
atte Fryth, who was subsequently appointed king's armourer in 1396, was
accused of making illegal alterations to a tenement in the parish of St Augustine by Paul Gate in the late 1370s, where manufacturing was undertaken to
the considerable consternation of the neighbouring residents.[19]

In some instances armourers who were engaged most closely in royal
service also had properties provided for them by the crown. Tout regarded
these as workshops and there is no reason to doubt this conclusion. The
quantities of finished goods supplied by John de Colonia and other leading
armourers suggest that sizeable premises were needed to accommodate the
number of employees required to produce and to store them before trans-
portation by cart to the Tower of London or elsewhere. Exchequer records
refer to the property provided to de Colonia for his 'office', that is to say,
for carrying out his armour-related commissions from the king, and as space
provided for workmen to make the king's armour.[20]

By the early fourteenth century the London community of armourers
comprised both English and foreign craftsmen. In the overwhelming majority
of cases it is not possible to determine nationality or ethnic origin with
complete certainty. Only a proportion of armourers can be identified by an
occupational name such as Le Armurer, Le Heaumer, and Le Hauberger.
Even these cannot be trusted absolutely. Former apprentices often adopted
the names of their masters. A significant number of identifications are only
made through a chance reference to that individual as armourer. Furthermore,
London armourers appear infrequently in documentary sources, more often
than not as names in property deeds, or in litigation as one of the opposing

---

[16] *CLBL* E, p. 97. The dual use appears in particular legal disputes: *London Assize of Nuisance 1301–1431*, ed. H. M. Chew and W. Kellaway (London Record Society, 1973), p. 164.

[17] *CLBL* F, p. 204. Sparke was also associated with John de Colonia, who was a witness to the lease, quite possibly as one of the armourers to whom the latter subcontracted business.

[18] Jane Geddes, 'Iron', in *English Medieval Industries: Craftsmen, Techniques, Products*, ed. J. Blair and N. Ramsay (London, 1991), pp. 174–8.

[19] *London Assize of Nuisance*, pp. 160–1: *CPR 1392–96*, pp. 718, 722.

[20] E 404/2/11; E 361/2/7, 3/30; E 101/389/14; Tout, *Chapters in Administrative History*, iv, 389–90.

parties in a dispute, or as jurors. In a great many instances they simply remain names.

There were a number of significant armourers who were almost certainly British. The name William de Skelton, for example, suggests he had probably originated in Yorkshire. Skelton, although not one of the king's armourers, even supplied armour and other equipment to the great wardrobe for the royal tournament in 1329–30.[21] Similarly, John, Thomas and Walter de Kesteven probably came from Lincolnshire. It has been proposed that they were members of the same family.[22] Some armourers came from further afield. Simon le Heaumer (also known as le Armurer) was probably the Scottish prisoner in Exeter Castle between 1307 and 1309. Le Heaumer appears to have been in royal service by this stage and the circumstances of his incarceration are unknown.[23] Nevertheless, he was subsequently part of a group of men who worked the king's mines in Devon. By 1318 at the latest he had relocated with his wife Matilda to Fleet Street in London, where he had established himself as an armourer.[24]

There was also, however, an established group of armourers from the Low Countries and Germany. The extent of mercantile contact between Low Countries armourers, London, and the royal court, based on evidence from English documents, has yet to be determined. Nevertheless, it seems likely that these groups not only manufactured armour in London but also imported quantities from the continent as well. There is firm evidence of contact from the Low Countries from the reign of Edward I onwards. Manekin le Heaumer appears to have come from the Low Countries and was an active member of the community of armourers. He had a brother Peter. Whether Peter de Bruges, who subsequently became a king's armourer under Edward III, is the same man can only remain a matter of conjecture. A Peter le Armurer was certainly active in London from at least 1326–27 and appears on the London Subsidy Roll of 1332.[25] It is probable that Hugh le Armurer of Bruges is the same armourer who acquired property in Fleet Street in the parish of St Brides by 1318. Hugh had provided a number of consignments of armour to Edward II in 1312–13. He became an active member of his local community in London and his name appears as a juror in coroner's

---

21 E 361/3; G. Unwin, *Finance and Trade under Edward III* (Manchester, 1918), p. 72. A Robert de Skelton is identified as an armourer in 1338–89: Ekwall, *London Subsidy Rolls*, p. 290.

22 E. Ekwall, *Studies on the Population of Medieval London* (Stockholm, 1956), pp. 175–6.

23 *CCR 1309–13*, pp. 12, 119.

24 One of the witnesses to this lease was a Hugh Le Armurer. It is uncertain, but not impossible, that this was the same Hugh le Armurer of Bruges: *CFR 1307–19*, pp. 126, 141–2, 144; *CLBL* E, p. 97. Other armourers resident in Fleet Street included a Gerard le Armurer in 1348: *CW*, i, 558. An Adam le Fourbour, who died in 1314, was operating there in the early fourteenth century: *CW*, i, 251.

25 *CPR 1324–27*, p. 326; *Calendar of Memoranda Rolls Exchequer, Michaelmas 1326 – Michaelmas 1327*, ed. R. A. Latham (London, 1968), p. 381; Unwin, *Finance and Trade under Edward III*, p. 71.

inquisitions.[26] Another Flemish supplier, Bartholomew le Armurer of Bruges, was also active in London towards the end of Edward II's reign.[27] Although more difficult to identify, there also appears to have been an active group of French armourers. In about 1276, for example, the armourer William de St Denis complained of the theft of a hauberk and other items by Walter Hervy, bailiff of the city of London. While it is more than likely that he was a French armourer, nothing is known of his activities as a craftsman.[28] There was also a John le Clerk of Dinan practising from at least 1315. This was probably the same John le Clerk who was assessed on the Subsidy Roll of 1332 as a resident in Farringdon Within.[29]

The maintenance and custody of the king's armour under Edward I and Edward II

Surviving evidence suggests that a more formal relationship developed between particular armourers and the crown during the first two decades of the fourteenth century. This also coincides with the moment when the label 'armourer of the king' enters the bureaucratic lexicon. This is not to suggest, of course, that there had been no tradition of service to the crown by London armourers before that time. There is documentary evidence for a number of armourers active in and around London in the late thirteenth century.[30] Moreover, it had long been the custom for the crown and the aristocracy to retain armourers for military service within the British Isles and abroad.[31] In 1242 Reginald le Hauberger had been granted 5 marks for the maintenance of his wife and household while he was serving with Henry III overseas.[32] These relationships become more evident by the late thirteenth century. Foremost amongst these armourers was Manekin le Heaumer of London. Manekin and his brother Peter supplied armour to the crown and also participated in military campaigns. Manekin first appears in records of the Mayor's Court in London in 1298 but seems to have maintained a presence within the London community of armourers for at least thirty years thereafter.[33] He was part of a

---

[26] *CCR 1307–13*, p. 526; *Calendar of Early Mayors' Court Rolls*, ed. A. H. Thomson (London, 1924), pp. 110, 200. He seems to be the same armourer still active in 1338–39: Ekwall, *London Subsidy Rolls*, p. 309.

[27] E 122/70/1 m. 4r.

[28] *The London Eyre of 1276*, ed. M. Weinbaum (London, 1976), nos 189, 508.

[29] E 403/176 m. 8; Unwin, *Finance and Trade under Edward III*, p. 89.

[30] Also active in London at this time was Druettus le Armurer who, in 1296, was demised the manor of Chalk in Kent by William de Charleton, the keeper of the priory of Bermondsey. Another London armourer, John de Hereford, was granted the priory's lands in Birling, near Maidstone, in Kent: *CPR 1292–1301*, pp. 224–5. John was possibly connected to William de Hereford: ibid., p. 106.

[31] In 1321 Andrew le Armurer was retained by John de Hastynges as one of his attorneys in Ireland: *CPR 1317–21*, p. 559.

[32] *CPR 1232–47*, p. 282.

[33] *CPR 1301–07*, p. 392; *Calendar of Early Mayors' Court Rolls*, p. 20.

group of at least six London citizens who had lent money for the king's wars in Gascony. As part of the pledge to repay the money, the considerable sum of £150 8s 5d, jewels had been delivered as security to the house of Manekin for safe keeping in July 1301.[34] Manekin was also associated with some of the leading nobility of England, including Henry de Lacy, earl of Lincoln, who intervened on his behalf in 1305 when he was indicted for committing various trespasses.[35]

In some instances London armourers led contingents of men and provided armour for the king's wars. In 1318 William le Hauberger was amongst those who undertook to find soldiers to serve in Scotland.[36] Moreover, one of the two centenars leading these men was to be Manekin le Heaumer.[37] London armourers, manufacturers and suppliers were actively called upon to provide armour for the wars of Edward I and Edward II in Scotland. In 1322 John de Kesteven, John le Clerk, Henry de Herepol and Geoffrey de Rothinge supplied large quantities of aketons, bascinets and gloves to the Sussex gentry, Henry Hussee and Richard Seyntes, for use north of the border.[38] Nicholas le Clerk supplied 100 aketons, 100 bascinets and 100 pairs of gloves in 1325, which were subsequently received into store by the constable of the Tower, John de Weston.[39] However, it was clear that domestic supply was insufficient to meet the crown's increasing demand. Supplies were therefore purchased from abroad. At the same time as Nicholas le Clerk was delivering his goods to the Tower, the Italian merchant Boniface, of the Peruzzi company, was also providing significant quantities of aketons, bascinets, vambraces, aventails and gloves.[40]

The first clear evidence for the presence of an armourer in the king's household appears to be Hugh de Bungay, who is described as a sergeant in 1310.[41] Certainly, from the reign of Edward I, men with particular levels of expertise were being retained in royal service and assigned the rank of a sergeant within the king's household. The term sergeant did not have the almost exclusively military implications of the modern 'sergeant'. Many

---

[34] *CPR 1292–1301*, p. 602.
[35] *CPR 1301–07*, p. 392. Possibly also known as Edmund, he had been committed to Newgate gaol in 1300: *CPR 1292–1301*, p. 555. Two other armourers, Thomas le Armurer and Philip le Armurer, were associated with leading nobles, in this case Henry III's son, Edmund: *CPR 1266–72*, p. 203, *CPR 1272–81*, p. 160.
[36] Le Hauberger subsequently became one of Edward III's king's armourers. He was William le Hauberger, senior, who appears on the 1332–33 Subsidy Roll for London. This was presumably to distinguish him from another William Le Hauberger: Ekwall, *London Subsidy Rolls*, p. 299.
[37] *CLBL* E, pp. 94, 99.
[38] *CLBL* E, pp. 170–1.
[39] E 403/217 m. 6
[40] E 403/217 m. 8. Le Clerk was not identified on the 1332 London subsidy as an armourer. He died in 1348 and directed that he be buried in the church of St Mary le Bow where he held property. He also held property in St Margaret Lothbury and in the county of Buckinghamshire: Ekwall, *London Subsidy Rolls*, p. 300; *CW*, i, 539.
[41] *CPR 1307–13*, p. 278.

were allocated to various household departments, and had largely domestic duties. Under Edward I there were about seventy sergeants in the mid-1280s, falling to about forty-five in 1300 and approximately thirty by the end of the reign. During the course of the fourteenth century the number of sergeants within the different offices of the household continued to vary across time.[42]

It is entirely possible that de Bungay was part of the household establishment even earlier than 1310. He had served as armourer to Prince Edward of Carnarvon as early as 1303 when, in preparation for war with Scotland, he had organized amongst other items the production of banners, aketons, spurs, mail collars, swords and scabbards.[43] Virtually nothing is known about de Bungay, however. The surname can be found at this time in East Anglia as well as London but the paucity of evidence means that it is unclear whether Hugh originated from the former or the latter, or whether the two were connected. What is apparent, though, is that the relationship between prince and armourer was maintained after his accession as Edward II to the throne in 1307.[44] It was de Bungay, in his capacity as king's armourer, who subsequently provided particular items for the monument of the king's favourite, Piers Gaveston.[45]

It would seem that de Bungay worked under the direction of the great wardrobe. By the mid-thirteenth century this department had acquired accommodation in the Tower of London. While the king's wardrobe remained an itinerating organization and was established wherever the king happened to find himself, it had already become customary by this stage for the great wardrobe to be permanently located in the Tower and to be used as a storehouse for the range of non-perishable goods and materials required by the king and his household. Initially this list included furniture, tapestry and hangings, clothing, cloth and other materials, and non-perishable groceries. During the later thirteenth century it had expanded its custodianship to include arms, armour, artillery and ammunition. From a logistical as well an administrative and accounting perspective, it made sense that de Bungay would work under the auspices of the great wardrobe.[46]

It was not until the second decade of the fourteenth century, however, that the role of the king's armourers and their relationship with the king's household

---

[42] Prestwich suggests that armourers and saddlers were being retained in this way, although the documentary evidence he quotes does not mention either armourers or saddlers: M. Prestwich, *Edward I*, new edn (New Haven and London, 1997), pp. 148, 152. For the later fourteenth-century household see C. Given-Wilson, 'The Court and Household of Edward III, 1360–1377', University of St Andrews PhD thesis (1976), pp. 8–10.

[43] E 101/363/18 fols 9d, 10. See also S. Phillips, *Edward II* (New Haven and London, 2011), p. 92.

[44] Ekwall, *Population of Medieval London*, p. 4. In the account he rendered in May 1317 for items supplied de Bungay was only called armourer: *CCR 1318–23*, pp. 439, 643. A Robert de Bungay, probably a tailor, was paid for eighty-one days' work in the great wardrobe accounts of Thomas de Useflete in 1324–25: E 101/380/15.

[45] E 403/172 m. 6

[46] Tout, *Chapters in Administrative History*, iv, 352, 439–41.

becomes clearer. Their relationship continued to evolve primarily through the great wardrobe; and as the great wardrobe gradually moved out of the Tower and established its presence more firmly within the city, it would appear that the majority, if not all, of those designated king's armourers remained resident outside of the Tower's walls too. The place of king's armourers within the structure of the household was defined by the York Ordinances of 1318, which reorganized the structure of the king's wardrobe. King's armourers were now treated as part of a clearly defined group of artificers permanently attached to the establishment of the great wardrobe. Along with the king's tailor, pavilioner and confectioner of spices, the armourers were subject to the authority of the clerk-purveyor of the great wardrobe. According to Tout, the reorganization of the wardrobe in 1318 had marked one of the 'chief administrative developments' up to that point in Edward II's reign and was primarily an attempt to codify the 'sounder customs of the previous generation' as well as to remedy existing abuses within the household.[47]

The close relationship between king's armourers and the great wardrobe was perhaps a reflection of the duties that they were expected to perform for the crown.[48] The activities undertaken by king's armourers and other craftsmen in the king's service suggest a continuing degree of flexibility in the duties they undertook. Up until the first half of the fourteenth century the preferred skills of king's armourers were tailoring skills. If metal products were required he could either purchase them or subcontract to specialist metal-working armourers in order to fulfil a particular commission. King's armourers supplied, either through their own manufacture or by purchase from a third party, quantities of arms and armour to the king through the wardrobe of the household, the great wardrobe, or subsequently the privy wardrobe. The first known king's armourer, Hugh de Bungay, was referred to as 'tailor' and 'tailor and armourer' as well as just 'armourer'. Records demonstrate that he supplied armour to the crown as well as repairing items when commissioned to do so.[49]

Alongside king's armourers there also appears to have been a supplementary group of armourers who were associated with the crown, generally through the subcontracting of work, without being formally retained within the king's household. This is demonstrated by the occasional references in the records of both the great and privy wardrobes. Thus, in the account of expenses of Thomas Usefleet for 1324–25 there was a one-off payment to the linen armourer, Robert de Lindsay, who had worked on the production of aketons. In 1329 Agnes, the wife of Richard le Heaumer, was paid for

---

[47]   Ibid., ii, 207, 246–7; iv, 387–90.
[48]   The same principle can be applied to king's tailors. They not only produced clothing for the royal household, they might also purchase armour for the king, and were even responsible for binding the king's books: ibid., iv, 388.
[49]   E 403/217 m. 8.

supplying a range of items for the king's use including a helmet and a leather box for his bascinet. In the same account William de Skelton (possibly working in conjunction with William le Hauberger) was paid for supplying armour for the joust and tournament. Neither supplier was formally attached to the king's household, however.[50] Despite the limitations imposed by the survival of documentary evidence, there were clearly armourers who were employed to supply equipment for the king's personal needs as well as those who were primarily contracted to supply the requirements of his military forces or to refurbish existing stores.

Until the emergence of the privy wardrobe from the late 1330s onwards, the Tower remained just one of a number of depots for the storage of the king's goods.[51] Certain king's craftsmen and artisans such as the attilator (supplier or maker of artillery), bowyer, fletcher and smith did have accommodation at the Tower and were routinely described in official documents such as the Exchequer Issue Rolls as 'smith of the king in the Tower of London' or 'attilator of the king in the Tower of London'. Until this point in time there is no evidence to suggest that king's armourers were regarded in the same way as other artificers.[52] The accommodation of the king's artificers was spread across different parts of the Tower complex. In the early 1330s the attilator Nicholas Conrad was based in one of the north-eastern Towers close to the queen's wardrobe.[53] Nevertheless, it would seem likely that most king's artificers were located in close proximity to the royal accommodation, in and adjacent to the Wakefield Tower. This is lent added confirmation in later grants to king's artificers. During the mid-fifteenth century the king's fletcher had a dwelling 'used of old for the said office' between that of the clerk of works and the Wakefield Tower, while the king's bow maker was provided with accommodation between the Wakefield and Westsmithfield Towers.[54]

The relatively small quantities of armour stored at the Tower at this stage seem to suggest that most king's armourers, other than those that were part of the king's household establishment and who might reasonably be expected to be in attendance upon the king for particular periods of time, were probably not based regularly inside. Tout dates the relationship of armourers (and smiths) with the Tower back to at least 1273 and seems to have regarded them

50 E 101/380/15; E 361/3. A Hugh Scot, armourer (probably a linen armourer), was also paid for producing seven aketons in 1342: E 101/389/14.
51 R. Storey, 'The Tower of London and the *garderobae armorum*', *Royal Armouries Yearbook* 3 (1998), 177–8.
52 These were normally carpenter, smith, crossbow maker, and *attiliator*. See, for example, E 403/99 m. 1.
53 J. Ashbee, 'The Tower of London as a Royal Residence', University of London PhD thesis (2006), p. 281. Nicholas was the son of the longstanding *attiliator* and *balistarius*, William Conrad. The Conrads formed a dynasty of artillery and crossbow makers from the late thirteenth century onwards: E 403/90 m. 1.
54 *CPR 1446–52*, pp. 523, 556.

as similar types of craftsmen. He asserted that 'There is no doubt that from an early time the Tower, where the king's armourers had their workshops, was the permanent place of wardrobe deposit, especially for the deposit of arms and armour.'[55] The presence of the king's smith within the Tower certainly meant that there were workshop facilities where metal-working activities could take place when that was deemed necessary. In fact, those armourers employed to undertake work at the Tower during the first two decades of the fourteenth century were probably retained to do specific tasks at particular moments in time and provided appropriate accommodation. John le Armurer, for example, who otherwise had no discernable link to the Tower, was paid for cleaning thirty hauberks in the Tower of London in 1323.[56]

King's armourers under Edward III

By the beginning of the reign of Edward III, king's armourers, especially those who were also sergeants in the royal household, probably had a twofold purpose: first and foremost, to make and supply armour for the king, his household and members of the wider royal affinity; and second, to help procure additional quantities of armour for military campaigns. And in this second role there was no real difference from other armourers periodically employed by the crown to supply armour. In common with these other armourers, the items were then delivered to the keeper of the king's arms and armour.

From 1323 the keepership of the king's armour was undertaken by the wardrobe clerk, John Fleet. This was to have a significant impact on the relationship of king's armourers with the Tower and the crown as the fourteenth century progressed. There had been identifiable custodians of the king's armour within his household from at least the 1270s. In about 1278–79 this function appears to have been entrusted to an esquire called Albin. He was the king's yeoman, Albin de Bevery, who was later granted lands in Lincolnshire and Somerset by the king in 1307. Household accounts make it clear that Albin was entrusted with making purchases, and arranging for the repair and refurbishment of the king's arms and armour. There is also some evidence to suggest that he, in turn, had a deputy at the Tower.[57]

There were, therefore, already established arrangements for the custody of the king's armour at the Tower before the rise of the privy wardrobe. With the emergence of the privy wardrobe these seem to have been revised. The privy

---

55 Tout, *Chapters in Administrative History*, ii, 53, n. 1; ibid., iv, 445; E 403/222 mm. 1, 2.
56 E 403/205 m. 7. It seems that by the late fourteenth century the king's armourer did have a house and workshops within the Tower. By this stage, however, king's armourers were metal-working specialists and had separated from the linen armourer, now a separate office: *CPR 1405–08*, p. 409; *CPR 1408–13*, p. 460.
57 E 36/201 fol. 27r; *Liber Quotidianus Contrarotulatoris Garderobiae, 1299–1300*, ed. J. Topham (London, 1787), p. 226; *CPR 1301–07*, p. 514; Tout, *Chapters in Administrative History*, iv, 445. The deputy was known as Alexander: C 47/4/5 m. 2d.

wardrobe had its roots in both the king's wardrobe and the king's chamber. Initially it was where the king kept his personal belongings, including armaments, as distinct from those required for the wider royal household. However, when the court was travelling it also took responsibility for the household's armaments. As the privy wardrobe developed its own identity at the Tower of London during the 1330s, it made sense for the custody of the king's arms and armour to be combined with the keepership of the privy wardrobe as well. In 1339 John Fleet was being described as keeper of the king's armour in the Tower. Subordinate to him were a number of yeomen of the king's armour who undertook much of the practical administration surrounding supply and delivery.[58] Nevertheless, as late as 1337 William de Standerwick, one of the king's armourers, could still be referred to as keeper of the king's armour, and it is possible that particular king's armourers remained closely associated with the custody of the king's arms and armour until Fleet became permanently established at the Tower as keeper of the privy wardrobe after 1338.[59]

Precisely where the king's stores of armour were being kept at the Tower of London is unclear. From at least 1241 the king's wardrobe had been situated on the ground floor of the Wakefield Tower. This placed it directly underneath the king's great chamber. By the mid-1330s this space was being used to store the goods of the great wardrobe and at this stage it still made sense for king's armourers to take a prominent role in the custody of the king's personal arms and armour. It is entirely plausible that the king's armour (both for his own personal use and for supplying royal forces) was also being stored here.[60] Moreover, until Fleet's arrival there are strong grounds for regarding king's armourers as the essential link between the king and his armed forces. In January 1335, for example, Sayer Bonet (also known as Sayer de Valence) was provided with letters of protection and sent from Scotland to fetch armour for the king from York, London and Dover.[61] Enrolled wardrobe accounts provide evidence of the number of days that king's armourers spent away from court during the period of that account. The longest spells naturally corresponded with the king's own absences from court campaigning against his enemies in Scotland and across the English Channel as well as attending tournaments. His longstanding metal-working

---

58 It would appear that some of these, such as John de London, were also armourers: *CPR 1354–58*, p. 11; E 361/4 m. 27.

59 *CCR 1337–39*, p. 24. This had perhaps been a reflection of the great wardrobe's continuing involvement in the custody of arms and armour in the itinerating *garderoba armorum*. The expenses for the *garderoba armorum* were still being charged to the great wardrobe as late as 1328: E 101/383/19.

60 At the same time, though, storage of arms and armour for the king's forces had begun to occupy rooms in St Thomas's Tower, on the south side adjacent to the wharf: Ashbee, 'Tower of London', pp. 279–81. Arms and armour are certainly stored in the same areas in the late fourteenth century: *CPR 1399–1401*, p. 214.

61 *CPR 1334–38*, p. 57.

armourer, William le Hauberger, for example, spent a total of 210 days at court and 155 days away from court during 1330–31. For time at court he was paid 7½d per day and for time away 12d per day.[62]

As the privy wardrobe became the dominant institution which managed the procurement, supply and distribution of arms and armour to the king's forces under Edward III, along with the establishment of the Tower as permanent storehouse, king's armourers naturally came to enjoy a closer relationship with Fleet and his subordinate yeomen.[63] This is not obvious, however, from surviving privy wardrobe accounts. The enrolled account of Robert Mildenhale for the period 1345–52 included William le Hauberger, who was given one pair of pauces[64] and braces[65] and two coifs for the tournament by gift of the king, yet he was not identified as a king's armourer despite his status. In fact, particulars of account for the privy wardrobe are inconsistent in their identification of individuals and do little to highlight the continuing importance of king's armourers or the role that they played in supplying the needs of the king and court.[66] Instead, the continuing role of king's armourers and their relationship with the crown is only made clear by a systematic scrutiny of the much more extensive records of the great wardrobe during this period. Nevertheless, like all armourers contracted to supply goods to the king, king's armourers delivered their finished goods to Fleet or his deputies. The language used in the indentures of receipt shows that a formal viewing of the items took place when they were delivered before being placed in storage.[67]

Linen armourers remained particularly prominent during the early part of Edward's reign, supplying the needs of the court, especially equipment for the king's tournaments.[68] At the beginning of the new reign the number

---

[62] E 361/3 m. 32d.
[63] There is even evidence to suggest that at least some of the yeomen working under Fleet's authority were also armourers. This would naturally have made them more skilled in the procurement and reviewing processes. One example was Adam le Hauberger (also referred to as a yeoman of the chamber) who was active in travelling, making purchases, and ensuring their delivery to the Tower: E 101/386/15, 16; E 101/387/10.
[64] Originally used to denote the lower part of a hauberk and subsequently a breastplate: C. Blair, *European Armour circa 1066 to circa 1700* (London, 1958), p. 80 n.
[65] Otherwise known as vambraces.
[66] E 372/198 m. 34. The gift to Le Hauberger perhaps represented a continuing chivalric and military aspect to the function of king's armourers. The accounts of Henry Snayth for 1360 and 1365 include the names of the city armourer, John Payn, and the king's armourer, John de London (also a king's yeoman), yet the status of William Glendale, also a king's armourer, is ignored: E 101/392/14; 394/14.
[67] Tout, *Chapters in Administrative History*, iv, 448; *CCR 1339–41*, p. 83; E 361/3 m. 34d.
[68] The beginning of the new reign marked a significant point in the development of the organization of the tailors and linen armourers. In 1327 they had received their first charter authorizing them to hold a guild once a year and 'to make rules and regulations for the ordering of their mistyeries by view of the mayor'. The following year, in common with other crafts and trades, they had also adopted the practice of appointing leading members to oversee the regulation of their 'mistery'. Four linen armourers were among the twenty wardens appointed to govern the craft. Significant connections were maintained throughout the reign between the crown, royal servants, and tailors

of armourers attached to the royal household rose dramatically.[69] There are perhaps several interlinked reasons for the sudden increase. On the one hand there was the new king's obvious interest in chivalric and martial pursuits. Linen armourers were particularly important in supplying the practical as well as luxury and decorative items needed for tournaments.[70] Secondly, alongside the resurgence in interest in these activities there was also an apparent desire to promote and encourage the domestic production of armour for the king's use. In turn this was perhaps also linked to an increased desire by the new king to retain the skills of foreign armourers directly.

In the immediate aftermath of Edward III's accession, Edward II's principal armourer, Thomas de Copham, continued to serve the new king, at least in the short term. De Copham had apparently succeeded Hugh de Bungay as Edward II's principal armourer towards the end of the reign.[71] Copham had been the armourer responsible for providing equipment for both the funeral of Edward II and the coronation of Edward III. Surviving accounts of the great wardrobe show Copham (and de Bungay in what was presumably his last major commission) organizing the activities of a substantial number of tailors and other artisans for the coronation.[72] Copham, however, died on 5 March 1332, thus paving the way for a new group of armourers to enter royal service.[73]

Not only did Copham's death coincide with increased royal demands for chivalric equipment, it might also have paved the way for the new king to establish closer relationships with London armourers like the metal-working specialist William le Hauberger. Tout had already noted that several armourers were often employed at the same time in the king's service 'but they were not, apparently, all of equal standing'.[74] Yet he did not consider when that change had taken place or when 'king's armourer' was first consist-

---

and linen armourers: *CPR 1327–30*, p. 29; *CLBL* E, p. 234; Davies and Saunders, *Merchant Taylors*, pp. 12–13.

[69] In 1327 the Exchequer Memoranda Rolls named Nicholas de Wright, John de Colonia, William le Hauberger, Thomas Copham and Peter de Bruges as king's armourers. By 1330 Nicholas de Wright, John de Colonia, Thomas Copham, Peter of Bruges, William le Hauberger, William de London and William Galeys were called king's armourers. De Wright and de London, were, however, tailors: *Calendar of Memoranda Rolls Exchequer, Michaelmas 1326 – Michaelmas 1327*, ed. R. A. Latham (London, 1968), p. 376.

[70] For the tournament armour produced see J. Barker, *The Tournament in England 1100–1400* (Woodbridge, repr. 2003), pp. 166–8.

[71] De Bungay seems to disappear from records shortly after the accession of Edward III. He is present, for example, in the great wardrobe account of Thomas Usefleet in 1327–28 and is still named as a sergeant. Thereafter, there are no obvious references to him: E 101/383/3.

[72] E 101/383/3 mm. 1–2. There has been no systematic identification of these individuals. Occasionally, however, it seems possible to make an identification. John de Estwyk, for example, was a tailor (not a chandler as Ekwall suggests), resident in Farringdon Within. William de Kent, on the other hand, was probably a tailor from Cripplegate: Ekwall, *London Subsidy Rolls*, pp. 259, 277, 324.

[73] *CLBL* F, p. 62.

[74] Tout, *Chapters in Administrative History*, iv, pp. 389–90.

ently used to identify those armourers favoured by the crown. In fact Tout did not seem to understand that while the term king's armourer was applied to those armourers favoured by the king, only the most favoured of those subsequently entered the royal household as sergeants.

Contemporary records suggest a periodic turnover of membership of the group of king's armourers during the first three decades of Edward III's reign. The king's marriage to Philippa of Hainault might have reinforced a developing preference for Low Countries armourers skilled in the production of both linen armour and metal armour. Amongst the new group of king's armourers were John de Colonia, Peter de Valenciennes and Gerard de Tournay. As his name suggests, John de Colonia was from the Rhineland. Peter de Valenciennes and Gerard de Tournay were, of course, from the queen's own homeland.[75] Expertise was also acquired from other European centres as well. Sayer de Bonet, otherwise Sayer de Valence, for example, was almost certainly from the centre of armour production in France based around Lyon.[76]

For most of the period between 1327 and 1357 the king's two principal armourers were probably the linen armourers John de Colonia and William de Standerwick, both of whom were provided with workshops in the city of London and who employed sizeable numbers of workers to undertake royal commissions.[77] Despite his apparent prominence and importance to the crown, William de Standerwick remains an elusive character. He was perhaps originally from Standerwick in Somerset, but little of substance can be made of his career. In 1338 de Standerwick had been pardoned for marrying Margery, the widow of the Surrey landowner Walter de Matham, without the king's licence.[78] De Standerwick was apparently succeeded briefly by John de Standerwick, probably his son, who also became a king's armourer (as well as king's yeoman and sergeant), and who was active from the late 1330s onwards. John, however, had died by 1345.[79] De Colonia, on the other hand,

---

[75] The principal king's armourers (although not all) can be found accounting to the great wardrobe in E 361/3. See also Mortimer who, citing E 101/388/13 mm. 2–3, suggests that James of Liege, Gottschalk and Arnold of Cologne, and Herman Keplyn were also armourers in the king's service: I. Mortimer, *The Perfect King: The Life of Edward III Father of the English Nation* (London, 2008), p. 116. They seem, however, to have been merchant armourers rather than craftsmen. In the same document cited by Mortimer above, Keplyn, for example, is also called an arblaster. This would suggest he traded in projectile weapons too. James of Liege appears elsewhere as a yeoman of the king's armour: E 372/198 m. 34d.

[76] Blair, *European Armour*, p. 108.

[77] John de Colonia is only apparently referred to as a linen armourer in one document, dated to 1359: SC 8/247/12310. Another king's armourer, Peter of Bruges, was also supplied with a workshop: E 361/3 m. 32d.

[78] *CPR 1338–40*, p. 51. It is not surprising that there is some evidence of debts owed to William de Standerwick, such as the £10 by William de Castelacre: *CCR 1337–39*, p. 413.

[79] *CCR 1343–46*, pp. 233, 341. 595. John kept the king's gardens at Westminster where he also held property, complaining in 1335 about the robbery of crops and other goods from his houses by other local residents. Furthermore, he apparently held some land at Staines in Surrey. Little else is known about him: *CPR 1334–38*, p. 217; *CPR 1343–45*, p. 448; *A Calendar of Feet of Fines*

was clearly an influential armourer with a wide-ranging network of contacts in the city. He first appears in the enrolled accounts of the great wardrobe for 1328–29;[80] though the brevity of the entry and the small quantity of items supplied in contrast to other armourers of the king, two aketons and two caps of beaver for the king and his brother John of Eltham, would suggest that the relationship was still in its infancy at this stage.[81]

By the mid-1330s John de Colonia seemed to be the dominant figure amongst this group, although this impression might be distorted in part by the survival of evidence weighted in favour of linen armourers. Precisely when de Colonia first arrived in England or started to supply armour to the crown is unknown. The earliest reference to him as 'armourer of the king' is in the Memoranda Roll for 1326–27. There does not appear to be any evidence whatsoever that de Colonia was supplying the needs of Edward II but this cannot, of course, be ruled out. The lack of evidence of any activity before 1327 lends some weight to the notion that de Colonia entered a service relationship with the new regime rather than the old. It is tempting to see de Colonia first entering the service of Queen Isabella and Roger Mortimer, earl of March, before subsequently transferring his allegiance to Edward III in 1330.[82] Their relationship was cemented, it would seem, after the king seized power back from his mother, Queen Isabella, and her lover, Roger Mortimer, earl of March. Within a short space of time he had become the principal supplier of armour and chivalric equipment to Edward III. It was de Colonia who supplied richly decorated aketons to those who had supported the young king's coup in 1330.[83]

De Colonia was an acknowledged member of the group of leading craftsmen in the capital upon whom the crown relied. In 1337 de Colonia, now a king's yeoman, was given permission to crenellate his premises in Cornhill.[84] Not only did this serve to identify de Colonia as one of the leading members of the armourer's craft and trade, it also emphasized his relationship to the

---

for London and Middlesex, Richard I to Richard III, ed. W. J. Hardy and W. Page (London, 1892), p. 119.

[80] He also benefited from the death of John de Standerwick, receiving the latter's former office of sealing sacks of wool and wool-fells to be shipped from London and the rights to maintenance from the Abbey of Beaulieu: *CPR 1343–45*, p. 446; *CCR 1343–46*, p. 558.

[81] *Calendar of Memoranda Rolls, 1326–1327*, p. 376; E 361/3 m. 24d.

[82] Roger de Colonia, brother of John de Colonia, held land at Mereworth near Maidstone in Kent from the Mortimers: *Calendar of Inquisitions Post Mortem, Edward III*, IX (London, 1935), p. 35. John de Colonia's property holding in Nettlestead placed him in the proximity of the royal castle of Leeds. His presence there, however, brought him into conflict with other members of Edward III's affinity. In 1342 Sir Philip de Pympe of Nettlestead acknowledged a debt to de Colonia of £40. De Colonia and Pympe had been in dispute locally over the presentation to a local benefice: *CCR 1341–43*, p. 672.

[83] C. Shenton, 'Edward III and the Coup of 1330', in *The Age of Edward III*, ed. J. S. Bothwell (York, 2001), pp. 23–4, 30–4.

[84] *CPR 1334–38*, p. 505.

crown.[85] His connections within the capital and adjacent counties included the great and the small. In 1339, for example, he acknowledged a debt for £80 in chancery to John de Colchester, the wealthy London goldsmith.[86] De Colonia and his family also took an active interest and role in the local affairs of Cornhill, where he was an influential figure. De Colonia's brother, Roger, a tailor, was one of the mainpernors in a case disputing the legality of a house reputedly built on royal land in the parish.[87] John de Colonia also took part in the business activities of other minor London armourers resident in the area. When William Sparke took out a lease for a shop on Birchin Lane in Cornhill, de Colonia witnessed the deed. Sparke was quite possibly one of the armourers to whom de Colonia subcontracted business.[88]

De Colonia's place within the royal household led to regular commissions from the royal family and the nobility. Amongst his most significant commissions were multiple items for the king's new chivalric fraternity, the Order of the Garter.[89] His particulars of account for 1331–32 illustrate the nature and extent of his connections within the linen armourer and tailoring crafts. In order to fulfil his commissions he employed a range of London artisans to undertake the production of different items. Certain workers are to be consistently found throughout the accounts whilst others appear only occasionally.[90] Contact with other linen armourers is demonstrated quite clearly through his employment of other well-known linen armourers such as Stephen Savage.[91] Stephen had previously worked for the king's armourer, Thomas de Copham, and was presumably related to Roger Savage, one of the overseers of the tailors and linen armourers.[92]

To meet those growing requirements the king clearly retained the services of metal-working specialists in addition to John de Colonia and William de Standerwick. This group included John Daundeigne, Gerard de Tournay and William le Hauberger. Daundeigne was the king's first identifiable helmet maker. Upon his death he was apparently replaced by de Tournay. William le Hauberger, as his name implies, supplied metal armour.[93] It has been suggested that king's armourers were capable of producing fine-quality

---

[85] Ibid., p. 57. In 1335 de Colonia was one of those craftsmen who provided pledges for those men going to serve the king in Scotland: *CLBL* E, p. 5.

[86] *CCR 1339–41*, p. 226. In 1341 he acknowledged a further debt to William de Edyngdon for £200: *CCR 1341–43*, p. 139.

[87] *Calendar of Plea and Memoranda Rolls*, pp. 201–2.

[88] *CLBL* F, p. 204.

[89] N. Harris Nicholas, 'Observations on the Institution of the Most Noble Order of the Garter', *Archaeologia* 31 (1846), 33–56, 119–24.

[90] E 101/385/7.

[91] Ekwall, *London Subsidy Rolls*, p. 299.

[92] E 101/383/3. Roger de la March, a London armourer, was employed by Thomas de Copham at the beginning of Edward III's reign. He was possibly a king's yeoman of the same name employed to go across the Channel on the king's business in 1332: E 101/384/2 no. 10; C 241/128/39; *CPR 1330–34*, p. 277.

[93] *CPR 1334–38*, p. 57; E 101/387/15 nos 67, 68.

armour (at the Tower) by the 1370s. Yet perhaps such a statement needs a modicum of refinement and clarification. King's armourers were already capable of producing prestigious pieces of linen armour by the early fourteenth century. In the wake of Edward III's victory over the Scots at Halidon Hill in 1333, for example, the king ordered a range of richly decorated tournament armour. One suit of armour for the king was to be embroidered with baboons and other animals. Similarly, four aketons were to be made of red cloth adorned with diverse heads and leaves.[94] There is perhaps a case for suggesting that king's armourers like Gerard de Tournay were capable of producing quality pieces of metal armour by the 1330s and 1340s. In 1334 de Tournay supplied a furbished helm for the tournament with the eyes gilded. Moreover, in his particulars of account for 1337–41 he was also recorded delivering amongst other items one bascinet from Lombardy polished and garnished, which suggests further decoration and embellishment.[95]

It is possible that by concentrating upon those king's armourers who were linen armourers and who remained resident outside of the Tower during the first half of the fourteenth century, the presence of metal-working armourers within the Tower has been overshadowed. Although items of metal armour were supplied by William de Standerwick and John de Colonia, these items were clearly identified in accounts because they were 'purchased' rather than manufactured.[96] Nevertheless, with the establishment of the privy wardrobe at the Tower and the increased need for those skills on-site, it made sense for specialist metal-working king's armourers to be present on a more regular basis. By the 1350s there is firm evidence that armour repair and manufacture was being conducted on-site by the king's armourer John de London. Presumably he had a workshop, although there is no clear evidence to substantiate this until 1374, when another king's armourer, William Snell, was recorded purchasing tools for a workshop on-site.[97]

Conclusion

In June 1357 John de Colonia died after a career in royal service spanning thirty years.[98] During the course of his career in royal service the nature of the armourer's craft had continued its gradual evolution from a situation where linen armourers dominated to one where metal-working specialists were becoming increasingly important. The capital was home to a burgeoning group of armourers who were craftsmen, merchants or both. There were also

---

[94] E 101/386/18 m. 58; Mortimer, *The Perfect King*, pp. 114–15.
[95] Richardson, 'Armour in England', p. 317; Mortimer, *The Perfect King*, p. 116; E 101/386/18 no. 41, 388/11. A note of caution is advised, however, as these accounts make it apparent that de Tournay was also covering or re-covering armour.
[96] *CPR 1334–38*, p. 57; E 101/387/15 nos 67, 68.
[97] E 361/4 m. 27.
[98] Davies and Saunders, *Merchant Taylors*, p. 13.

domestic and foreign specialists established in the city. Moreover, as the reign of Edward II progressed, a number of individuals emerge from the gloom who obviously enjoyed a closer relationship to the crown and who were capable of manufacturing and supplying finished articles. Amongst this group there were also armourers within the king's household establishment who provided an important link between court and city.

It is about the time of the accession of Edward III that the most favoured men begin to be referred to as king's armourers. During the first half of Edward III's reign the king's armourers were resident in the city of London, a reflection of their close relationship to the great wardrobe, which had largely moved out of the Tower. Some were even provided with workshops by the crown in which to conduct their business. De Colonia, and quite possibly the other king's armourers, provided a vital link to the crown in securing the services of other craftsmen. With the emergence of the privy wardrobe at the Tower, their relationship began to shift back towards it too. More-over, with the passing of de Colonia and other armourers of his generation by the mid-fourteenth century, so apparently declined the dominance of the linen armourers within the ranks of the king's armourers. As the century progressed, and as metal superseded cloth as the principal ingredient in the manufacture of armour, metal-working armourers finally emerged as clearly defined individuals at the Tower.[99] Provided with designated space within the Tower and much closer to the stores and personnel of the privy wardrobe, the king's armourers had returned to the royal fold.[100]

[99] By the end of the fourteenth and beginning of the fifteenth century there was even a formal separation of linen armourers from metal-working armourers. Although still referred to as king's armourers on enrolled wardrobe accounts, these men were overwhelmingly metal-working specialists. The skills and services of the linen armourer were not completely sidelined, however, as armour continued to be covered with fabric throughout the second half of the century. A separate appointment was now made, though their identity becomes harder to determine. In 1408 it was Philip Cheppestowe: *CPR 1405–08*, p. 409.

[100] By 1360 William Glendale was being described as 'armator pro corpora domini regis', suggesting a much closer association with the production of armour for the person of the king. Tout, *Chapters in Administrative History*, iv, 390. In 1399 when John Dounton was appointed 'armourer of the body within the Tower of London' his facilities consisted of a workshop with a dwelling chamber, kitchen, and woodshed attached: *CPR 1399–1401*, p. 162. These were the same that had been provided to Stephen atte Fryth in 1395: *CPR 1391–96*, 618, 722; *CPR 1413–16*, p. 199. In 1360 another king's armourer, John de London, was granted the keeping of the gate of the Tower with an allowance for himself and a yeoman when they were making the king's armour there: *CPR 1358–61*, p. 511. However, as the 1437 appointment of John Beauchamp demonstrates, the sergeant and yeoman armourers of the body were no longer skilled metal-working armourers by the early fifteenth century: *CPR 1436–41*, p. 99.

IN THE BEST INTEREST OF THE QUEEN: ISABELLA OF FRANCE, EDWARD II AND THE IMAGE OF A FUNCTIONAL RELATIONSHIP

Lisa Benz St John

Recent scholarship on medieval queenship has developed a paradigm for the relationship between the late medieval king and queen. In this paradigm, the office of queenship is an essential part of the crown and of the king's exercise of sovereignty. Both the king and queen benefited from this relationship, with the queen actively involved in creating, upholding and performing the roles of queenship (intercession, motherhood, patronage and so on), and the king manipulating them to legitimize and strengthen his own rule.[1] In this way, a partnership, albeit an uneven one, was created for the benefit of the crown.

Surprisingly, this very paradigm of a functional, royal marriage can be found in one of the most notoriously dysfunctional marriages in late medieval history – that of Edward II, king of England, and his queen, Isabella of France. If we focus on the more salacious aspects of their marriage, it becomes clear why it is often viewed as highly ineffectual. Isabella married Edward II at Boulogne-sur-Mer in 1308 and from the beginning their marriage was plagued with conflict. Edward II had a penchant for favouritism, and so he bestowed his patronage on his friend Piers Gaveston. The nobility of England reacted in 1311 by drawing up a list of Ordinances by which the king was to abide. One of these Ordinances required Gaveston's exile, his third exile since 1307. However, he returned to England sometime between December 1311 and January 1312. Edward II, Gaveston and Isabella fled north to avoid the nobility's anger, but in the summer of 1312 Gaveston was captured and murdered. It was not long before Edward found a new favourite, Hugh Despenser, the younger, and once again the nobility called for the favourite's exile. Their request was granted, but it did not prevent civil war from breaking out in 1321. Hugh Despenser returned from exile shortly thereafter. Relations between Edward and Isabella deteriorated quickly and Edward seized all of Isabella's lands, granting them to Despenser in 1324.

In 1325, despite these strains in their marriage, Edward sent Isabella as an ambassador to the French court to defend English interests in the disputed

[1] J. Laynesmith, *The Last Medieval Queens: English Queenship, 1445–1503* (Oxford, 2004), pp. 22, 30–6, 73, 129, 131, 179–80, 219, 242, 263–5; L. B. St John, *Three Medieval Queens: Queenship and the Crown in Fourteenth-Century England* (New York, 2012), pp. 57–63, 81, 94, 97, 100–1, 107, 165–9.

Liza Benz St John

territory of Gascony. By the summer of 1326, Isabella had succeeded in negotiating a truce with Charles IV with the condition that Edward II would come to France to pay homage to him. Initially, Edward agreed, but he had changed his mind by the time he reached Dover, supposedly at the urgings of Hugh Despenser. He sent his son, Edward of Windsor, instead. It was at this point that Isabella began to seek support for an invasion of England. She travelled to the Low Countries and secured this support from William, count of Hainault, on the agreement that Prince Edward would marry William's daughter, Philippa. It was around this time that Isabella became involved with the exiled English knight, Roger Mortimer. By January 1327, Isabella and Mortimer, with the help of William of Hainault's brother John, succeeded in leading a coup against Edward II, gaining control of government and initiating the deposition of the king in favour of the young Prince Edward.

After their coup, Isabella and Mortimer had to consolidate and stabilize their control of the realm. In order to do this, they had to justify their actions, both political and extramarital. It has been argued that they did so through propaganda, which claimed that Edward might become violent towards Isabella if she returned to him and that Edward's favouritism towards Despenser had led to the deterioration of their marriage.[2] W. M. Ormrod has argued that another element may be added to Mortimer and Isabella's propaganda. He asserts that they perpetuated rumours that Edward II's relationships with his favourites were homosexual in nature in order to cast 'doubt on the heteronormativity of her marriage' to Edward II.[3] However, from 1308 to 1324 Isabella and Edward's marriage had fulfilled the functions a royal marriage was designed to and Isabella did her best to maintain this relationship. This study will demonstrate that they consciously exploited their relationship as husband and wife, king and queen, in an attempt to maintain their power, their authority and the integrity of the crown. The examination of Edward and Isabella's marriage reveals how fully reliant late medieval kings and queens were on each other. The nature of their relationship was truly symbiotic.

Contemporary evidence for interpreting Isabella and Edward's marriage as dysfunctional appears almost immediately after their marriage. These sources express criticism of Edward's attention to Gaveston. Yet it is striking that much of the criticism laid at Gaveston's door does not mention Isabella among those who felt neglected by the king, and the few that do are tainted by hindsight. A newsletter survives from the spring of 1308, which many scholars have used to support claims that a coalition consisting of Philip IV, Isabella and the barons had formed against Gaveston.[4] However, this letter never

---

[2] R. M. Haines, 'The Stamford Council of April 1327', *EHR* 127 (2007), 142, 144.
[3] W. M. Ormrod, 'The Sexualities of Edward II', in *The Reign of Edward II: New Perspectives*, ed. G. Dodd and A. Musson (York, 2006), p. 42.
[4] P. C. Doherty, 'Isabella, Queen of England, 1296–1330', University of Oxford PhD Thesis (1977), pp. 29–33; J. S. Hamilton, *Piers Gaveston, Earl of Cornwall, 1307–1312: Politics and*

actually mentions Isabella directly, or implies any mistreatment of her by Edward. It was the 'regina Regis defuncti' or the queen of the deceased king whom the letter directly connected with the earls of Lincoln and Pembroke.[5] Thus, only Queen Margaret, the consort of the late Edward I, is specifically implicated with those listed as part of this plot. It is Edward II's grant of Ponthieu and Montreuil to Isabella shortly after this letter was written that historians have used as evidence to connect Isabella with this coalition. The *Annales Paulini* include a description that a number of French magnates, including Louis of Evreux and Charles of Valois, Philip IV's brothers, cooperated with these opposition barons.[6] Thus, it is possible that Isabella may have been involved by association, but there is nothing directly connecting her with this coalition.

It was also in the spring of 1308 that the monks of Westminster Abbey cited Isabella as an opponent of Gaveston. In January 1308, Richard Kedyngton was elected as abbot of Westminster Abbey. A faction of the monks at Westminster resented his election because they believed that he had received this appointment unfairly through Gaveston's patronage. They believed that Isabella would support their plan to replace Kedyngton with their own candidate because of her purported hatred for Gaveston.[7] An enrolment of two letters that outline their plot survives in the Westminster Abbey Muniments, claiming that whatever hurt Gaveston 'the queen and earls, even the pope and cardinals and even the king of France desired'.[8] Katherine Allocco argues that these enrolled letters were a correspondence between Isabella and the monks.[9] However, this is not the case. These letters were not written to or by Isabella. They cannot be used as evidence that Isabella actually felt this way, only that she was perceived to have done so. The monks of Westminster may have manipulated rumours of Isabella's alleged animosity towards Gaveston to strengthen their complaints against him.

It is even more remarkable that the chronicles, for the most part, did not mention Isabella in their discussion of Edward and Gaveston.[10] The

---

Patronage in the Reign of Edward II (Detroit, 1988), p. 50. J. R. Maddicott, *Thomas of Lancaster, 1307–1322: A Study in the Reign of Edward II* (Oxford, 1970), pp. 82–6, 335–6.

5 St John, *Three Medieval Queens*, pp. 33–64.

6 *Annales Paulini*, in *Chronicles of the Reigns of Edward I and Edward II*, ed. W. Stubbs, 2 vols, RS 76 (London, 1882–83), i, 258.

7 Maddicott, *Thomas of Lancaster*, p. 89.

8 [Westminster Abbey Muniments] WAM 5460.

9 K. Allocco, 'Intercessor, Rebel, Regent: The Political Life of Isabella of France', University of Texas at Austin PhD Thesis (2004), p. 124.

10 *The Anonimalle Chronicle, 1307–1334: from the Brotherton Collection MS 29*, ed. W. Childs and J. Taylor (Leeds, 1991); *Gesta Edwardi de Carnarvan Auctore Canonico Bridlingtoniensi* [Bridlington Chronicle], in *Chronicles of the Reigns of Edward I and Edward II*, ed. W. Stubbs, ii; Geoffrey le Baker, *Chronicon Galfredi Le Baker De Swynebroke*, ed. E. M. Thompson (London, 1889); *Chronicon de Lanercost*, ed. Joseph Stevenson (Edinburgh, 1839); 'Annales Londonienses', in *Chronicles of the Reigns of Edward I and Edward II, Annales Paulini*; *Chroniques de London*, ed. G. J. Aungier, Camden Society, Old Series 28 (London, 1844);

Vita Edwardi Secundi, for example, makes assertions that Edward's love for Gaveston 'is said to have surpassed the love of women', but it does not clearly link their friendship to any particular harm done to Isabella.[11] The chroniclers who did believe that Isabella was in some way harmed by Edward's favouritism of Gaveston, mainly John de Trokelowe, Robert of Reading and Ranulph Higden, wrote after 1327 or 1330 and tended to be pro-baronial in tone. They used the events of 1308 to 1312 as a tool for foreshadowing and for building momentum in the narrative towards Isabella's coup in 1326. Trokelowe's *St Albans Chronicle* may have been written after the death of Edward II, perhaps as late as 1330. He claims that Isabella did not receive enough affection and includes accounts of Isabella's complaints to her father about Gaveston's status with the king.[12] Higden, writing sometime in or after 1327, claims that Edward neglected Isabella.[13] Robert of Reading's contribution to the *Flores Historiarum* is strongly opposed to Gaveston and in favour of Thomas of Lancaster. It includes a scene in which Isabella begs Edward not to follow Gaveston's counsel.[14] Reading wrote soon after the deposition and before 1330. He may have been writing at the behest of Isabella and Mortimer and there is strong evidence that his purpose was to justify the deposition of Edward II by creating the impression that Isabella's relationship with Edward was dysfunctional from the start.[15]

Hatred for Gaveston in general, whether justified or not, was widespread, and blaming him for the neglect of the queen could be a powerful attack, one which the monks at Westminster and later chroniclers utilized to their advantage. While this analysis of the newsletter from Philip IV discounts Isabella's direct involvement with any coalition against Gaveston, the chronicle evidence and the letters surrounding the Kedyngton affair do indicate that some contemporaries may have believed that Gaveston prevented Isabella from fulfilling some of her duties as queen and Isabella may even have believed this herself. However, a detailed examination of Isabella's actions indicates that despite any opinion to the contrary, she was able to fulfil the duties associated with the office of queenship successfully.

One of the major expectations of both kingship and queenship was the perpetuation of the dynasty. If Edward's relationship with Gaveston was

W. Dene, 'Historia Roffensis', in *Anglia Sacra*, 2 vols, ed. H. Wharton (London, 1691), i; *Adae Murimuth Continuatio Chronicarum; Robertus de Avesbury de Gestis Mirabilius Regis Edwardi Tertii*, ed. E. M. Thompson, RS 93 (London, 1889); *Vita Edwardi Secundi, The Life of Edward II*, ed. and trans. W. R. Childs (Oxford, 2005).

[11] *Vita Edwardi Secundi*, pp. 52–3.

[12] *Johannis de Trokelowe et Henrici de Blaneford Chronica et Annales*, ed. H. T. Riley, RS 28 (London, 1866); Antonia Gransden, *Historical Writing in England c. 1307 to the Early Sixteenth Century* (London, 1982), pp. 5–8.

[13] *Polychronicon Ranulphi Higden Monachi Cestrensis*, ed. C. Babington and J. R. Lumby, 9 vols, RS 41 (London, 1882), viii, 300–1; Gransden, *Historical Writing*, p. 44.

[14] *Flores Historiarum*, ed. H. R. Luard, 3 vols, RS 95, iii (London, 1890).

[15] Gransden, *Historical Writing*, pp. 17–23.

a homosexual one, it might have affected Isabella's access to the king's bed. However, Isabella's procreative functions were not impeded by any of Edward's possible extramarital sexual practices. Isabella and Edward actually spent a great deal of time together, or at least as much as can be expected for a king and queen with itinerant households. From Isabella's itinerary, we can see that she was with the king for significant periods of these early years, and Isabella's household accounts demonstrate that when the king and queen were not together they corresponded with each other.[16] There are also records of gifts exchanged, which may indicate actual affection, but could also be indicative of traditional practice between husband and wife.[17] Isabella gave birth to four children and when her itinerary can be reconstructed, it places her with Edward around the right time for conception. Prince Edward was born on 12 November 1312, John of Eltham was born on 15 August 1316, Eleanor was born on 18 June 1318, and Joan was born on 5 July 1321. There is no suggestion in the chronicles that any of Isabella's four children were not Edward's. Edward also had a bastard son named Adam.[18] Therefore, Edward had sex with women, though perhaps not exclusively.

It is true that Isabella did not have children while Gaveston lived, but Isabella's age at her marriage may provide an explanation for the lack of a sexual relationship with Edward prior to 1311. Isabella was about twelve when she married Edward and common Plantagenet practice was to consummate when the queen reached twelve and to begin conjugal relations at the age of fifteen.[19] Although the exact age of menarche is difficult to determine, it is likely that Isabella would not have been able to conceive during the first years of her marriage.[20] Thus, it was probably not Gaveston who prevented Isabella from sexual access to the king early in their marriage, but the queen's own age. Gaveston returned from his third exile in late December 1311 or early January 1312 and Prince Edward was probably conceived around the end of February 1312. Isabella would have been around fifteen or sixteen at this time. Isabella and Edward had probably only begun their sexual relationship when Gaveston returned from his exile, so their prior lack of children was not necessarily an indication of Edward's indifference or his preoccupa-

---

[16] Blackley and Hermensen, *Household Book of Queen Isabella*, pp. 208–9, 214–15, 216–17, 218–19, 220–1; E 101/375/9 fols 33, 33v, 34; E 101/375/19; E 101/376/20; SC 1/35/29.

[17] E 101/375/8 fols 8, 27, 27v.

[18] C. Given-Wilson and A. Curteis, *The Royal Bastards of Medieval England* (London, 1984), p. 136; C. T. Wood, 'Queens, Queans and Kingship', in *Joan of Arc and Richard III: Sex, Saints and Government in the Middle Ages*, ed. C. T. Wood (Oxford, 1988), pp. 12–28.

[19] J. C. Parsons, 'Mothers, Daughters, Marriage, Power: Some Plantagenet Evidence, 1150–1500', in *Medieval Queenship*, ed. J. C. Parsons (New York, 1998), pp. 63–78.

[20] Aline Horniday asserts that menarche occurred between the ages of fourteen and sixteen in the twelfth century, although she does not cite any authorities: A. G. Horniday, 'A Capetian Queen as Street Demonstrator: Isabelle of Hainaut', in *Capetian Women*, ed. K. Nolen (New York, 2003), p. 83.

tion with Gaveston. In fact, their first son was conceived even while Gaveston was present in the king's household.

Intercession was another official duty of queenship and one that required the general support of the king.[21] A thorough analysis of Isabella's intercessory activity between 1311 and 1321 demonstrates that she was able to undertake this official role of queenship. The only time she was unable to act as an intercessor was when Edward's royal prerogatives were challenged. It also allows us to see that Isabella was constantly protecting the king and in doing so maintaining their joint power. There were two ways in which a queen could practise intercession: she could petition the king verbally or she could approach the crown through formal and official petitionary channels. Verbal requests most often took place in private and there are very few records of these kinds of acts.[22] Part of this access included a sexual relationship with the king, which the queen could use (and was indeed sometimes urged to use) in order to influence him.[23] If Isabella took advantage of her uniquely close relationship with the king to secure his patronage for others, she had the opportunity to do so despite any other sexual relationships, homosexual or otherwise, that Edward may have had. However, Isabella's private verbal interactions with the king are generally not recorded, so we have no way of knowing whether or not Isabella was able to intercede with Edward himself at this time.

The closest method of reconstructing any verbal interactions the queens may have had is through chronicle accounts. However, using these accounts as strictly factual sources is problematic: first, while these accounts record verbal acts of intercession, the examples of intercession the chroniclers chose to record are still public performances, and so they do not represent any discussions that might have gone on in private settings; second, since intercession was categorically expected of the queen, the chroniclers may not have had any qualms about representing Isabella as a mediator in these events, even if she was not historically present. Evidence for Isabella's mediations between the barons and Edward comes from the *St Albans Chronicle*, the

---

[21] St John, *Three Medieval Queens*, p. 42.

[22] Ibid., pp. 35, 42, 51–7; Paul Strohm, *Hochon's Arrow: The Social Imagination of Fourteenth-Century Texts* (Princeton, 1992), p. 107.

[23] In the thirteenth century, Thomas of Chobham claimed 'that no priest is able to soften the heart of a man as is a woman … She should address her husband in the bedroom, coaxing him in the middle of his embraces and if he is, for example, a harsh, unmerciful oppressor of poor men she ought to encourage him to compassion' (author's translation): Thomas of Chobham, *Summa Confessorum*, ed. R. Broomfield (Paris, 1968), p. 375. Christine de Pizan advised her female readers that a wife should bring things to her husband's attention when they are alone together. Christine de Pizan, *The Treasure of the City of Ladies or the Book of the Three Virtues*, trans. Sarah Lawson (London, 1985), p. 64. J. C. Parsons, 'The Pregnant Queen as Counsellor and the Medieval Construction of Motherhood', in *Medieval Mothering*, ed. J. C. Parsons and B. Wheeler (New York, 1996), pp. 42, 45, 46, 52–5; J. C. Parsons, 'The Queen's Intercession in Thirteenth-Century England', in *Power of the Weak*, ed. J. Carpenter and S. Maclean (Urbana, Ill., 1995), p. 158.

Vita Edwardi Secundi and the *Annales Paulini*.[24] There is no direct external evidence to verify any of the accounts of Isabella's mediation on behalf of Edward and the barons as portrayed in these chronicles. The accuracy of chronicles is always debatable and their agendas must always be kept in mind, especially when they are the only source available. The most recent editor of the *Vita*, Wendy Childs, points out that much in the *Vita* has been confirmed by other sources, even if this particular incident is not, and Childs believes that the author was too politically aware and informed to be far from the centre of court. Scholars have differing opinions on the historicity of the *Annales Paulini*. Antonia Gransden cites a few examples of accounts in the *Annales* that may have truth to them, but H. G. Richardson presents a harsh view of the accuracy of the 1307 to 1308 portion of this text.[25] Likewise, the historical exactness of Trokelowe's *St Albans Chronicle* is problematic. This article has already pointed out that its construction and composition may very well be tainted by hindsight, yet the account of Isabella's mediation may have been derived from eyewitness accounts, since the papal envoys sent to aid in the mediation between Edward and the barons in 1313 to 1314 lodged at St Albans. These texts may reflect actual events, but they do so within the chronicler's personal agenda and indicate what the chronicler believed to be a categorical truth, not necessarily what modern readers would consider factual accuracy. Thus it is the historian's task to tease out the function of the queen's intercession in these sources, keeping in mind that it may reflect actual events, hearsay of these events, or the chronicler's perception of what could have happened.

The only method of quantifying the queen's intercession is through records of chancery issues that were dispensed at the request of the queen. These represent the outcome of a queen's petition to the chancellor, who acted in the interests of the crown. In these cases, the chancellor would release a chancery issue, which would have initiated an action to be taken on behalf of the queen. The issue would then be recorded on the chancery rolls. It is these records in the chancery rolls that represent the queen's successful acts of intercession; they are the only surviving documents recording actual intercessory activity performed successfully by fourteenth-century queens and they represent a second avenue for the queen's intercession, petitions to the crown as an institution.[26] The chancery records six acts of intercession in Isabella's first year as queen and four, six and five acts in 1309, 1310 and 1311, respectively.[27] However, in 1312, the year in which Gaveston was captured and

---

[24] *Trokelowe*, pp. 80–1; *Vita Edwardi Secundi*, pp. 152–3; *Annales Paulini*, p. 297.
[25] Gransden, *Historical Writing*, pp. 2–3, 6, 8–9, 22, 25–9; H. G. Richardson, 'The *Annales Paulini*', *Speculum* 23 (1948), 630–8.
[26] St John, *Three Medieval Queens*, pp. 9–12, 18, 20, 34–46, 50–1, 62–4, 65–94, 127–31, 134–8, 161–3, 165–9.
[27] *CPR 1307–13*, pp. 36, 138, 150, 177, 190, 208, 212, 311, 349, 378, 379, 393; *CCW 1244–1326*, pp. 37, 321; *CChR 1300–26*, p. 123.

executed, Isabella's recorded acts of intercession decline to only three acts of intercession.[28] It is true that these three acts of intercession occurred in the autumn and winter of 1312, after Gaveston's execution, potentially indicating that his return from exile hindered Isabella's access to Edward and that his death allowed her to intercede again. However, Isabella's lack of intercessory activity was not due to Edward's renewed attention to Gaveston, but rather to the enforcement of the Ordinances and the political crisis created by the flight of Edward, Isabella and Gaveston through the north of England. No matter how scholars view the strength of the late medieval queen's agency, they tend to agree that it in some way depended on the person of the king and/or the institution of the crown. In the event of a disruption to Edward's access to authority, or – worse – his capture or death, Isabella's own position of power would be compromised; this is exactly what occurred in 1311 and 1312.

In her unpublished PhD thesis on Isabella, Katherine Allocco claims that the queen was involved in the writing of the Ordinances because she corresponded with the Lords Ordainer, mainly the earls of Gloucester, Hereford, Warenne, Lancaster and Pembroke in 1311.[29] Yet the Ordinances weakened Isabella just as much as they did Edward, and so it is highly doubtful that she was involved in their orchestration. In general, anything that limited the king's prerogatives hurt the queen. Under the Ordinances, a temporary check was placed on the king's power to grant gifts, liberties and offices. His rights of issuing protections and pardons were also restricted, except in cases in which he could give grace.[30] All of these limitations on the king's power blocked one path to intercession for the queen. Isabella could only hope that those holding crown administrative offices – now under control of the baronage – would be amenable to her requests. This was not the case in the spring of 1312. By 1312 there were two rival governments: Edward's in the north and the Ordainers' government in the south. The Ordainers effectively controlled Westminster and the exchequer, and Edward controlled the chancery at York. Any attempts by Edward to exercise authority in the exchequer were ignored, and the chancery only issued writs with great caution as they waited for the outcome of this contest.[31] Attempts at verbal mediation with the king would have been futile, not because Edward disregarded them, but because he could only act on them as far as his limited authority in the north allowed. It was also likely that if the Ordainers closed their eyes to Edward's efforts at government, they also ignored any petitions that Isabella

---

[28] *CCR 1307–13*, p. 433; *CCW 1244–1326*, p. 148.

[29] Allocco, 'The Political Career of Isabella of France', p. 123; Blackley and Hermensen, *Household Book of Queen Isabella*, pp. 206–7, 208–9, 210–11, 214–13, 218–19.

[30] J. C. Davies, *The Baronial Opposition to Edward II* (Cambridge, 1918), pp. 368–82 for a discussion of the specific Ordinances.

[31] T. F. Tout, *The Place of the Reign of Edward II in English History* (Manchester, 1914), 97–9; T. F. Tout, *Chapters in the Administrative History of Medieval England*, 6 vols (Manchester, 1920–33), ii, 199.

sent directly to Westminster. Given the limitations the Ordinances placed on Isabella as well as the king, it is more likely that the correspondence between Isabella and the barons in 1311 cited by Allocco were attempts on Isabella's behalf to mitigate the anger of the earls and soften the blow of the Ordinances – though, in this instance, her efforts were in vain.

In 1313 Isabella's recorded number of intercessions rises again to eleven, then ten and nine in the subsequent two years.[32] This increase was representative of Edward's movements to stabilize his authority in reaction to Gaveston's execution, which in turn allowed Isabella to rebuild her intercessory power: first, Edward made sure that he could defend himself militarily, politically and diplomatically; second, Lancaster was away from court, estranged from the king and several of the other barons, breaking down any unified baronial opposition; third, at the end of 1312 a tentative peace treaty between Edward and the barons was negotiated, which, for the moment, did not mention the Ordinances, although it would be another year before it was fully realized; and finally Isabella gave birth to a son and heir, the future Edward III.[33]

During this period after the death of Gaveston, Isabella was drawn into the political conflicts between Edward and his barons in an effort to preserve the relationship upon which her status depended. Not only was there a significant rise in intercessory activity recorded on the chancery rolls, but the chronicles also provide descriptions of her intercession between Edward and the barons. In these chronicle accounts it is clear that she was trying to maintain an already functioning marriage, rather than hide a deeply dysfunctional one. Consequently, even though Edward's instability after Gaveston's execution allowed access to public politics, as Sophie Menache has pointed out, this insecurity was not a positive situation for the queen.[34] The author of the *St Albans Chronicle* describes Isabella's mediation between Edward and the barons following Gaveston's death. He claims that Isabella, Gilbert de Clare and the bishops convinced the earls to humble themselves before the king during parliament and to ask for mercy for the ways in which they had offended him.[35] It is revealing that Trokelowe's Isabella urges the earls to humble themselves before the king, thereby defending his interests rather than challenging his position against the barons.

Between 1315 and 1316 Thomas, earl of Lancaster, took control of the administration of government and this was as harmful to Isabella as it was to Edward II. Lancaster's enforcement of the Ordinances and his attempts

---

[32] *CCR 1307–13*, p. 4; *CPR 1307–13*, pp. 519, 522, 577, 579, 582; *CCR 1313–18*, p. 246; *CPR 1313–17*, pp. 80, 82, 119, 166, 169, 201, 223, 254, 305, 336, 352, 370; *CPR 1313–21*, p. 45; *CCW 1244–1326*, pp. 389, 406; *CFR 1307–19*, pp. 253, 255.

[33] Tout, *Chapters in Administrative History*, ii, 201.

[34] Sophie Menache, 'Isabella of France Queen of England: A Reconsideration', *JMH* 10 (1984), 109–10: Menache argues that it was positive.

[35] Trokelowe, pp. 80–1.

to regulate the king's household created the same situation for Isabella as in 1311 and 1312 when the Ordinances were first published.[36] It is no coincidence that the number of her acts of intercession dropped in 1316, and Paul Doherty has found evidence that her household revenues also declined under Lancaster.[37] By 1317, when Lancaster had removed himself from court because he could not control Edward as he wanted, Isabella's recorded acts of intercession climb to thirteen. It is during this time that Isabella is portrayed as a significant mediator between Edward and Lancaster by the chroniclers. The *Vita*'s description of Isabella's part in the negotiation of the Treaty of Leake (1318) is very concise, but it clearly shows a queen trying to ease the tensions between the king and his barons: 'the agreement between Edward and Lancaster was achieved at the request of the lady queen, the earl of Hereford, and other nobles whom the earl of Lancaster accounted faithful to him'.[38] This passage highlights not only Isabella's concern for the king and crown, but the strength of her influence with the crown's opponents.

By 1321 the barons faced another threat to their power, Edward's new favourite, Hugh Despenser. Again Isabella is portrayed as the actor, who brings stability to the crown, court and realm. Isabella's final act of mediation between Edward and the barons was during the call for Despenser's exile. The Pauline Annalist tells the reader that 'even the lady Isabella, queen of England, bowing on her knee and telling the king about the petitions of the lords and barons, interceded for the common people'.[39] In this depiction of mediation, she acts on behalf of the *populus*, indicating that she was the spokesperson for the people of England and for the leaders of the people – the earls – and thus for the realm, but she acts in a manner that recognizes the king's authority. This article will go on to demonstrate in detail that Isabella did not feel threatened by Despenser in 1321 any more than she had been by Gaveston. Instead, her plea for his exile was merely another attempt to prevent further interference in royal government by the barons because those were the times that proved to be most harmful to the collective power of the king and queen.

The administrative documents clearly show that Isabella was successful as a queenly intercessor and that the level of her success correlates directly with the king's stability. If the chronicle depictions of Isabella's mediations can be taken as historically accurate, they show a queen acting to preserve the stability of the king and crown by supporting the king, the nobles and the realm. In this way, she preserved royal authority while building her own strength and power. If they are not historically accurate, then it can be said that medieval writers perceived Isabella as acting in this manner. Isabella did

---

[36] Maddicott, *Thomas of Lancaster*, pp. 162–200.
[37] Doherty, 'Isabella, Queen of England', pp. 60–3.
[38] *Vita Edwardi Secundi*, 152–3.
[39] *Annales Paulini*, p. 297.

not support the Ordinances, nor did she advocate Gaveston's execution, nor was her request for Despenser's exile in retaliation against Edward. Instead she tried to create a harmonious environment in which the barons would not feel the need for such constraints upon royal authority.

In addition to securing grants through the king or chancellor, the queen's own landholdings were an important source of patronage for her. Another popular argument among historians for a dysfunctional relationship is that Edward was unable to provide sufficient dower for Isabella because of his heavy-handed grants to Gaveston.[40] The chronicle evidence and the French newsletter discussed above seem to support this interpretation. Nevertheless, while Edward's friendship with Gaveston may have intensified the problem, it was the possession by the dowager queen, Margaret of France, of the queen's customary dowerlands that was likely to have been the central cause of Isabella's dearth of land.

Scholars have demonstrated that queen consorts were traditionally assigned the same lands for their dower and that it was not unusual for a king to have difficulties providing for them.[41] In fact, Margaret was the first queen to hold her dower during her husband's lifetime and so it is no surprise that this custom, brand new during the reign of Edward II, created some problems for the new king when he married Isabella. Margaret lived as dowager queen for almost ten years after Isabella and Edward's marriage, holding lands that were needed to support the new consort. Several draft valors of Margaret and Isabella's dowerlands from July 1299 indicate that some attempt to remedy this situation was made under Edward I. In these draft valors, Margaret and Isabella each receive completely different land assignments.[42] However, the final dower granted to Margaret in September 1299 does not completely replicate the lands listed in the valor of July 1299. Many of the lands that had been proposed for Isabella in July were actually assigned to Margaret in September; for example, Leeds Castle, the manors of Ospring and Middleton, and the town of Hereford.[43] Thus there was some recognition early on that dowering both Margaret and Isabella would be problematic, and there seems to have been some attempt to provide separate dower assignments to each of

---

[40] Doherty, 'Isabella, Queen of England', p. 28; P. Doherty, *Isabella and the Strange Death of Edward II* (Oxford, 2003), p. 47; Haines, *Edward II*, p. 71: Haines claims that Philip IV withdrew his opposition to Gaveston when Edward granted Ponthieu and Montreuil to Isabella. Maddicott, *Thomas of Lancaster*, pp. 83–5; McKisack, *The Fourteenth Century*, pp. 7–9: McKisack believes Edward only granted Ponthieu and Montreuil to Isabella to hasten the return of Gaveston from exile; Chaplais, *Piers Gaveston*, p. 10: Chaplais argues that Edward 'took Isabella's welfare very much to heart'.

[41] H. Johnstone, 'The Queen's Household', in Tout, *Chapters in Administrative History*, v, 269; J. C. Parsons, *Eleanor of Castile: Queen and Society in Thirteenth-Century England* (London, 1995), pp. 69–81; Anne Crawford, 'The King's Burden: The Consequences of Royal Marriage in Fifteenth-Century England', in *Patronage, the Crown and the Provinces in Later Medieval England*, ed. R. Griffiths (Gloucester, 1981), pp. 41–2.

[42] E 142/4 mm. 1–2.

[43] *CPR 1292–1301*, p. 451.

them. Yet in the end, Edward I and his administration abandoned this possibility and simply passed on the problem to his son.

When Edward II became king and married Isabella, it quickly became clear to him that it would be in his best interest to settle Isabella's dower. The Treaty of Montreuil, under which his father's marriage to Margaret and his own marriage to Isabella had been arranged, contained a clause that stated that if Edward II were unable to provide Isabella with adequate dower from lands in England, he would assign English lands in France to Philip IV.[44] This may have been a ploy on Philip's part to absorb English lands in France back into the French crown, and it would certainly not have been to Edward's advantage to assign English lands in France to Philip IV.[45] Consequently, Edward did take steps to provide for Isabella early in their marriage. Edward had promised to assign Isabella half her dower in England and the other half in Ponthieu, Montreuil and Agen, and indeed letters patent were issued in May 1308 granting Isabella the whole of the lands of Ponthieu and Montreuil for her personal expenses.[46] Isabella used these lands as a source of patronage: the chancery rolls record grants and assignments made by Isabella from her lands in Ponthieu.[47] For example, in 1311 she granted, by her own letters patent, the custody of her castle of Corley to William de Bonneval.[48]

Edward continued to grant Isabella lands and income when he was able. In 1309 Edward granted Isabella the manor and hundred of Macclesfield (£175 8s), the manor of Overton (£126) and Rosfeyer (£170); in 1311 she received the manor of Eltham, and all the lands in Cray and Catford; in 1313 she received the manor and castle of High Peak (£291 13s), and the manors of Tropel and Upton (£100); in 1314 she received the manor of Maundeville; and in 1317 she received the shrievalty, castles, towns, manors, lands and tenements in Cornwall (£1,094 1s 4d) and the manors of Wallingford and Walery (£300).[49] In augmentation of these crown grants, Edward granted Isabella the minority of Thomas Wake and the minority and marriage of John Bohun.[50] It is not possible to value all of the lands Isabella held in dower prior to Margaret's death, but from the landholdings for which an approximate value can be determined, she held upwards of £2,256 by the time Cornwall was granted to her in 1317.[51] If the counties of Ponthieu and

[44] *Foedera* I, 904–7.
[45] Doherty, *Isabella of France*, pp. 10–11.
[46] Ibid., p. 26; *Foedera*, II, i, 44; *CPR 1307–13*, p. 74.
[47] *CPR 1307–13*, pp. 134, 323, 359, 362.
[48] *CPR 1307–13*, p. 323.
[49] *CPR 1307–13*, p. 101; *CPR 1307–1313*, p. 398; *CCR 1313–18*, p. 144; *CPR 1313–17*, p. 641; *CPR 1313–17*, p. 668, *CPR 1317–21*, pp. 8–9. *CPR 1313–17*, p. 111: Margaret held Leeds at this time and it seems, from the entry on the patent roll and the original letter patent, that Isabella was meant to receive Leeds Castle after Margaret's death, but not before.
[50] *CPR 1307–13*, pp. 330, 398.
[51] *CPR 1317–21*, pp. 5, 8–9; B. P. Wolffe, *The Royal Demesne in English History: The Crown Estate in the Governance of the Realm from the Conquest to 1509* (London, 1971), pp. 230–9.

Montreuil, the minorities of John Bohun and Thomas Wake, and the other unvalued manors and lands are added to this inventory, her total estimated landed value must have been approaching the customary £4,500.

It is true that some of the lands that Isabella received during this period had been held by Gaveston. Nevertheless, Edward did not grant these lands and incomes to her immediately, which shows that while these lands were eventually used to augment Isabella's dower, Edward was not directly taking from his queen to endow his favourite. Gaveston had held the manors of Torpel, Upton and High Peak, and the minority of Thomas Wake, as well as the honour of Wallingford and the earldom of Cornwall.[52] Gaveston surrendered the manors of High Peak, Torpel and Upton in August 1309 and Isabella did not receive them until 1313.[53] High Peak was considered part of the traditional queen's dowerlands; it had made up a portion of the dower of Eleanor of Castile, Edward I's first wife.[54] Thus, in this case it may be said that Edward had dipped into the queen's rightful dower in the same way that he may have given lands intended for his half-brother to Gaveston.

The status of Torpel and Upton as dowerlands is unclear during the early fourteenth century. These manors were 'acquired' by Eleanor of Castile in 1280. Until Edward I dowered Margaret of France during his own lifetime, the queen only received her dower at the king's death. In order to compensate Eleanor, Edward I encouraged her to purchase land until she could have her dower.[55] As a result, Torpel and Upton may not have been considered part of the queen's traditional dower. Although they were initially among the lands listed in the July 1299 draft valor of Isabella's dower, they were not among those given to Margaret in September 1299. Their ambiguous status might explain why they were not included in Margaret's dower, why they were then given to Gaveston, and why they were not immediately granted to either queen at Gaveston's death. Likewise, Gaveston surrendered the minority of Thomas Wake in December 1309 and William Trent held the minority throughout 1310 until it was granted to Isabella in 1311.[56] Gaveston was executed in 1312, but Isabella did not receive Wallingford or the county of Cornwall until 1317.[57] This may have partly been due to the fact that Gaveston's widow, Margaret de Clare, held a significant portion of the county of Cornwall in 1316.[58] Torpel, Upton, Wallingford, Cornwall and the minority of Thomas Wake were not part of the initial 1299 valor, nor do they fall under Eleanor of Castile's grants of lands, acquisitions or dower. In his attempt to provide for his wife while his stepmother still lived, Edward saw the avail-

---

[52] Hamilton, *Piers Gaveston*, p. 37.
[53] Ibid., pp. 37, 53, 75.
[54] Parsons, *Eleanor of Castile*, pp. 164, 184; E 142/4 m. 2.
[55] Parsons, *Eleanor of Castile*, p. 123.
[56] *CPR 1307–13*, pp. 218–19.
[57] Cornwall was taken into the king's hands from 1312 to 1317: *CIPM 1316–27*, no. 85, 62.
[58] *CPR 1313–17*, pp. 576–9; Hamilton, *Piers Gaveston*, p. 100.

ability of these lands and income as opportunities to further enhance those lands he had already granted to his consort. With the possible exception of High Peak, this was not a case of Edward returning lands to Isabella that made up the queen's traditional dower but which he had granted to Gaveston.

Edward's patronage of Gaveston may have indirectly exacerbated his inability to dower Isabella, but it was not the primary factor. Edward did his best to solve the conundrum, inherited from his father, but it is clear that he was waiting for Margaret's death to release land for Isabella's maintenance. Margaret died on 14 February 1318. Between February and October 1318, Isabella received the bulk of her dowerlands, of which about three-quarters had been held by Margaret, as well as reconfirmation of those lands already assigned to her.[59] Further evidence that Edward II had been waiting for Margaret's death to complete Isabella's dower assignment can be found in a chancery issue, which states 'assignment of dower to queen Isabella *in fulfil-ment* of the arrangement made, under the supervision of Pope Boniface VIII, between Philip, then king of France, her father, and king Edward I for her marriage to his son Edward, the king that now is, to the value of £4,500'.[60] In other words, Margaret's death allowed Edward to *fulfil* his obligations to dower his wife. Strikingly, among those lands that were reconfirmed in 1318 was the county of Cornwall in addition to the shrievalty. This was done only months after the crown denied Hugh de Audley's petition for the entire earldom, which he claimed through his wife, Gaveston's widow, Margaret de Clare.[61] Despite Edward's overpowering love for Gaveston, Isabella and Edward had a normative royal marriage in all aspects. They had children together, Edward found the means to provide for her household, and she was both able and encouraged to partake in the intercessory culture of the period. Isabella actively worked to maintain the integrity of the crown and thereby her own stability.

The maintenance of a cooperative relationship was also beneficial for the king. Not only did Isabella's ability and desire to mediate between the king and the barons work in Edward's favour, but he was also able to exploit his queen's status as a widely acknowledged representative of the crown. Since Isabella's diplomatic missions have been covered elsewhere, this study will not go into great detail about the way in which Edward took advantage of Isabella's natal ties during negotiations with France in 1314 and 1320.[62] Instead it will focus on two domestic examples, the 1317 election of the bishop of Durham and the Leeds Castle incident of 1321. In 1317 Edward supported Isabella's candidate to the bishopric of Durham as a means of demonstrating

---

59 E 42/544; E 159/93 m. 96; *CPR 1317–1321*, pp. 108, 115–16, 453.
60 *CPR 1317–21*, p. 115 (italics added).
61 *CPR 1317–21*, p. 233, Hamilton, *Piers Gaveston*, pp. 100–1; J. R. S. Phillips, *Edward II* (New Haven and London, 2010), pp. 335, 338.
62 St John, *Three Medieval Queens*, pp. 33–4, 59–60, 62–3.

his royal power to his detractors. Bishop Richard Kellawe had died on 9 October 1316. As his replacement, the cathedral priory monks put forward the prior of Finchale, Henry Stamford, while the king proposed Thomas Carleton, a clerk of the secret seal, and Thomas of Lancaster supported John Kynardsey. Queen Isabella recommended her kinsman, Louis de Beaumont, the brother of Henry de Beaumont, earl of Buchan and Isabella de Vescy, both of whom had been removed from court by the Ordinances. Edward switched his support to his queen's candidate, Beaumont, and referred the matter to the decision of Pope John XXII, who agreed to quash the monks' election, and elevated Beaumont to the see on 9 February 1317. By shifting his support to a member of the Beaumont family, Edward signalled to Lancaster that he would continue to support the Beaumonts despite the Ordinances' order for them to be removed from royal favour. Because Louis was Isabella's candidate, Edward could simultaneously put Lancaster in his place and also deny this as his true motive. It seemed that the monks of Durham picked up on this subtlety when they made Isabella the scapegoat in their version of the event. In their *Historia Dunelmensis*, the monks claim that Isabella told the king that if he loved her he would make Louis de Beaumont the bishop of Durham, and at this 'the king was so conquered by her prayers that he wrote to the curia on behalf of Louis'.[63] The monks described Edward as having been 'incantatus per Regina', evoking the negative stereotypes of queens with too much power. By manipulating queenly stereotypes and his queen's allegiance to the Beaumonts in this fashion, Edward was able to make what could be argued was a sophisticated political play. Without Isabella's initial proposal of Beaumont as bishop of Durham, Edward would not have been able to develop this strategy.

The Leeds Castle incident of 1321 is a prime example of the case that Edward and Isabella viewed their cooperative relationship as mutually beneficial and of how they manipulated that relationship. During the Leeds Castle episode Edward exploited his relationship with Isabella both as husband and wife and as king and queen, as well as the connections she had established with the barons during her previous mediations. By the autumn of 1321 Thomas of Lancaster and the Marcher lords had left court in protest at Edward's rising favourites. Bartholomew Badlesmere, who had hitherto been a firm supporter of Edward, also left court and allied himself with Lancaster and the other rebel barons.[64] In October 1321 Isabella, on her way to Canterbury, demanded entrance into Leeds Castle, which was controlled by Bartholomew Badlesmere. Margaret Umfraville, Badlesmere's wife, held the castle in her husband's absence and refused Isabella entrance. Allegedly skirmishes broke out between Isabella's servants and the castle garrison. Badlesmere sent reinforcements to Leeds to defend it, and in response Edward besieged the castle.

---

[63] *Historiae Dunelmensis Scriptores Tres*, ed. J. Raine, Surtees Society 9 (London, 1839), p. 98.

[64] Haines, *Edward II*, pp. 132–3; Maddicott, *Thomas of Lancaster*, pp. 293–4.

It fell at the end of October 1321. The incident was a slight to Isabella and by extension the king and intensified the friction between Edward and the rebel barons. It set the stage for civil war.

The motivations behind both Badlesmere's and Edward's actions as well as the extent to which Edward premeditated the entire incident to draw the rebel barons into open hostilities have been debated. Scholars agree that it was the refusal of Badlesmere's wife to allow Isabella entrance to the castle that provided Edward with the justification for the attack. However, only a few historians have examined the incentive for Isabella to participate and, with the exception of Paul Doherty, these attempts have been cursory.[65] Sophia Menache claims that despite assertions that Isabella wanted her honour to be avenged, the attack on Leeds Castle was in Edward's best interest, not Isabella's. Haines implies that Isabella might have been angry because Leeds Castle ought to have been part of her dower, but went to Badlesmere instead. Katherine Allocco argues that Isabella was being used in a larger political scheme by the barons to send a message to Edward II. Doherty's treatment of the subject offers the most in-depth discussion. According to Doherty, Isabella actively participated in a plan that Edward and Despenser devised to punish the barons for Despenser's exile, in order to keep peace in the realm and because her fortunes lay with the king. Still, Doherty does not take this idea any further. He does not explore what Isabella had to gain and why she still felt as if her fortunes lay with the king. Ironically, the Leeds Castle incident allowed Edward to provoke a civil war, which he would win, thereby initiating a period of 'tyranny' and Isabella's decline in political influence.[66]

Nevertheless, Isabella had much to gain from participating in such a plan. In 1321 Isabella's position seemed stable: she had held her full dower grant for three years and doubtless believed that Despenser was no more of a threat to her than Gaveston had been, even if Despenser were eventually to return. Yet despite Despenser's exile, there was still a group of nobles who had withdrawn from court, and Isabella's previous experience had shown her that this baronial hostility was the greatest threat to the crown's strength. The peace of the realm alone was not her chief concern. Under the Ordinances in 1311, 1312 and 1316 Isabella had learned that an unstable king meant instability for her as well. The demise of the rebel barons might end the political factions, and her own position at court would be stabilized. Edward, in turn, saw the queen as the appropriate person to provoke Badlesmere. The *Annales Paulini*

---

[65] Haines, *Edward II*, p. 132; Maddicott, *Thomas of Lancaster*, p. 33; Tout, *Edward II*, p. 133; McKisack, *The Fourteenth Century*, p. 64; Davis, *Baronial Opposition*, p. 106; N. Fryde, *The Tyranny and Fall of Edward II, 1321–1326* (Cambridge, 1979), pp. 50–1; Doherty, 'Isabella, Queen of England', pp. 81–5; Menache, 'Isabella of France', pp. 108–10; Allocco, 'The Political Life of Isabella of France', pp. 154–5.

[66] Simon J. Harris, 'Petitioning in the Last Years of Edward II and the First Years of Edward III', in *Medieval Petitions: Grace and Grievance*, ed. W. M. Ormrod, G. Dodd and A. Musson (York, 2009), pp. 173–92.

assert that the insult to the queen inspired a huge response to the king's summons, and men who had been Badlesmere's closest allies joined the king against him. If this is true, then the insult against the queen was a unifying factor for the court factions.[67] The king recognized this unifying power that the queen possessed as a result of her previous acts of intercession with the barons and he exploited it.

Isabella and Edward worked together for a common purpose. Prior to 1322 not only did they actually have a functional, normative relationship, but they both actively worked to maintain and exploit it for their mutual benefit. Nevertheless, their relationship did deteriorate. For Isabella's volte-face we must turn to her ambassadorial mission to France in 1325, when it became obvious to her that Hugh Despenser created an entirely different situation than Gaveston had presented.[68] Hindsight has allowed later medieval and modern historians to see that 'the younger Despenser controlled royal patronage and policy in a way Gaveston never imagined', but as the Leeds Castle incident has demonstrated, Isabella may not have been completely aware of this. Gaveston had not been a hindrance to her ability to exercise queenship, and perhaps she viewed Despenser as another Gaveston, an annoyance to be endured.[69] Edward's seizure of Isabella's lands and estates in September 1324 has always been pointed to as a sign of Edward's alienation from her and often viewed as a major source of her hatred of Despenser; undoubtedly it gave her some idea of Despenser's power over Edward, but I would argue that it was not the final straw. However, only four months later preparations were made for her ambassadorial mission to France, indicating to Isabella that, despite Edward's predilection for Despenser, the king still viewed her as an integral part of the crown. Edward sent Isabella because Charles IV communicated that if Edward did so, Charles would agree to a peace.[70] There was no preconceived plan on the part of Isabella for rebellion, nor any plot concocted by Charles, the exiled barons or papal envoys.[71] Both

---

[67] *Annales Paulini*, pp. 298–9; Menache, 'Isabella of France', p. 110; Tout, *Edward II*, pp. 132–3.

[68] Hamilton, *Piers Gaveston*, pp. 38, 139–40; Chaplais, *Piers Gaveston*, pp. 99–104; Phillips, *Edward II*, p. 367.

[69] Hamilton, *Piers Gaveston*, p. 12.

[70] Haines, *Edward II*, p. 324, refers to a letter in which Edward writes to the pope recounting that the king of France has told him he would agree to a peace if Edward sent Isabella to France. Haines does not cite a reference for this letter, so it is not clear if this letter still survives or if it is recorded in the chronicles that Haines then goes on to evaluate.

[71] Fryde, *Tyranny and Fall of Edward II*, p. 147, argues that there is no reason to assume that Isabella went to France to join Roger Mortimer, but she believes that Isabella had some ulterior motive for going to France. Doherty, 'Isabella, Queen of England', pp. 109, 113, believes that it was a 'ruse', concocted by the papal envoys and Charles, so she could flee Despenser and regain her position and status through a successful diplomatic mission. F. D. Blackley, 'Isabella and the Bishop of Exeter', in *Essays in Medieval History Presented to Bertie Wilkinson*, ed. T. A. Sanquist and M. R. Powicke (Toronto, 1968), p. 235, argues that while Isabella may have been dissatisfied with her treatment in England, she was not in league with her husband's enemies. Haines, *Edward II*, p. 325 does not believe that the 'outcome' of the trip was planned because that would have meant that everyone in England was blind to the possible dangers of sending Isabella to England.

kings were aware of the influence Isabella had as the wife of one king and
the sister of the other, and were hoping to duplicate the success of Isabella's
negotiations in 1314.[72] This demonstrated to Isabella that Edward still relied
on her, and consequently she believed that Despenser's tyranny would be
temporary.

However, by the summer of 1325 it became clear to Isabella that her relationship with Edward had been fractured: Edward failed to re-establish her
landed estates and to uphold his end of the treaty she had worked so hard to
broker. The negotiations between England and France in the spring of 1325
were difficult and lengthy and it seems that Edward's presence was one of
the key components to the settlement. Charles IV was to keep Aquitaine until
he received Edward's homage on 15 August and it was agreed that if either
king were unable to make the meeting in Beauvais, they would immediately inform the other.[73] According to the Rochester Chronicle, the question
arose at the English parliament in June as to whether or not Edward should
renounce his proxies (Isabella being one of them), thereby rendering the
treaty they had made null and void, or travel to France and pay the homage.
It was decided that he must go.[74] In the end, of course, Edward, fearing for
his safety or at least fearing the trustworthiness of the French, sent his son
instead, an arrangement to which Charles IV agreed.

Prince Edward, who had been accompanied to France by Walter Stapeldon,
bishop of Exeter and John Stratford, bishop of Winchester, paid homage to
the French king in September 1325. In October 1325 Stapeldon and Isabella
had a disagreement, which caused his hurried departure to England. This
quarrel made it apparent to Isabella that she no longer benefited from her
relationship with Edward. It had been important that Isabella arrived in
France with a well-financed household because it was also a way for the
king to show his might and power.[75] Before her departure for France, her
treasurer was given £1,000 for her expenses and permission to borrow more
from the Bardi in Paris.[76] However, Edward did not return the estates he
had taken from her in 1324 and it should be noted that her allowance from
the exchequer prior to her visit to France was £1,000. Thus the only thing
that she gained in February 1325 was permission to borrow from the Bardi.
One surviving letter from October 1325 from Isabella to Stapeldon after his
return to England expressed her irritation that he departed without leaving
the money that he had been charged to give her.[77] When Stapeldon arrived
in France with monies, it must have been clear to her that she was not going

---

[72] St John, *Three Medieval Queens*, pp. 59–60.
[73] *Foedera*, II, i, 601–2.
[74] Haines, *Edward II*, p. 327; Pierre Chaplais, *The War of Saint-Sardos*, Camden Third Series 87
       (London, 1954), pp. 277–8.
[75] St John, *Three Medieval Queens*, p. 79.
[76] Blackley, 'Isabella and the Bishop of Exeter', p. 228.
[77] SC 1/49/118.

to regain her estates. A monetary allowance was not the same as having control of lands from which she could dispense patronage. Isabella may have expected to regain her estates now that a settlement with France had theoretically been achieved. Edward had claimed that that Isabella's French origins made her a liability during the war of St Sardos when he confiscated her lands in 1324.[78] Of course, Isabella was not the only target of Edward's policies against the French in England: Edward had ordered that 'all French persons living within the realm of England, including members of the households of the king or the queen consort, be taken and their lands and goods and chattels seized into the king's hands'.[79] However, Isabella's success in France once again proved her allegiance to and place within the crown of England, as it had in 1314 and in 1320. She may have believed that her success would ensure that she should no longer be considered a liability and Edward would restore her estates. It was not Isabella's financial loss that made Edward's seizure of her estates without a quid pro quo transaction so detrimental to her ability to practise queenship. It was the loss of her ability to use her estates to dispense patronage through appointments and to attract a retinue, in essence to act in the same manner as a male magnate, that was so damaging to her agency.[80] Edward II had stripped Isabella of an important source of power and authority and now it was clear that he would not return it.[81]

The impact on Isabella of Edward's sudden refusal to come to France to pay homage to Charles IV must also be considered in Isabella's final break with Edward. If the rumours that Despenser was behind the king's failure to pay homage in person reached Isabella, these rumours, in combination with the realization that she would not receive her estates, must have been the ultimate sign to Isabella that Despenser had supplanted her in a way that Gaveston never had.[82] It seems likely that Stapeldon himself relayed Despenser's involvement to Isabella. In December 1328 Edward II sent a letter to Isabella addressing each of her grievances, which he claims to have learned about when John Stratford returned to England with her letters.[83] The greater part of the letter describes his incredulity that she should fear Despenser and says that she should return to England immediately. He also makes a vague promise as to her income or estates: 'as to her expenses, the king will, when she has returned to him as a wife ought to do to her husband, ordain so that she shall have no lack of things appertaining to her, whereby neither the king nor she may be dishonoured in any wise'.[84] Edward merely states that she shall have 'no lack of things appertaining to her', which could

---

78 *CCR 1323–27*, p. 223; *CFR 1319–27*, pp. 300–1.
79 C 61/36, m. 24d.
80 St John, *Three Medieval Queens*, pp. 72–92.
81 Ibid., pp. 88–9.
82 Rumours are recorded in *Murimuth*, p. 44 and *Vita Edwardi Secundi*, pp. 234–5.
83 *CCR 1323–27*, p. 580; Blackley, 'Isabella and the Bishop of Exeter', p. 232.
84 *CCR 1323–27*, p. 580.

imply her dower since a queen's dower pertains to her, but the promise is not specific. This letter was clearly written to address the grievances Isabella outlined in the letters she sent to Edward via Stratford. I would therefore argue that Isabella and Stapeldon quarrelled over the money that he brought for her and over Despenser's involvement in Edward's decision not to come to France. After Stapeldon's departure, Isabella wrote letters to the king expressing her complaints, which Stratford delivered.

Edward made some attempt to maintain their relationship into the winter of 1326: despite Isabella's adamant refusals to return to England, Edward continued to issue letters of protection for her men until February 1326 and he sent further letters to Prince Edward and Charles IV, urging her return.[85] However, it was also at this time that Edward realized that Isabella had begun to 'take the counsel' of his enemies. Edward mentioned that Isabella was 'adopting the counsel of Roger Mortimer', his 'notorious enemy and rebel', in a letter to the sheriff of Northampton in February 1326.[86] In March 1326 Edward also ordered the arrest of John of Brittany, who was with Isabella and likewise refused to return home, and in June he seized Brittany's lands.[87] In his letter to Isabella in December 1325, Edward had warned her against 'transgress[ing] the king's commands'. In his letter to his son in March 1326, he made several mentions that Isabella's duty was to love and maintain the estate of the king's crown and that she had not conducted herself towards the king, as her lord, as she ought to have done.[88] For Edward, the final break in his relationship with Isabella occurred when it became clear to him that she no longer behaved in a manner that recognized his authority.

It had been in both Isabella's and Edward's interests to guarantee that their relationship functioned, and at the beginning it did. Edward ensured that Isabella was able to perform all the necessary duties associated with her office because it benefited him to do so. While a cooperative marriage was advantageous for Edward, it was a necessity for Isabella. Her very status relied on the king and his ability to rule effectively. She continued to ally herself with the king in order to maintain her greatest source of power. This interdependent relationship reveals itself so strikingly in this specific royal alliance because of the political turmoil of the early fourteenth century. Likewise, the breakdown of this relationship also demonstrates how integral the queen was to the crown. Edward's refusal to pay homage to Charles IV was an implicit rejection of Isabella's efforts on the crown's behalf. Her invasion and coup in the autumn of 1326 was swift and met with very little opposition. It was so successful precisely because it was the queen who was leading the invasion, or was at least its figurehead. If a queen who had fought so hard

[85] *CPR 1324–27*, pp. 178, 180, 185, 213; *CCR 1323–27*, pp. 578–9.
[86] *CCR 1323–27*, p. 543.
[87] *CCR 1323–27*, p. 552; Blackley, 'Isabella and the Bishop of Exeter', p. 234.
[88] *CCR 1323–27*, pp. 578–9.

to maintain the king and the institution of the crown, of which she was an integral part, was the leader of this open rebellion, it must have signalled to contemporaries that the crown was fractured and damaged as a result of the king's political incompetence. It was for this reason that supporters flocked to her cause. Nonetheless, despite the political crises that plagued most of their marriage, until 1326 Edward and Isabella's relationship was conventional for a king and queen. Isabella was able to fulfil her duties as a queen and wife, and Edward was able to fulfil his duties as a royal husband.

THE FIRST ENTRY OF THE BISHOP: EPISCOPAL *ADVENTUS* IN FOURTEENTH-CENTURY ENGLAND

Katherine Harvey

In August 1310, Walter Reynolds wrote a short letter to John de Wyke, prior of Worcester. Reynolds had recently been appointed chancellor of England, but his letter did not relate to royal business; rather, he was writing in his capacity as bishop of Worcester. His enthronement as bishop, he wrote, had been long delayed, and he was now anxious to remedy this; within a fortnight, he wrote again, this time to fix the date for his installation.[1] The ceremony, which finally took place in late September 1310, was essentially a ritual in three stages: the first was the bishop's entry into his cathedral city, the second the service of enthronement in the cathedral church, and the third the celebrations which followed. Together these rituals formed the final stage of the bishop-making process, the culmination of months or even years of discussions, disputes and ceremonies, and the only stage of this process not to be tightly controlled by the demands of canon law.[2] This paper will explore the nature and significance of these ceremonies, as they were conducted and understood in England during the long fourteenth century.

The preparations for the enthronement of a new bishop were set in train when he despatched a letter to the dean or prior of his cathedral, in which he announced his intention to be enthroned. The bishop and the cathedral chapter first had to agree when the ceremony would take place; usually, but not always, the service would be held on a Sunday.[3] Whilst its obvious religious significance made Sunday a fitting day for the installation of a bishop, more pragmatic concerns were also taken into consideration. In the 1430s, Prior Wessington encouraged Robert Neville of Durham to be enthroned at

---

[1] *Liber Albus*, fol. 45d, nos 502–3. For Reynolds' career, see J. Wright, *The Church and the English Crown, 1305–1334: A Study based on the Register of Archbishop Walter Reynolds* (Toronto, 1980).

[2] K. Harvey, *Episcopal Appointments in England, c. 1214–c. 1344: From King John's Freedom of Election Charter to Papal Provision* (Farnham, 2014); Véronique Julerot, 'La première entrée de l'évêque: réflexions sur son origine', *Revue historique* 338 (2006), 635–6.

[3] The dates of the enthronements of the English bishops of this period (where known) are included in J. le Neve *et al.*, *Fasti Ecclesiae Anglicanae 1066–1300*, 11 vols (London, 1968–) and *Fasti Ecclesiae Anglicanae 1300–1541*, 12 vols (London, 1962–65). Of the forty-eight dated enthronements held between 1300 and 1400, thirty took place on a Sunday, seven on a Monday, one on a Tuesday, none on a Wednesday, four on a Thursday, two on a Friday and four on a Saturday. Sunday was also the most popular day for enthronements in fifteenth-century France: see Julerot, 'La première entrée', p. 644.

Christmas, pointing out that he would save money by combining his enthronement with the major feast of the year.[4] It is probably no coincidence that at
least eight fourteenth-century bishops made their first entry on one of the
great Marian feasts,[5] whilst three others were enthroned during Holy Week.[6]
Attendance was also an issue: the schedules of important guests were taken
into consideration, and one of the benefits of Sundays and religious festivals
must surely have been that if the masses were not at work, there was no good
reason why they should not come to welcome their new bishop.[7]

Once the date had been set, there were many further preparations to be
made. Invitations had to be issued to important guests,[8] and preparations
made for their arrival. Chief amongst these preparations was the assembly of
large amounts of food and drink. Most of the provisions were sourced from
the episcopal manors (when William Raleigh was enthroned at Winchester in
November 1244, grain, game and stock were sent from virtually every manor
on the Winchester estate),[9] but these might be supplemented by the purchase
of extra supplies,[10] and by gifts.[11] Guests might also contribute: when John
Pecham summoned the bishops of his province to his enthronement as archbishop of Canterbury in 1279, he requested that they send the traditional
presents of venison and game for the enthronement feast.[12] It might also be
necessary to make repairs to the episcopal residence: before John Sandale
arrived at Winchester in 1317, three workmen were employed for three weeks
to repair the gutters and roof of Wolvesey Castle, and further payments were
made 'for cleaning the Hall, chambers, kitchen and other buildings'.[13]

---

4   R. B. Dobson, *Durham Priory, 1400–1450* (Cambridge, 1973), p. 228.
5   The eight were William de la Zouche (York, 1342); John Thoresby (York, 1354); Simon Langham
    (Canterbury, 1367); John Barnet (Ely, 1367); John Waltham (Salisbury, 1388); Thomas Arundel
    (York, 1389); Richard Mitford (Salisbury, 1396); John Burghill (Coventry and Lichfield, 1398).
6   Wulstan Bransford (Worcester, Easter Sunday 1339); John Sheppey (Rochester, Maundy Thursday
    1353); Simon Sudbury (Canterbury, Palm Sunday 1376).
7   B. Harvey, 'Work and *Festa Ferianda* in Medieval England', *Journal of Ecclesiastical History*
    23 (1972), 289–306.
8   See, for example, Archbishop Pecham's request for Edward I to attend his enthronement in 1279:
    'Sire, sachez ke la feste de nostre entronizement sera ordene le second dimanche apres la seint
    Michel, u jeo ateng l'oneur de vostre presence, solum ceo ke vus m'avez premis, vostre merci.'
    Recueil de lettres anglo françaises, ed. F. J. Tanqueray (Paris, 1916), no. 21.
9   N. Vincent, 'The Politics of Church and State as Reflected in the Winchester Pipe Rolls, 1208–
    80', in *The Winchester Pipe Rolls and Medieval English Society*, ed. R. Britnell (Woodbridge,
    2002), p. 167.
10 See *The Register of John Pecham, Archbishop of Canterbury 1279–92*, ed. D. Douie, 2 vols, CYS
    64–5 (1968–69), i, 12–13 for a contract to purchase wine, oxen and other animals for Pecham's
    enthronement feast.
11 Lady Alicia de Neville sent Bishop Braybrooke of London a pipe of wine for his enthronement
    feast in January 1382. See M. Erler, *Women, Reading and Piety in Late Medieval England*
    (Cambridge, 2002), p. 53.
12 *Register of John Pecham*, i, 37–8.
13 *The Registers of John de Sandale and Rigaud de Asserio, Bishops of Winchester (A.D. 1316–
    1323)*, ed. F. J. Baignent, Hampshire Record Society 8 (London, 1897), p. xxxviii.

The bishop himself had to travel to his cathedral city. When he arrived, he would usually spend the night before his enthronement a short distance outside the city walls, either at one of the episcopal residences or at a local religious house. At Lincoln, for example, the bishop traditionally stayed at St Katherine's Priory, a short distance to the south of the city;[14] at Worcester, the early fourteenth-century bishops favoured the episcopal manor of Kempsey, nearly four miles from the cathedral.[15] Rising early in the morning,[16] the bishop would ride towards the city. Pausing outside the city gates closest to the cathedral (often at another religious house), he would dismount, remove his shoes, and from there process to the main door of the cathedral. At some stage on his procession (exactly where varied from diocese to diocese) he would be met by the prior and convent or dean and chapter, dressed in their processional copes, and the bells would be rung to announce his arrival.

When the bishop came to the cathedral door, the second stage of the ceremony began. In the early stages of the ceremony, before the actual enthronement took place, he would swear an oath of fidelity to respect and defend the rights and liberties of the cathedral church. From the door, two of the most senior chapter members (including either the abbot or dean, as appropriate) would lead him in procession to the high altar. Here the bishop prostrated himself, whilst a series of prayers were said. The bishop then rose, and was led to the episcopal throne, where he was formally enthroned. There were then more chants and prayers, before the bishop blessed the congregation. He then retired to the vestry, to prepare himself to celebrate mass. Mass having been said, the service of enthronement was complete, and the festivities could begin. The bishop and his guests would repair to the episcopal palace for the enthronement feast. The next two or three days were taken up with further celebrations, and with various matters of business relating to the installation.

There were, then, standard rituals of episcopal entry and enthronement in place in late medieval England; the above account of the installation process would certainly be recognized as such by a late medieval bishop. However, given that enthronement was the one stage of the bishop-making process which was not strictly controlled by detailed legal prescriptions, it was inevitable that each see would develop its own rituals and tradition. At Worcester,

---

[14] *Statutes of Lincoln Cathedral*, ed. H. Bradshaw, 3 vols (Cambridge, 1892–97), iii, 273.

[15] *The Register of the Diocese of Worcester during the Vacancy of the See, usually called Registrum Sede Vacante*, ed. J. W. W. Blund (Oxford, 1897), p. 52; *Liber Albus*, f. 45d, no. 504; a translation is included in *The Worcester Liber Albus*, ed. J. Wilson (London, 1920), pp. 100–2.

[16] This and the next paragraph are based on a combination of several cathedral *ordos* and statute books, each of which includes the order of service for the reception of a new bishop: *Lincoln Cathedral Statutes*, iii, 273–4; *Ceremonies and Processions of the Cathedral Church of Salisbury*, ed. C. Wordsworth (Cambridge, 1901), pp. 104–9; H. E. Reynolds, *Wells Cathedral: Its Foundation, Constitutional History and Statutes* (Leeds, 1881), pp. 91–2; *Registrum Statutorum et Consuetudinum Ecclesiae Cathedralis Sancti Pauli Londoniensis*, ed. W. S. Simpson (London, 1873), p. 11; *The Statutes of the Cathedral Church of Durham*, ed. A. H. Thompson (London, 1929), pp. 74–7.

for example, the prior and several of the monks went to Kempsey, nearly four miles outside the cathedral city, to escort the bishop on his procession.[17] At Salisbury, the dean and canons prepared for the bishop's arrival by performing the processions which were customarily made on a double feast, before meeting their new prelate at the great north gate of the cathedral close.[18] At Lincoln, the dean and chapter went no further than the western door of the cathedral,[19] and the prior and convent of Durham received their bishop at the north door.[20] Likewise, when English practices are compared with continental *adventus* rituals, many similarities are found: the *adventus*, procession and enthronement were repeated across Europe.[21] There are, however, some striking differences: the great Florentine celebrations, which included the symbolic marriage of the bishop to the abbess of San Pier Maggiore,[22] make English enthronements seem rather understated, whilst the bishop's oath to the cathedral, customary in England from the thirteenth century onwards, did not appear in Spain until the sixteenth century.[23]

Having established what happened when a bishop arrived in his cathedral city for the first time, we must now turn our attention to the significance and purpose of these events. Episcopal entry processions evoked a wide range of similar celebrations performed by a wide range of figures, from Jesus' entry into Jerusalem on Palm Sunday, to the triumphal processions of Roman emperors, and the entry processions frequently performed by medieval popes, emperors and kings.[24] There were also many historical precedents for

---

[17]	*Reg. Sede Vacante*, p. 52; *Liber Albus*, f. 45d, no. 504.

[18]	*Ceremonies and Processions*, p. 104.

[19]	*Lincoln Cathedral Statutes*, iii, 273.

[20]	*Durham Cathedral Statutes*, pp. 74–5.

[21]	See J. Tyler, *Lord of the Sacred City: Episcopus Exclusus in Late Medieval and Early Modern Germany* (Leiden, 1998), pp. 123–50; Julerot, 'La première entrée', pp. 635–75; J. Maciejewski, 'Nudo Pede Intrat Urbem: Research on the *Adventus* of a Medieval Bishop through the First Half of the Twelfth Century', *Viator* 41 (2010), 89–100.

[22]	The Florentine *adventus* rituals have been the subject of several papers: M. Miller, 'The Florentine Bishop's Ritual Entry and the Origins of the Medieval Episcopal *Adventus*', *Revue d'histoire ecclésiastique* 98 (2003), 5–28; M. Miller, 'Why the Bishop of Florence Had to Get Married', *Speculum* 81 (2006), 1055–91; M. Miller, 'Urban Space, Sacred Topography, and Ritual Meanings in Florence: The Route of the Bishop's Entry, c. 1200–1600', in *The Bishop Re-Formed: Studies in Episcopal Power and Culture in the Central Middle Ages*, ed. J. Ott and A. Trumbore-Jones (Farnham, 2006), pp. 237–49; S. Strocchia, 'When the Bishop Married the Abbess: Masculinity and Power in Florentine Episcopal Entry Rites, 1300–1600', *Gender & History* 19 (2007), 346–68.

[23]	Julerot, 'La Première entrée', p. 674.

[24]	The literature on these topics is too large to be listed in full. For Palm Sunday, see Matthew 21:1–11; Mark 11:1–11; Luke 19:28–44; John 12:12–19. On the late antique and early medieval evolution of the *adventus* ritual, see E. Kantorowicz, 'The King's Advent and the Enigmatic Panels in the Doors of Santa Sabina', *Art Bulletin* 26 (1944), 207–31; S. MacCormack, 'Change and Continuity in Late Antiquity: The Ceremony of *adventus*', *Historia* 21 (1972), 721–52; P. Buc, *The Dangers of Ritual: Between Early Medieval Texts and Social Scientific Theory* (Princeton, 2001), pp. 37–44. For papal *adventus* rituals, see Sible de Blauaw, 'Contrasts in Processional Liturgy: A Typology of Outdoor Processions in Twelfth-Century Rome', in *Art, cérémonial et liturgie au Moyen Age*, ed. N. Bock (Rome, 2002), pp. 357–94; S. Twyman, 'Papal *Adventus*

bishops making splendid public entrances into their domains, although early medieval episcopal entries differed from the late medieval *adventus* in at least two significant respects. The earlier period made little distinction made between the first entry into the cathedral city and other episcopal entries; furthermore, because early medieval bishops were typically consecrated in their own cathedral, the ceremonies of consecration and enthronement were often merged.[25]

During the course of the twelfth and thirteenth centuries, the ceremonies of *adventus* and enthronement took on a new significance. The first entry of the bishop was now clearly distinguished from other episcopal entries: the Black Book of Lincoln Cathedral, the Statute Book of St Paul's London, and the Durham Cathedral Statutes all state that the bishop should only be received in such a manner on his first entry. Subsequently, he would receive a rather more subdued welcome. At Lincoln, he had to be away from his diocese for at least a quarter of a year before the bells should be rung to announce his arrival, and even then there should be no procession; at Durham, the bishop's arrival would be granted for any formal arrival, but there would only be a procession if he came to make a visitation.[26] The significance of the first entry was enhanced by the fact that bishops were now consecrated away from their diocese, either at the metropolitan's cathedral, or increasingly at the papal curia. Consequently, the service of enthronement became firmly separated from the consecration.[27]

At the same time, enthronement became an increasingly necessary part of the bishop-making process. Archbishop Thomas Arundel of Canterbury (1399–1414) went so far as to claim that, without lawful enthronement, a bishop was effectively an intruder; he argued that unenthroned bishops 'cannot in any manner enter their cathedral churches or personally exercise episcopal authority in them'. Only once he was enthroned could the bishop take full control of his diocese, assume responsibility for its administration, and perform important tasks such as appointing episcopal officials and undertaking visitations within his diocese.[28] There is, however, little evidence to support Arundel's claims, which were almost certainly politically moti-

---

at Rome in the Twelfth Century', *Historical Research* 69 (1996), 234–53; S. Twyman, *Papal Ceremonial at Rome in the Twelfth Century* (Woodbridge, 2002). On royal entry ceremonies, see B. Guenée and F. Lehoux, *Les Entrées royales françaises de 1328 à 1515* (Paris, 1968); L. Bryant, *The King and the City in the Parisian Royal Entry Ceremony: Politics, Ritual and Art in the Renaissance* (Geneva, 1986); G. Kipling, *Enter the King: Theatre, Liturgy and Ritual in the Medieval Civic Triumph* (Oxford, 1998).

25 Miller, 'Florentine Bishop's Ritual Entry', pp. 10–15, which gives references to numerous early medieval episcopal entries.

26 *Lincoln Cathedral Statutes*, ii, 273–4; *Registrum Sancti Pauli*, p. 11; *Durham Cathedral Statutes*, pp. 74–5.

27 I. Churchill, *Canterbury Administration*, 2 vols (London, 1933), i, 273–5; Harvey, *Episcopal Appointments*, pp. 57–9, 144.

28 Churchill, *Canterbury Administration*, i, 278.

vated.[29] The canon law on this subject made clear that it was confirmation and consecration which made a bishop, and not the *possessio* or installation;[30] if enthronement was a legally significant process, it would surely have been better regulated. Furthermore, there is evidence to suggest that at least some bishops were involved in diocesan administration prior to their enthronement: Oliver Sutton of Lincoln (1280–99) examined candidates for benefices in his diocese following his consecration in May 1280,[31] and John Grandisson of Exeter (1327–69) also seems to have assumed episcopal duties immediately after his consecration.[32] Most striking of all is the case of Aymer de Lusignan of Winchester (1250–60), who was neither consecrated nor enthroned, but nevertheless appointed officials and exercised patronage.[33] However, none of this rules out the possibility that at least some medieval churchmen felt that one could not be a proper bishop without entering one's cathedral city, being enthroned, and thus taking 'corporal possession' of the cathedral and diocese.

Certainly most bishops were enthroned relatively quickly: in late medieval England, a bishop's enthronement usually took place within a few months of his consecration. This allowed sufficient time for the necessary arrangements to be made, and for the bishop to deal with any urgent business before travelling to his see.[34] However, some bishops delayed their first visit to their cathedral city for considerably longer; Walter Reynolds, for example, was enthroned almost two years after his consecration.[35] But such lengthy delays were frowned upon. Richard Clifford, consecrated as bishop of Worcester in October 1401, was enthroned in February 1403. Inviting the clergy of the diocese to attend his enthronement, he wrote that:

> He has been absent unwillingly and now the heavy necessity of ruling, together with gratitude for the liberality of all the clergy that he has experienced, and the law of seemliness especially, urge him to make haste to come nearer to those parts to see his fair spouse.[36]

---

29 Arundel's claims were made in the context of a dispute with John Trefor, bishop of St Asaph (1394–1410); Trefor supported the overthrow of Richard II, but quickly became disgruntled with the new regime. He joined Glyn Dŵr in 1404, and was deprived of the temporalities of his see in the following year. See J. Tait and R. Davies, 'John Trevor', *ODNB* and Glanmor Williams, *The Welsh Church: From Conquest to Reformation* (Cardiff, 1976), pp. 212–45.

30 R. Benson, *The Bishop-Elect* (Princeton, 1960), pp. 35–6, 358–9.

31 *The Rolls and Register of Bishop Oliver Sutton*, ed. Rosalind Hill, 7 vols (Woodbridge, 1948–86).

32 *Reg. Grandisson*, i, 330.

33 H. Ridgeway, 'The Ecclesiastical Career of Aymer de Lusignan, Bishop Elect of Winchester, 1250–60', in *The Cloister and the World: Essays in Honour of Barbara Harvey*, ed. J. Blair and B. Golding (Oxford, 1996), pp. 148–77.

34 See *Fasti Ecclesiae Anglicanae* for the dates of both consecrations and enthronements.

35 Reynolds was consecrated at Canterbury on 13 October 1308, and enthroned at Worcester on 21 September 1310.

36 *The Register of Richard Clifford, Bishop of Worcester, 1401–1407*, ed. W. Smith (Toronto, 1976), p. 114.

If a bishop delayed his enthronement for too long, his apparent lack of interest could cause tensions with the cathedral clergy. Robert Neville was translated from Salisbury to Durham in January 1438; two and a half years later he had still made no plans to travel to his new see, and so Prior Wessington wrote suggesting that he might be enthroned at Christmas 1440. Neville was eventually enthroned in April 1441.[37]

The new significance of the first entry and enthronement was a by-product of the changes in the methods by which bishops were appointed. The long-standing practice of election by the clergy and people, heavily influenced by secular rulers, was replaced by free capitular election in the years around 1200. Then, in the late thirteenth and early fourteenth centuries, episcopal election was gradually replaced by papal provision (the direct appointment of bishops by the pope). From the 1340s until the Reformation, every English bishop was provided by the pope.[38] This shift away from local involvement in the choosing of the bishop meant that, by the fourteenth century, the clergy and people, including the cathedral chapter, often saw their new bishop for the first time on the day of his enthronement. Nevertheless, many of the components of the first entry appear to be designed to maintain the fiction of assent: these people had very little or no say in the choice of their bishop, but they could still demonstrate their assent to the capitular or papal choice by participating in the rituals surrounding his appointment. This tendency is apparent throughout the bishop-making process, in the involvement of the people of the diocese in the preparations for election,[39] the popular acclamation of the capitular choice once the election had been held,[40] and the participation of the other bishops of the province in the consecration ceremony.[41]

The people demonstrated their acceptance of their new bishop when he entered the city for the first time by turning out to meet him; descriptive accounts of such entry processions refer to the large numbers of people present, and to the manner in which they welcomed him.[42] Véronique Julerot

[37] Dobson, *Durham Priory*, pp. 227–8.

[38] Harvey, *Episcopal Appointments*; J. Peltzer, *Canon Law, Careers and Conquest: Episcopal Elections in Normandy and Greater Anjou, c. 1140–1230* (Cambridge, 2008).

[39] For the role of the people of Canterbury in the election of the archbishop, see *The Historical Works of Gervase of Canterbury*, ed. W. Stubbs, 2 vols, RS 73 (London, 1870–80), ii, 117; R. Graham, 'Archbishop Winchelsey: from his Election to his Enthronement', *Church Quarterly Review* 148 (1949), 161–75; R. Haines, *Ecclesia Anglicana: Studies in the English Church of the Later Middle Ages* (Toronto, 1989), p. 27.

[40] *Gervase*, ii, 122–3; Graham, 'Archbishop Winchelsey', p. 166.

[41] Canon law required the presence of at least three bishops at an episcopal consecration: see Gratian D. 55 c. 5§1. In practice, the consecration of late medieval English prelates, especially archbishops, often attracted a considerably largely number of bishops than was strictly necessary; see Harvey, *Episcopal Appointments*, pp. 57–9.

[42] See, for example, *Liber Albus*, f. 45d, no. 504; *Reg. Sede Vacante*, pp. 52–3; *Registrum Ludowici de Charlton: episcopi herefordensis, A. D. MCCCLXI–MCCCLXX*, ed. J. H. Parry (London, 1914), pp. 4–5; M. P. D. Collinson, 'The Courtenay Cartulary from Powderham Castle, Devon', University of Exeter MA thesis (1972), p. 270.

has described French *adventus* ceremonies as consisting of 'a series of welcome ceremonies, of receptions',[43] and this description seems to sum up the English experience as well. For example, when William Gainsborough arrived at Worcester in June 1303:

> The Prior came in the morning to Kempsey with the Sacristan, Chaplain and other Monks and his servants, and told the Bishop it was time to go. The Bishop assented and stated that he desired to be enthroned if it could be done before the third hour, on account of the heat of the day and the crowd of people. Forthwith he was met by the Abbots of Evesham, Pershore, and Tewkesbury, and other officials, and by the Bishops of Hereford and Llandaff and various Archdeacons, and by Sir Thomas Berkeley and Sir Hugo de Vere ... It was estimated that more than 70 horsemen met the Bishop. The first procession met the Bishop at Red Hill. The second procession of the Friars Minors met the Bishop at the hospital of St Wulfstan ... Master Reginald de Bondone was there on behalf of the archdeacon of Canterbury ...

When the procession moved towards the church it was split into two halves, with the bishops and other officials following 'as soon as they could from the press of people'.[44] His arrival would also have been heralded by the ringing of the bells. William Gainsborough was appointed in difficult circumstances (he was provided by the pope after the archbishop of Canterbury refused to confirm the election of John de Sancto Germano, the monastic candidate),[45] but he seems to have been warmly received in his diocese, with large numbers of people turning up and actively greeting him.

Other aspects of the *adventus* celebrations were also designed to encourage unity and promote good relations between bishop and diocese. Unity was a theme of the enthronement service: the Salisbury *ordo* for the reception of a new bishop includes Psalm 133 ('Behold, how good and how pleasant it is for brethren to dwell together in unity'),[46] and bishops sometimes chose similarly focused texts for their enthronement sermon; William Gainsborough of Worcester preached on the text 'We are one body in Christ.'[47]

Prominent guests signalled their welcome by participating in the procession to the cathedral, by attending the enthronement service, and by accepting the bishop's hospitality at the festivities that followed. Chief amongst these celebrations was a banquet, and at this banquet individual nobles had the duty of performing certain services. The workings of this system are perhaps best illustrated by a charter issued by Archbishop Boniface of Canterbury to

[43] Julerot, 'La première entrée', pp. 650–1.
[44] *Reg. Sede Vacante*, pp. 52–3.
[45] R. M. Haines, 'William Gainsborough', *ODNB*.
[46] *Ceremonies and Processions*, p. 106.
[47] *Reg. Sede Vacante*, p. 54.

Richard de Clare, earl of Gloucester and Hereford, in 1258. This document set terms for Richard's tenure from the archbishop of seven Kentish manors; he must act as high steward and chief butler at enthronement feasts, although he would also receive an allowance for these services, including clothing, wine, wax, food and tableware.[48] By performing these services, in return for land, the aristocrats involved were bound to the bishop, and he to them. The relationship between the bishop and his tenants was also emphasized through the performance of homage in the days following the installation,[49] and through the presentation of lavish gifts to the newly installed prelate.[50]

Throughout his episcopate, one of the bishop's most important relationships would be with his cathedral chapter, and it is thus unsurprising that many of the *adventus* rituals were focused around the establishment of this bond. The chapter members, and especially their head, played an important role in the enthronement service, processing with the bishop, chanting and leading prayers;[51] sometimes the dean or abbot even enthroned the bishop.[52] But there are three features of the day that have particular relevance here. The first is the bishop's oath: throughout the later Middle Ages English cathedral chapters took this opportunity to demand from the bishop an oath of loyalty to their church, in which he promised to respect and defend its rights and privileges.[53] This oath gained particular significance in the age of papal provision, providing the chapter with some measure of protection against arbitrary treatment by a bishop who was not of their choosing.[54] The second significant feature is ritual kissing: at some point during the celebrations

---

48 Canterbury Cathedral Archives, DCc-ChAnt/A/28.

49 *Registrum Simonis Langham Cantuariensis archiepiscopi*, ed. A. Wood (Oxford, 1956), p. 116.

50 See *CLBL* F, p. 55 for the purchase of gifts, worth a total of £37 3s 4d, to be presented to the bishop of London on his enthronement.

51 *Ceremonies and Processions*, pp. 104–8; *Lincoln Cathedral Statutes*, iii, 273–4; *Reg. Sede Vacante*, pp. 52–4; *Reg. Charlton*, pp. 4–5; Salisbury Cathedral, Chapter Act Book of Dean Dunham, fols 80–4; *The Chronicle of John Stone, Monk of Christ Church Canterbury, 1415–71*, ed. W. G. Searle (Cambridge, 1902), pp. 62–3.

52 For example, Simon Langham was enthroned by the prior of Christ Church Canterbury in March 1367: *Reg. Simon Langham*, p. 115. Henry Wakefield of Worcester was jointly installed by the prior, Walter de Legh, and the bishop's official, Robert de la More, in 1376: *A Calendar of the Register of Henry Wakefield, Bishop of Worcester 1375–95*, ed. W. P. Marett (Birmingham, 1972).

53 *Ceremonies and Processions*, p. 105; *Lincoln Cathedral Statutes*, iii, 273–4; Salisbury Cathedral, Chapter Act Book of Dean Holme, fol. 44; *The Historians of the Church of York and Its Archbishops*, ed. J. Raine, 3 vols, RS 71 (London, 1879–94), ii, 423–4; *Anglia Sacra*, ed. H. Wharton, 2 vols (London, 1691), i, 450; *Calendar of the Patent Rolls of Edward III, 1367–70* (London, 1913), p. 154; Durham Muniments, Cartulary 1 fol. 118 r–v.

54 Dobson, *Durham Priory*, p. 230; K. Edwards, *The English Secular Cathedrals in the Middle Ages* 2nd edn (Manchester, 1967), p. 114. The oath was sometimes cited in disputes between bishop and chapter, as in the case of Alexander Neville. He was accused by the canons of York of being 'unmindful of his oath to God and St Peter on the day of his enthronement' when he attacked 'the ancient customs and liberties of the church.' See *Historians of the Church of York*, ii, 423–4; R. B. Dobson, 'The Authority of the Bishop in Late Medieval England: The Case of Archbishop Alexander Neville of York, 1374–88', in his *Church and Society in the Medieval North of England* (London, 1996), pp. 185–94.

(at Lincoln immediately after the enthronement, at Worcester at the chapter meeting the following day) the monks or canons would file up in order of rank to receive the kiss of brotherhood from the new bishop.[55] The third notable thing (which occurred only in cathedrals with a secular chapter) is the bishop's induction into the cathedral chapter, which typically took place the day after the enthronement.[56] In combination, these three practices made it quite clear to the new bishop that whilst he may have been placed over the monks or canons by papal authority, he was also one of their brethren, and as such he owed respect to them and their church.

Of course, the bishop also needed the chapter, along with the rest of his flock, to respect him, and one way to win their respect was to be a good bishop. Much of the enthronement service was taken up with prayers that the new prelate would be a good shepherd to his flock, that he should fulfil his duties and set a good example to his people.[57] Fortunately for the bishop, his entry celebrations included many opportunities for him to display the qualities and skills which made him fit to be a bishop, and thus to demonstrate the justice of his appointment. His humility, for example, was illustrated by his procession to the cathedral door, bareheaded, barefoot and dressed in simple robes, and by his prostration before the high altar.[58] His generosity to appropriate causes was displayed through offerings and acts of charity. New bishops presented lavish gifts at the altar of their cathedral: Antony Bek of Durham presented two canopies embroidered with scenes of the Nativity to decorate the high altar at Christmas, and William Gainsborough of Worcester offered three pieces of gold cloth.[59] Almsgiving was also a standard part of the installation procedure. At Lincoln and Exeter the carpet on which the bishop had walked in procession was cut up and given to the poor,[60] whilst at Rochester the poor brethren of St Bartholomew's Hospital received both alms from those who dined with the bishop, and the cloth which covered the dining table.[61]

---

[55] *Lincoln Cathedral Statutes*, iii, 274; *Reg. Sede Vacante*, pp. 54–5.

[56] This custom was most firmly established at Salisbury: *Ceremonies and Processions*, pp. 107–9. Accounts of the admission of Bishops Waltham and Mitford of Salisbury as canon and prebendary of Potterne are given in Dunham Chapter Book, fols 84–5 and Holme Chapter Book, fol. 45 respectively. Elsewhere the bishop's position as a canon was more contentious. On the bishop as a member of the cathedral chapter, and the difficulties this might cause, see Edwards, *Secular Cathedrals*, pp. 101–13.

[57] *Ceremonies and Processions*, pp. 104–7; *Registrum Sancti Pauli*, p. 11; *Durham Cathedral Statutes*, pp. 74–5.

[58] *Lincoln Cathedral Statutes*, iii, 273–4; *Ceremonies and Processions*, p. 104; *Extracts from the Cathedral Registers of the Diocese of Hereford, 1275–1535*, ed. E. N. Dew (Hereford, 1932), pp. 75, 120, 122.

[59] *Durham Annals and Documents of the Thirteenth Century*, ed. F. Barlow, Surtees Society 155 (1945), pp. 64–5; *Historiae Dunelmensis Scriptores Tres*, ed. J. Raine, Surtees Society 9 (1839), p. 70; *Reg. Sede Vacante*, p. 53.

[60] *Lincoln Cathedral Statutes*, iii, 273; M. Buck, *Politics, Finance and the Church in the Reign of Edward II: Walter Stapeldon, Treasurer of England* (Cambridge, 1983), p. 46.

[61] E. Hasted, *The History and Topographical Survey of the County of Kent*, 12 vols (Canterbury,

The bishop offered hospitality to his guests, feeding them at the enthronement banquet and often accommodating them in his palace.[62] The performance of spiritual duties, including the celebration of mass, the preaching
of a sermon and the blessing of the congregation were a standard part of
the enthronement service.[63] Some bishops also granted an indulgence to
those present at their first mass.[64] Pastoral skills were also on display, and
the celebrations following an enthronement often included large numbers
of confirmations.[65] There would be opportunities for the bishop to display
his administrative and management skills, whether by participating in a
chapter meeting,[66] appointing episcopal officials[67] or beginning preparations
for his first visitation.[68] Finally, the power and wealth of his exalted position were manifested in the scale of the celebrations, the number and status
of the guests, the splendour of the pontifical robes and the lavishness of
the entertainment. Indeed, by the mid-fourteenth century these celebrations
had become so grand that one chronicler complained that 'the festivals of
enthronement ... give rise more to ostentation and pomp than to honour'.[69]

The enthronement of a bishop, then, was meant to be a joyous occasion,
a celebration which brought together and bound together a vast range of
people, and an event which cemented the new prelate's position as the loving
shepherd of an obedient flock. When Richard Clifford, bishop of Worcester,
invited the clergy of his diocese to his enthronement in 1403, he wrote that:

1797–1801), iv, 213. For a useful recent consideration of the role of the cathedral in the provision
of alms, see David Lepine, 'Cathedrals and Charity: Almsgiving at English Secular Cathedrals in
the Later Middle Ages', *EHR* 126 (2011), 1066–96.

[62] *Reg. Sede Vacante*, p. 54; *Liber Albus*, f. 45d, no. 504; *Anglia Sacra*, i, 655; *Historians of the
Church of York*, ii, 415–16. For the scale of these banquets, see the menus for two fifteenth-
century enthronement feasts: John Chandler of Salisbury, in 1417 (*Two Fifteenth-Century
Cookery-Books*, ed. T. Austin, EETS OS 91 [1888], pp. 60–1) and George Neville of York, in
1465 (*The Antiquities of Canterbury*, ed. Nicolas Battely [London, 1703], Appendix, p. 29).
The splendid fish-based spread provided for William Warham's enthronement as archbishop of
Canterbury in 1504 demonstrated that Lenten observances did not always prevent the enjoyment
of a good dinner: *Antiquities of Canterbury*, Appendix, pp. 21–9). For a discussion of such feasts
in context, see Christopher Woolgar, 'Fast and Feast: Conspicuous Consumption and the Diet of
the Nobility in the Fifteenth Century', in *Revolution and Consumption in Late Medieval England*,
ed. M. Hicks (Woodbridge, 2001), pp. 7–25.

[63] *Ceremonies and Processions*, p. 107; *Lincoln Cathedral Statutes*, iii, 274; Reynolds, *Wells
Cathedral*, p. 92.

[64] St Hugh of Lincoln offered an indulgence of eleven days to all who attended his enthronement:
English Episcopal Acta 4: Lincoln, 1186–1206, ed. D. M. Smith (Oxford, 1986), nos 77–8, p. 204
n. 1. William Gainsborough gave a six days' indulgence to all who heard him celebrate the Mass
of St Wulfstan on the day of his enthronement: *Reg. Sede Vacante*, p. 54.

[65] Gainsborough confirmed boys at the house of the Friars Minor on the Monday after his
enthronement: *Reg. Sede Vacante*, p. 54.

[66] *Ceremonies and Processions*, pp. 107–8; *Reg. Sede Vacante*, p. 54.

[67] Thomas Lisle instituted a retinue of notable size and magnificence when he was enthroned at Ely
in 1345; see *Anglia Sacra*, i, 655.

[68] *Anglia Sacra*, i, 43.

[69] *Historia Roffenses*, cited by Haines, *Ecclesia Anglicana*, p. 35.

> Although he does not venture to promise luxurious entertainment, nevertheless the intercourse of so many friends as they come together will serve them with a greater enjoyment in place of luxurious fare, and afterwards, he hopes, they will have a merry countenance and a grateful heart.[70]

There were surely many enthronements that passed without mishap, and from which everyone went home happy; Clifford's enthronement was probably one such occasion. Given the scale of such celebrations, however, it is unsurprising to find that complications often occurred. Sometimes the difficulties began even before the celebrations, for enthronements were extremely costly affairs, and somebody had to pay. For a bishop who was already heavily burdened by the debts he had run up at the papal curia, securing his bishopric, this could be something of a problem. Archbishop John Pecham, for example, was already in financial difficulty when he borrowed 2,000 marks to pay for his enthronement at Canterbury in 1279.[71] Walter Stapeldon, enthroned at Exeter in 1308, complained that his consecration, his enthronement, and a lawsuit against an individual who had contested his appointment to the bishopric would together cost him three years' revenue.[72] At Worcester, when William Gainsborough returned from Rome in 1303 his finances were so depleted that he was unable to pay for his enthronement, and had to ask the prior and convent for financial assistance.[73] Unfortunately, they were also in debt; they had borrowed £60 from the King's Almoner, which they were unable to repay, and therefore could only give the bishop £20.[74] By the time of the enthronement, a tangled web of loans existed between the bishop, the chapter and the Almoner, who was threatening to 'take other means' to recoup his money if repayment was not forthcoming.[75]

Gainsborough's financial woes hardly amounted to an auspicious start to his episcopate, but compared to some bishops he was lucky. In December 1243, William Raleigh arrived at Winchester, having been translated there by the pope after a five-year electoral dispute between Henry III and the monks of Winchester. His provisions were seized (by an over-zealous royal official)[76] and the city gates were closed against him; he tried each in turn, but with no success.[77] Attempting to remain near his see, he found that the

[70] *The Register of Richard Clifford, Bishop of Worcester 1401–1407: A Calendar*, ed. W. E. L. Smith (Toronto, 1979), p. 114.
[71] D. Douie, *Archbishop Pecham* (Oxford, 1952), p. 66.
[72] *The Register of Walter Stapeldon, Bishop of Exeter*, ed. F. C. Hingeston-Randolph (London, 1892), p. 14.
[73] *Reg. Sede Vacante*, pp. 37, 46.
[74] Ibid., pp. 38, 40.
[75] Ibid., pp. 52, 55.
[76] *CPR 1232–47*, p. 438.
[77] *Annales Monastici*, ed. H. R. Luard, 5 vols, RS 36 (London, 1864–69), ii, 89, iii, 162; *Matthæi Parisiensis, Monachi Sancti Albani, Chronica Majora*, ed. H. R. Luard, 7 vols, RS 57 (London, 1872–83), iv, 266.

king had barred the local laity from trading with him,[78] and eventually he was forced into exile.[79] Richard Beauchamp, enthroned at Hereford in 1449, managed to enter his city but was clearly not made to feel welcome: he placed the churches of All Saints and St Peter's under interdict because they had failed to ring the bells upon his arrival, and only removed the interdict once they had submitted to him.[80] In the early 1330s, at Carlisle, John Kirkby was attacked 'with blasphemous words, arrows and stones', causing Archbishop Melton to place the city under interdict and excommunicate the perpetrators.[81] It is unclear whether this attack happened on the day of his enthronement or shortly afterwards, but it is certainly a salutary reminder that the goodwill which surrounded the first entry of the bishop was not always long-lived.

Enthronement-related disputes typically arose because one or more of the parties involved felt that their rights were being infringed. In the double see of Bath and Wells, for example, the two chapters agreed that the bishop should be installed in both cathedrals, but could not decide which should take precedence.[82] Bishop and chapter sometimes disagreed about where the latter should receive the former. In 1303, William Gainsborough refused to continue his journey into Worcester unless the prior came to meet him at Kempsey; on this occasion the prior agreed to do so, even though it was contrary to custom for him to go more than a mile outside the city, and Kempsey was approximately four miles from the cathedral.[83] Shortly after Walter Skirlaw was enthroned at Durham in 1390, the prior and convent compiled a list of the injuries which they had suffered at his hands, amongst them the improper manner in which the bishop had forced them to meet him at his installation, which they feared might be taken as a precedent.[84] Similarly, some bishops were reluctant to swear the customary oath; this was the cause of a bitter dispute between Bishop John Waltham of Salisbury and his chapter in 1388.[85]

The most common cause of disputes, however, was the question of who should enthrone the bishop. In theory, the answer to this question was straightforward: in the Canterbury province the archdeacon of Canterbury had the right to officiate, whilst the archdeacon of York claimed the same right in the Northern province. If the archdeacon was unable to perform the task in

[78] *CPR 1232–47*, p. 439.
[79] *Chronica Majora*, iv, 285; *Annales Monastici*, ii, 332.
[80] *Registrum Ricardi Beauchamp*, ed. A. T. Bannister (London, 1919), p. 6.
[81] *The Register of William Melton, Archbishop of York, 1317–40*, ed. R. Hill *et al.*, CYS 70–1, 76, 85, 93, 101 (Woodbridge, 1955–), i, 95.
[82] *Calendar of the Manuscripts of the Dean and Chapter of Wells*, ed. W. H. Bird and W. P. Baildon, 2 vols (London, 1907–14), i, 64, 118; *Anglia Sacra*, i, 567; *Annales Monastici*, iv, 553.
[83] *Reg. Sede Vacante*, p. 52.
[84] Durham Cathedral Muniments, Pontificalia 2.5.Pont.7.
[85] Dunham Chapter Book, fol. 57, fols 81–2.

person, he might delegate it to a proctor.[86] In practice, disputes were common; in some sees, they seem to have occurred at virtually every enthronement. Durham was one such see. When Antony Bek arrived at Durham in December 1285, he was already at odds with the monks, and had refused to greet the monastic delegation who had come to meet him when he entered the diocese. On the day of the enthronement, things seem to have gone smoothly until the point at which Antony stood, robed, before the episcopal throne, waiting to be installed, but then the prior of Durham and the official of the archdeacon of York began to argue over who had the right to perform this task. Fortunately, Antony's brother, Thomas Bek, bishop of St David's, was present, and the new bishop invited his kinsman to enthrone him, in order that no one's rights be prejudiced.[87] Throughout the fourteenth century the Durham bishops were enthroned by the prior (although not without challenges from the archdeacon of York and his representatives), and the dispute was still ongoing in 1441, when, the day before Bishop Neville's enthronement, Prior Wessington received a visit from two archidiaconal proctors who tried to browbeat him into resigning his right to enthrone. He refused.[88]

Such disputes were echoed across the country; the question of who should enthrone the bishop was one which exercised most cathedrals at some point during the later Middle Ages. Occasionally, the bishop himself might object to the officiant. This happened at Ely in 1302, when Robert Orford refused to be enthroned by the archdeacon of Canterbury, on the grounds that he owed his see to papal provision.[89] Even when the identity of the officiant was not called into question, there might be disagreement over the gifts he was to receive. At one early fourteenth-century enthronement, the archdeacon of Canterbury's proctor 'took from the Bishop his palfrey and saddle; he also took his cape, cap, shoes and cup. He also claimed besides the cup ten marks for his expenses, and he was not satisfied.'[90] Given that the canon law forbade payment to be made in return for enthronement,[91] the proctor in question made himself rather vulnerable to claims that he was at best greedy, and at worst corrupt. When the bishop questioned whether it was customary for

---

[86] Churchill, *Canterbury Administration*, i, 276.
[87] *Durham Annals*, pp. 64–5; *Scriptores Tres*, pp. 69–70; Constance Fraser, *A History of Antony Bek* (Oxford, 1957), pp. 42–3.
[88] Dobson, *Durham Priory*, pp. 228–9.
[89] B. Thompson, 'The Fourteenth Century', in *Ely: Bishops and Diocese, 1109–2009*, ed. P. Meadows (Woodbridge, 2010), p. 74. It was probably not irrelevant to the situation that the archdeacon of Canterbury was one John Langton, Orford's erstwhile rival for the bishopric of Ely.
[90] *Reg. Sede Vacante*, p. 53.
[91] *Decrees of the Ecumenical Councils*, ed. N. P. Tanner, 2 vols (London, 1990), i, 214–15 (c.7). It nevertheless remained standard practice for those who installed heads of religious houses and inducted parish clergy to receive or demand gifts; see M. Haren, *Sin and Society in Fourteenth Century England* (Oxford, 2000), p. 98 and M. Burger, *Bishops, Clerks and Diocesan Governance in Thirteenth-Century England* (Cambridge, 2012), pp. 130–1.

the archdeacon to receive more, the official therefore had little choice but to back down.[92]

If the ceremony itself passed off without incident, the banquet that followed still offered opportunities for conflict. In each diocese, certain members of the aristocracy held lands from the bishop in return for performing services at the enthronement feast, and the right to perform these services was as jealously guarded as the right to enthrone the bishop. The significance of such positions is reflected in the fact that they were considered valuable enough to be used as an occasional source of royal patronage,[93] and in the complex arrangements which were made for another member of the family to act as the tenant's proctor if he was unable to be there in person.[94] Another indication of the prestige attached to such arrangements is the willingness of the individuals concerned to disrupt the *adventus* celebrations in order to defend their rights; such disturbances occurred at no fewer than three fourteenth-century enthronements. At Exeter, in 1307, the enthronement of Walter Stapeldon was disrupted by a dispute between the new bishop and Sir Hugh Courtenay, who held the manor of Slapton in return for acting as steward at the enthronement feast. Courtenay claimed an exceptionally large fee in return for his services, and the dispute was not resolved for nearly three weeks, at the end of which period a lengthy agreement was formulated, by which Courtenay was granted a fee in excess of that received by the earl of Gloucester for performing the same services at Canterbury.[95] Two decades later, the services performed by the earl of Gloucester at Canterbury themselves became the focus of a dispute. When Simon Meopham was enthroned in 1328, the country was politically divided following the recent deposition and murder of Edward II, and these divisions came to the fore in the allocation of services at the enthronement feast. Gilbert de Clare had been killed at Bannockburn, and thus a replacement steward had to be found, but Meopham did not wish Hugh Audley (husband of one of the Gloucester co-heiresses and lord of the relevant manor) to take de Clare's place, probably because of his association with the Lancastrian faction. Consequently, the role was performed by Sir Henry Cobham. At the same feast, Lady Badlesmere claimed the role of chamberlain, guarding the doors of the archbishop's chamber, but because she had defended Leeds Castle against Edward II, the

---

[92] *Reg. Sede Vacante*, p. 53.
[93] See *CPR 1441–6*, p. 159, for a grant to the king's sergeant, Robert Roos, of the right to act as chamberlain at the enthronement of the archbishop of Canterbury during the minority of Lord Roos.
[94] Exeter Cathedral, Dean and Chapter 2291.
[95] Collinson, 'Courtenay Cartulary, pp. 270–3. An English summary of this text is included in E. Cleveland, *A Genealogical History of the Illustrious Family of Courtenay* (Exeter, 1735), pp. 136–7. In the thirteenth century, the earl of Gloucester was rewarded with the archbishop's cup, seven scarlet robes, 30 gallons of wine, 30 lb of wax, provision for eighty horses, and three days' accommodation at one of the archbishop's manors while he recovered from the blood-letting necessitated by the celebrations. See Douie, *Pecham*, p. 66.

new archbishop would have nothing to do with her.[96] Even on this extremely
tense occasion, nobody threatened to use force to secure their rights. But
in 1356, one John de Caston, knight, claimed the right to perform services
at the forthcoming enthronement of Thomas Percy as bishop of Norwich.
When his claims were denied, he threatened 'to come with very many men
and take such fees there by force', and Edward III was obliged to intervene
to restrain him.[97]

An enthronement such as this one, at which discord rather than unity
was the order of the day, was clearly not what a medieval bishop aspired to
when he wrote to his cathedral chapter to inform them that he wished to be
enthroned. The ideal first entry was a far more harmonious occasion, during
the course of which the bishop took physical possession of his cathedral
church and thus completed the final stage of the long journey to a bishopric.
It was also supposed to be a joyous occasion, a time for the bishop and his
people to celebrate the fact that the widowed cathedral church, bereft by the
death of the last bishop, now had a new spouse, and that there was once again
a shepherd to take care of the flock. Inevitably, however, the reality was often
far more complex than the ideal. Historians have paid a great deal of attention to the complexities of the earlier stages of the bishop-making process,
especially the circumstances of the actual appointment, but the end of the
process – the *adventus* and enthronement – is all too often dismissed in little
more than a footnote. Such occasions are worthy of greater attention, not only
for the light which they shed on the bishop-making process as a whole, but
also as substantial, significant events in their own right.

---

[96] R. M. Haines, 'An Innocent Abroad: The Career of Simon Mepham, Archbishop of Canterbury,
      1328–33', *EHR* 112 (1997), 565–6.
[97] *CPR 1354–58*, pp. 454–5.

TEMPORALITIES BE TAKEN: EDWARD III, UNRULY ECCLESIASTICS AND THE FIGHT FOR THE BENEFICES OF EXETER, 1337–60

Charlotte Whatley

The anticlerical period often attributed to Edward III's reign saw a concerted royal effort to maintain control over a lower clergy that increasingly acted against the king and the interests of his realm. Papal provisions and English advowson rights had long been a subject of contention in English church–state relations.[1] The tumultuous political atmosphere of the mid-fourteenth century, coupled with attempts on both sides to consolidate resources, created a situation in England in which it was often difficult to know which party had legal claim to present to a benefice. The lower clergy took advantage of the opportunities provided by this confusion by ruthlessly seeking these offices, often to the detriment of the bishops and in derogation of the king's right. Cases of physical occupation and other forms of clerical dissent present in the plea rolls illustrate not only the lengths to which provisors were willing to go to secure their positions, but the subversive nature of their behaviour towards the will of Edward III. The king's increased litigation against these clerics in the mid-1340s was a direct response to these activities and an attempt to reassert his authority over the clergy in these matters. In the wake of the Black Death, Edward redoubled his efforts to control these unruly lower clergy through the Statutes of Provisors (1351) and Praemunire (1353). In so doing, Edward restored some semblance of order to the English lower clergy.

Historians have frequently cited the 1340 crisis with Archbishop Stratford and Edward's subsequent removal of ecclesiastics from his administration as a crucial moment in the political relations between the church and the English state. The dismissal of these ministers – and Edward's strident declarations that he would never again install a bishop as chancellor – marked the beginning of a period during which his agenda was driven by what some historians have termed 'anticlericalism'.[2] During the following years (1340–52),

---

[1] The right of advowson, or *ius presentandi*, allowed the holder to nominate to the bishop a suitable person to an ecclesiastical benefice within a parish.

[2] See S. Waugh, *England in the Reign of Edward III* (Cambridge, 1991) pp. 216–21; W. Jones, 'Bishops, Politics, and the Two Laws: The *Gravamina* of the English Clergy, 1237–1399', *Speculum* 41 (1966), 228; R. Palmer, *English Law in the Age of the Black Death* (Chapel Hill, 1993), p. 29; N. Fryde, 'Edward III's Removal of His Ministers and Judges, 1340–1', *Historical Research* 48 (1975), 150.

Edward clashed with the church over questions of jurisdiction and was at odds with both the pope and the English clergy on administrative, political and personal levels. Although much work has been done to show that the 1340s were perhaps not as volatile as previously thought,[3] there appears good reason to argue that ongoing crime, increasingly restrictive policies towards the clergy, and the looming war with France contributed to a turbulent political atmosphere in England. At the same time, a growing concern among the clergy held that if Edward continued to present the powerful and loyal men that he did to these offices, the general fabric of the clergy would favour the king and his agenda over the pope and his. This turbulence seems to be something to which the clergy responded negatively, as the plea rolls show distinct upward trends in litigation concerning violence and trespasses between and against clerics.[4] Moreover, these trends show an increasingly unruly clergy. These clerics were not only concerned by the actions taken by the monarchy, but had the potential to cause serious trouble for Edward. The king's reaction, which was increasingly strident litigation, ordinances, and eventually statutes, seems at first an attack on the English clergy as a whole. This period of persistent litigation has been analysed in a variety of ways: for decades, the prevailing narrative suggested that Edward was staging an attack on papal influence within England,[5] while others have argued that the papacy, particularly under Clement VI (1342–52), was attempting to make inroads into the king's jurisdiction.[6] Still others have understood this conflict and the statutes it produced as mere political machinations rather than a true conflict.[7] More recently, scholars have argued that Edward and Clement must have enjoyed a more amicable relationship for a number of reasons, most notably because the pope consistently installed and confirmed those clerics that Edward nominated to him.[8]

The evidence supports this final argument on a superficial level, but a detailed examination of the legal record suggests that while Edward and

---

3   See *Before the Black Death: Studies in the 'Crisis' of the Early Fourteenth Century*, ed. B. Campbell (Manchester, 1991).

4   Over the course of the 1320s and 1330s, there was a relatively slow increase in the number of cases involving clerics or clerical violence. Such cases were much more common in the 1340s, and P. Saunders made the important connection between the increase in clerical violence with the increase in Edward's attempts to expand his jurisdiction over advowsons. See P. Saunders, 'Royal Ecclesiastical Patronage in England, 1199–1351', University of Oxford PhD thesis (1978), p. 332.

5   See W. Capes, *The English Church in the Fourteenth and Fifteenth Centuries* (London, 1900), p. 86; J. MacKinnon, *History of Edward III* (Woodbridge, 1974), pp. 244–5; J. Ellis, 'Anti-Papal Legislation in Medieval England (1066–1377)', Catholic University of America PhD thesis (1930), pp. 112, 120.

6   A. Deeley, 'Papal Provision and Royal Rights of Patronage in the Early Fourteenth Century', *EHR* 43 (1928), 497.

7   W. Waugh, 'The Great Statute of Praemunire', *EHR* 37 (1922), 175–6; M. McKisack, *The Fourteenth Century, 1307–1399* (Oxford, 1959), p. 281.

8   R. Fitzgerald, 'Community and Conflict: The English Church, 1350–1381', Duke University PhD thesis (1976), p. 151; W. Pantin, *The English Church in the Fourteenth Century* (Toronto, 1980), pp. 55–6.

Clement may have been willing to compromise on episcopal appointments, discord arose over the distribution of benefices for the lower clergy.
Clement VI and later Innocent VI (1352–62) generally allowed Edward's
chosen clerics to be installed into the bishoprics to which he nominated them,
especially after 1344. Prior to 1344, bishops tended to be elected to their
posts and subsequently confirmed by the pope.[9] Over the course of the 1340s
this ceased to be the case in practice, if not in fact, and after 1344, all of the
bishops installed and consecrated to offices within England were granted
their benefice by papal provision, most of them through nomination by the
king.[10] However, while Edward and the pope filled episcopal benefices with
some level of cooperation, the same was not true for the minor benefices
and ecclesiastical offices of England. This article examines the issue of royal
presentation versus papal provision on a different level: that of the lower
clergy.

Research into this topic has hitherto focused upon bishops' registers and
the calendared rolls while largely ignoring key legal sources found in the plea
rolls of the King's Bench and the court of common pleas. These sources alter
the current narrative of Edward's relationship with the clergy by demonstrating
the vigour and aggression with which each party engaged in legal battles over
advowson rights and papal provisions.[11] These documents, which have not
previously undergone a thorough examination or been transcribed, provide a
new perspective on these conflicts: one in which Edward's legal battles with
the clergy could hardly be considered an indiscriminate attack on the clergy,
but rather as focused attempts to subdue those clerics attempting to under-
mine monarchical power.[12] These legal contests were particularly vigorous in
the diocese of Exeter, where Bishop John Grandisson, in attempting to pacify
the provisors who hounded him, found himself in a tug of war between the
provisors, the king and the pope that culminated first in his excommunication
and then in the seizure of the temporalities of his bishopric.

[9]   Waugh, *England in the Reign of Edward III*, p. 145.
[10] Pantin, *English Church in the Fourteenth Century*, pp. 55–6.
[11] The documents referenced in this article have been transcribed and translated in full from
      their original manuscripts here for the first time. Three cases, out of the approximately eighty
      transcribed, were featured in the Year Books, though none in its entirety. All of the others can
      be found only in the plea rolls for the King's Bench or the Court of Common Pleas. Citations to
      TNA documents (CP 40, KB 27) refer to the digital archive assembled by Robert C. Palmer and
      Elspeth K. Palmer, The Anglo-American Legal Tradition, available at aalt.law.uh.edu/aalt.html,
      hereafter AALT.
[12] In *The Legal Significance of the Statute of Praemunire of 1353* (Cambridge, 1929), Edgar Graves
      examined approximately 30 per cent of the Rex Rolls of the King's Bench. The Rex Rolls
      themselves represent only a small percentage of the total records included in the King's Bench
      plea rolls. Palmer, *English Law in the Age of the Black Death*, has also completed a significant
      examination of plea rolls for this period; however, his investigation was not focused on advowson
      and benefice litigation in Exeter, but rather the on larger societal and legal changes wrought by
      the Black Death.

Advowson rights and papal provisions had been a source of conflict in England ever since the Norman Conquest, when the first proprietary churches were founded as part of William I's redistribution of English lands.[13] William ordered that churches be built in areas of dense population (one hundred or more) and that the baron responsible for that portion of land also be charged with procuring and maintaining a priest for the church. The maintenance of the priest could be accomplished, in this initial form, in any of three ways: by a fixed income via a stipend, by allowing him a portion of the tithe, or by assigning him glebe lands. This living provided by the patron of the church came to be called a benefice, and by the fourteenth century such benefices not only represented a highly sought after and potentially lucrative means of support for clerics in England, but prestige and influence as well. As one of the temporal rights associated with proprietary churches, advowson rights allowed the benefactor of the church to present candidates to ecclesiastical positions within those churches. The Constitution of Clarendon more clearly defined the conflict in 1176, when it stated *inter alia* that any controversies between laymen over advowsons and church patronage must be handled in the king's court rather than in court Christian.[14] By the fourteenth century, the idea that 'the church in England and in all its states of prelacy was said to have been founded by the king and his nobility in order to provide services, alms, hospitality and instruction to the faith', served as a foundation for the revival of the regalian right, and was used to justify many of Edward's more questionable acquisitions.[15]

Lay patrons did not control every benefice, however, and conflict regularly arose between such patrons and clerics over the right to present to a particular benefice. The pope could intervene in English benefices through direct collation by providing a cleric to a named benefice via a papal bull, or he could grant a cleric the expectation of a benefice in a given church or office.[16] Advowsons became a growing source of conflict over the course of the thirteenth century as the papacy continually attempted, in the form of various decrees and changes to canon law, to increase its jurisdiction over the ecclesiastical benefices of England. First, in the mid-thirteenth century, Pope Clement IV's *Licet Ecclesiarum* (1265) laid claim to all benefices of clergy who died while at the papal curia.[17] John XXII's *Ex Debito* (1319) added to these appropriations the benefices of any clerics who perished within two days of Rome, as well as those of cardinals, curial officers, and bishops

---

[13] W. Salmon, *Churches and Royal Patronage: A History of the Royal Patronage in the Churches of England and Wales* (Cowbridge, 1983), p. 32.

[14] *Select Charters and Other Illustrations of English Constitutional History*, ed. W. Stubbs, 9th edn, rev. by H. Davis (Oxford, 1921), p. 166.

[15] A. Barrel, 'The Ordinance of Provisors of 1343', *Historical Research* 64 (1991), 265.

[16] Deeley, 'Papal Provision and Royal Rights', 498.

[17] Peter Heath, *Church and Realm, 1272–1461* (London, 1988), p. 126.

consecrated in Rome.[18] While these decrees were not directed at England alone, they signalled that the papacy did not approve of the strength of lay influence in the distribution of ecclesiastical offices.

Meanwhile, like other lay patrons, the king held rights to present to benefices within his own holdings and could present to benefices other than his own under specific circumstances. The king could provide to a benefice in cases in which the custodianship of a minor child, and thus any temporalities associated with that ward's lands, was in his hands.[19] Similarly, if for some reason a bishopric was voided – usually in the case of a death, but rarely due to the bishop's excommunication – the king took control of the temporalities until a new bishop could be elected and consecrated.[20] In turn, the bishops themselves often had rights to provide clerics to benefices within their own bishopric; however, some required special dispensation by the pope.

Despite these very specific circumstances, Edward III and his legal ministers worked diligently to expand the benefices to which Edward could present. His reinterpretations of legal doctrine, particularly the idea that time did not run against the king, meant that he was able to use the common law to acquire significant numbers of benefices for his presentation.[21] Edward III's threefold increase in presentations over those of Edward I created friction with the papacy even under the pontificates of John XXII (1316–34) and Benedict XII (1334–42), both relatively restrained in their provisions to ecclesiastical offices.[22] His attempts to provide to as many benefices as possible in the early years of his reign are well documented, but the advent of Clement VI and his far more abundant provisions made it difficult for Edward III to maintain such numbers. Clement's thwarting of Edward's presentations, calculated or not, amplified tensions between king and pope at a time when England was entering a pivotal phase in its relationship with France.

---

[18] Ibid., p. 127.

[19] For example, CP 40/355, AALT 4070 (1348), http://aalt.law.uh.edu/E3/CP40no355/aCP40no355mm1toEnd/IMG_4070.htm in which Edward III recovered the right of advowson to the church of Southill on account of the wardship of Nicholas being in the hand of Edward I during the last time there was a presentation.

[20] KB 27/189 AALT 1493 (1297), http://aalt.law.uh.edu/AALT1/E1/KB27no189/aKB27no189fronts/IMG_1493.htm in which the temporalities of the bishopric of Lincoln were in the hands of the king due to the vacancy occasioned by the death of Oliver Sutton.

[21] *Nullum tempus occurrit regi*. This was a legal concept that Edward III used extensively to acquire the advowson rights to certain benefices. It was the idea that the king could bring cases that would not normally have been viable for a common litigant. He typically did this by stating that because a vacancy occurred during the wardship of a minor in the time of his grandfather Edward I (or sometimes his great-grandfather, Henry III), the right to present to the benefice now fell to him. He used this argument successfully to acquire the right to present to the church of Southill from Ralph, Baron of Stafford. See CP 40/355, AALT 4070, n. 19.

[22] In 'Royal Ecclesiastical Patronage in England', Saunders completed a painstaking statistical analysis of the number of royal presentations during several reigns, along with how the king justified those presentations, clearly demonstrating both the rise of provisions to benefices, and the distinct changes in the justifications for those presentations.

The political atmosphere during this period, particularly the intensifying tensions between England and France, added another dimension to the advowson issue. In England, the French connections to the papacy, and to any non-English benefice-holders by proxy, were considered increasingly suspect. Because the livings attached to ecclesiastical offices and benefices had the potential to be worth significant sums of money, the English population was uncomfortable with the idea of a French pope closely tied to the French monarchy providing foreign clerics to the wealth of English benefices. Ecclesiastics provided by the pope to a benefice below the rank of abbot paid *annates*, the first year's income from the benefice, back into the papal coffers.[23] The sheer number of provisions made by Clement VI in the early years of his pontificate meant that the *annates* of a substantial number of benefices, and thus large sums of money, could potentially be funnelling into the French war effort via the papal coffers in Avignon. Having acted as a counsellor in King Philip VI's court, as well as spending his ecclesiastical career in various positions within France before becoming the archbishop of Rouen, Clement VI's loyalties came under attack amongst the English people despite the fact that he had been born a subject of the English crown.[24] In the *Continuatio Chronicarum*, Adam Murimuth cautioned that 'the cardinals and the *curiales* ... hold the better benefices of the kingdom' and that it 'seems likely that the riches which go from England to the papacy and aliens exceed the annual income of the king, and that out of this money the king's enemies are for the large part supported'.[25]

Whether or not Murimuth's chronicle revealed the true state of the English clergy at the time, it is clear that there was at least some fear among the English populace that it did. Edward was happy to use the resulting agitation in parliament and among the population to his advantage. In 1337 and again in 1346 Edward issued decrees removing *alienigenae* from English benefices and redistributed those religious houses among trusted members of the clergy and his favoured barons for safe-keeping.[26] These seizures allowed Edward the opportunity to provide English clerics for dozens of ecclesiastical offices throughout England. Particularly in the diocese of Exeter – which at the time consisted of the counties of Devon and Cornwall – this policy would have explosive effects.

Although Edward took steps to annul papal provisions in both 1342 and

---

[23] Heath, *Church and Realm*, p. 128.

[24] G. Mollat, *The Popes at Avignon, 1305–1378* (Edinburgh, 1963), p. 37.

[25] *Adae Murimuth Continuatio Chronicarum*, ed. E. Thompson, RS 93 (London, 1889), pp. 175–6; Pantin, *English Church in the Fourteenth Century*, p. 71.

[26] J. Bothwell, *Edward III and the English Peerage: Royal Patronage, Social Mobility and Political Control in Fourteenth-Century England* (Woodbridge, 2004), p. 58. Bothwell argues that the confiscation of the alien priories, an act that spurred a significant number of the conflicts over benefices during this period, was a cunning method devised by Edward to provide annuities and wealth to his newly made earls.

1343, it was not until the mid-1340s that the most aggressive legal battles began. The consecration of Clement VI in 1342 led to the emergence of a decidedly more luxurious, and markedly more French, papacy.[27] Clement's extravagance extended to providing for his lesser clergy, and chroniclers reported that he called to Rome all those members of the clergy in search of a post, triggering a massive influx of benefice-seekers flocking to Avignon.[28] While the figure of 100,000 reported by Peter of Herenthals can be dismissed, historians tally nearly 1,600 papal provisions made by Clement during his papacy, and suggest that his penchant for providing one cleric to as many benefices as were necessary to achieve a particular income was a practice wholly new and particularly troublesome.[29] Clement designed his policies regarding provisions to place as many clerics as possible within the benefices available to him. Edward's similar goal led to a truly astonishing amount of litigation, nearly all of which was handled in England's common law courts.

Traditionally, legal questions concerning provisions had been handled in the papal court, but starting around 1300 these cases moved almost exclusively into the common law courts.[30] Under the English common law, a lawsuit over advowson rights would typically start with a simple writ of darrein presentment: a legal remedy introduced in 1179 that the courts used to determine what party had last presented to the benefice if there was a complaint. A writ of prohibition removed cases concerning advowsons from church courts to the king's courts in accordance with the Constitution of Clarendon.[31] Once there, the rather more severe *quare impedit* put the case before a jury of countrymen whose duty it was to determine the vacancy of the benefice during a certain period in time.[32] Often, the rival patron would have a writ of *ne admittas* sent to the bishop, which was intended to keep him from installing another person in the benefice until a judgment was made in the court. If the bishop ignored the *ne admittas*, a writ of *quare incumbravit* questioned why he had encumbered the benefice with the incorrect provisor, despite the writ that should have stayed his hand. Rarest and most severe, the *quare non admisit* was brought only when all other remedies had been exhausted. This was the most powerful tool in the king's legal arsenal and could result in the taking of the bishop's temporalities.[33] This writ called the

---

[27] Pantin, *English Church in the Fourteenth Century*, p. 81.
[28] Mollat, *Popes at Avignon*, p. 38; Heath, *Church and Realm*, p. 126.
[29] Heath, *Church and Realm*, p. 127.
[30] R. H. Helmholz, *The Oxford History of the Laws of England* (Oxford, 2004), p. 479.
[31] Ibid., p. 478.
[32] KB 27/342, AALT 0428 (1345), http://aalt.law.uh.edu/AALT1/E3/KB27no342/aKB27no342fronts/IMG_0428.htm: a *quare impedit* brought against the Prior of Tywardreath (Cornwall) concerning the vicarage of St Andrew of Tywardreath.
[33] KB 27/360, AALT 4605 (1349), http://aalt.law.uh.edu/E3/KB27no360/aKB27no360fronts/IMG_4605.htm: a *quare impedit* brought against John Grandisson concerning the archdeaconry of Cornwall, and ibid.: a *quare non admisit* brought against John Grandisson concerning the church of Southill.

bishop to court to answer why he impeded the king's presentation. From 1342 to 1352 the king rarely lost these cases; even if the evidence worked against him, these conflicts were argued in the common law courts in front of what were almost certainly stacked juries.[34] This put Edward's bishops in an untenable position: between Edward III's significant legal power within England and the pope's power of excommunication.

John Grandisson, bishop of Exeter (1327–60), found himself on both sides of this conflict over papal provisions and experienced the worst penalties either side had to offer. Already in 1342, Grandisson and his fellow bishops faced an overabundance of avaricious provisors clamouring for livings. In October, a group of bishops met at Canterbury to discuss the issue of papal provisions.[35] The consensus of the group, which Grandisson relayed to Pope Clement VI, was one of frustration – due largely to the dubious quality of the clerics travelling to the Roman curia to present themselves for bene-fices. The best ecclesiastics, they argued, stayed at home in England to tend their congregations, and thus remained unnoticed and without the lucrative benefices that could widen their influence. The bishops held this meeting mere months after Clement's accession, however, and the frustrations of the clergy described in Grandisson's letter illustrate the precarious nature of the bishops' situation even in the early years of Clement's pontificate.

By 1344, Grandisson was embroiled in a legal battle concerning the vicarage of Ermington (Devon). Unlike many of Edward's bishops in 1344, Grandisson owed little to Edward personally; consecrated in 1327, well before Edward fully controlled his throne, Grandisson had been a clerk to John XXII during his papal administration and educated in Paris by Jacques Fournier, later Benedict XII.[36] His loyalties would almost certainly have lain with the papacy first, rather than the king. That having been said, when the presentation to the vicarage of Ermington was being contested, Grandisson refused to admit the pope's candidate, John Crokhull, to the benefice.[37] Crokhull then took his case to the Roman court and returned with documents that described the pope's excommunications of Grandisson, all the canons of Exeter, the ministers and justices of the court, and John Stonor, the chief justice of the court of common pleas.[38] The king learned of Grandisson's

---

34 Heath, *Church and Realm*, p. 124.
35 *Reg. Grandisson*, iii, 111–12.
36 Palmer, *English Law in the Age of the Black Death*, p. 41.
37 See KB 27/349, AALT 2908 (1347), http://aalt.law.uh.edu/E3/KB27no349/aKB27no349fronts/ IMG_2908.htm.
38 See ibid.: 'Item per tertiam bullam manifeste liquet quod sententias ad excommunicandi archiepiscopum Cantuari, episcopum Exonie, omnes canonicos ecclesie Exonie, Willelmum de Hathelsay vicariam ecclesie de Ermyngton per regis ad eandem presentatum necnon dominum Johannem Stonore militem, ac Walterum de Strecthelegy, necnon alios parochianos dicte ecclesie de Ermyngton, ac contradictores quoslibet et rebelles, qui eidem Johanni Crokhill, seu eius procuratori super permissis se opposuerunt, vel impedimentum prostabunt, per se vel per alium, aut consilium auxilium, vel favorem contra ipsum dederint publice vel occulte. Et dicit quod

excommunication in December 1346, and a record of it exists only because the king sued the men who returned with the bulls that described the excommunication for bringing papal instruments into the country.[39]

John Crokhull brought the papal documents detailing the excommunications of those associated with the Ermington decision into the country in December 1346. The sentence levelled was excommunication *latae sententiae*, a form of excommunication that took effect immediately the crime was committed. Ostensibly, such a sentence should have prevented Grandisson from performing many of his administrative and ecclesiastical duties, even though by the fourteenth century the penalties associated with excommunication *latae sententiae* had softened significantly in comparison to their original form.[40] The bishop's registers make clear, however, that Grandisson continued to fulfil his episcopal duties, as entries concerning the installation and consecration of clerics appeared regularly throughout late 1346 and early 1347.[41]

Indeed, excommunication seems to have been a common penalty in this period, particularly the excommunication *latae sententiae*, which hypothetically would have been levelled against anyone who knowingly broke canon law.[42] Just before the battle of Crecy in 1346, a rector promulgated a sentence of excommunication on Edward III himself.[43] In July 1347, Grandisson levelled a sentence of excommunication on several messengers of the king. Two years earlier, in 1345, several royal messengers – William Wyke, Robert Kirkham and Elias Wilde – had delivered a writ of prohibition to Grandisson to stop him from hearing suits in his court regarding a presentation to the church of Kilkhampton, which were in derogation of the king's right.[44] For their interference, Grandisson fulminated a sentence of

---

ista sententia lata fuit per Oliverum de Cerreto decanum ecclesie Sancti Hillarii Pictaviensis, auditore curie Rome anno pontificatus Clementis pape quarto'. In the third bull with which Crokhull returned, it was made clear that the *latae sententiae* form of excommunication has been fulminated upon the archbishop of Canterbury, Bishop Grandisson, and all the other king's ministers and canons involved, by Oliver de Cerreto, dean of the church of Saint Hilary of Poitiers.

[39] I have found no references to this excommunication in any of the secondary sources relating to Grandisson, contemporary chronicles, or anywhere in his register.

[40] E. Vodola, *Excommunication in the Middle Ages* (Berkeley, 1986), pp. 28–9.

[41] *Reg. Grandisson*, iii, 1355–63.

[42] Vodola, *Excommunication in the Middle Ages*, pp. 28–9.

[43] Palmer, *English Law in the Age of the Black Death*, p. 29.

[44] KB 27/342, AALT 0402 (1345), http://aalt.law.uh.edu/AALT1/E3/KB27no342/bKB27no342 dorses/IMG_0402.htm. 'Dominus rex per Johannem de Lincoln qui sequitur pro eo optulit se quarto die versus Johannem episcopum Exonie de placito quare, cum dominus rex nuper accipiens quod idem episcopus in Willelmum Wyke, Robertum de Kirkham, Eliam Wilde, et Johannem Dobyn pro eo quod ipsi tanquam nuncii regis quandam prohibicionem regis ne Thomasiam que fuit uxoris Roberti de Kirkham super hiis quorum cognito ad regem pertinuit coram eo in curia Christianitas responsurus evocari nec quicquam quod in derogationem iuris corone cedere valeret attemptaret seu faceret aliqualiter attemptari eidem episcopo liberarunt sententiam excommunicationis fulminavit.'

greater excommunication on the group of messengers, who returned to the king to inform him of Grandisson's actions. When the messengers returned, they did so with writs prohibiting the bishop from proceeding against the messengers.[45] Grandisson, angered by the king's interference, had Wyke and his associates beaten and their belongings taken.[46] Wyke and the others were held in chains for fifty-three days before being released.[47] Grandisson's treatment of these messengers was openly rebellious, and his sentence of major excommunication against them was a serious one that could keep them from partaking of any of the ecclesiastical sacraments, if viable. Although perhaps not always this severe, excommunication seems to have been something of a hazard of doing business, given that the canons and justices of Cornwall, who were excommunicated by the pope in the course of the same case, continued to carry out business as usual.

Several factors contribute to the relative indifference with which these clerics and ministers reacted to these instances of excommunication. Though excommunication was the church's greatest weapon, it had to be enforced in order for it to offer any true discipline; such enforcement, after 1257, fell under the purview of the secular courts.[48] Often, the bishop of the diocese submitted the names of the excommunicate to the sheriff so that if they continued in their contumacy they could be brought to heel by the secular law. Perhaps more problematic in this case, though, was that the Constitution of Clarendon precluded the king's ministers from excommunication unless the king had reviewed and

---

45 Ibid.: 'eidem episcopo prohibitur rex ne quicquam pretextu liberationis huiusmodi brevis regis sibi facte contra eosdem Willelmus, Robertum, Eliam, et Johannem nec eorum aliquem quod in lesionem corone et dignitatis regis regio seu ipsorum Willelmi, Roberti, Elie, Johannis dampnum cedere valeret faceret aut fieri attemptaret aliquot modo.'

46 KB 27/345, AALT 5839 (1346), http://aalt.law.uh.edu/E3/KB27no345/aKB27no345mm1toEnd/ IMG_5839.htm. This action resulted in several lawsuits brought against Bishop Grandisson and a number of his associates by the king on behalf of the messengers in question, William Wyke, Robert Kirkham and Elias Wilde. 'Johannes episcopus Exonie, Johannes fitz Johannes atte Wode, Willelmus Rocomb, Johannes Fynamour, Ricardus de Gatepathe senior, Ricardus de Coppeshull, Johannes de Stonore, Michael de Aysthlegh, Johannes filius Walteri Horigge, Ricardus de Gatepathe junior, Johannes de Blakalre, Willelmus de Hosecomb, Petrus de Clyfford, Johannes Stille, Benedictus de Paston, Ricardus de Gummeshale, Johannes de Clyfford, Galfridus le Chamberleyn, et Willelmus Henry attachiati fuerunt ad respondendum Roberto Kirkham de placito quare vi et armis in ipsum Robertum apud Ayshporton insultum fecerunt et ipsum verbaverunt, vulneraverunt, et male tractaverunt et bona et catalla sua ad valenciam centum solidorum ibidem inventa ceperunt et asportaverunt et alia enormia etc. ad grave dampnum etc. et contra pacem etc.'

47 Ibid.: 'Et unde predictus Willelmus Wyke in propria persona sua queritur quod predicti episcopus et alii die Veneris proximo post festum Sancti Bartholomei Apostoli anno regni regis nunc decimonono vi et armis videlicet gladiis etc. in ipsum Willelmum apud Ayshperton insultum fecerunt et ipsum verberaverunt, vulneraverunt, imprisonaverunt videlicet per septem septimanas et quatuor dies tunc proximo sequenter et maletractaverunt et bona et catalla sua videlicet gladium, bokelarium, cultellum, pannos lineos et laneos ad valenciam etc. ibidem inventa ceperunt et asportaverunt contra pacem domini regis nunc unde dicit quod deterioratus est et dampnum habet ad valenciam mille librarum. Et inde producit sectam etc.'

48 Vodola, *Excommunication in the Middle Ages*, p. 189.

approved the sentence.[49] In this case the court, its ministers and justices simply carried on with the business at hand, perhaps because the king did not approve their excommunications, or possibly because they did not consider their work to be contrary to canon law or worthy of excommunication.

For a bishop, however, excommunication was certainly not a penalty to be taken lightly, especially as it was his duty to care for the souls of an entire diocese. Grandisson had acted against the pope in the Ermington case, and had jeopardized the eternity of his spiritual life and that of his flock in the process. Provisors continued to agitate for positions, despite the peril that Grandisson had endured. Clearly, siding with the king on such issues would be problematic. As a result, circumstances forced the bishop to alter his position.

Most bishops chose not to fight the king, instead sequestering the benefice in dispute until the parties reached a resolution, yet Grandisson was adamant in his course.[50] While a number of the cases involving Grandisson appear to have been resolved eventually through legal remedies with minor fanfare, a pair of cases brought in 1350 proved to be particularly troublesome for him. In that year, the king issued a writ of *quare impedit* against Grandisson concerning the archdeaconry of Cornwall. The conflict had begun in 1343 as two lay patrons – Ralph, Baron Stafford and John de Foreys – each claimed the right of advowson to the church of Southill in Cornwall, and each presented a cleric to the living.[51] Grandisson, because he could not determine who held the true right to present, refused to admit either candidate. Ralph appealed to the king for a writ of *quare impedit*, and in 1348 the case was removed to the king's courts. Although Ralph recovered the presentation to the benefice, in 1349 the king sued Ralph for the advowson right himself and won.[52] The king then presented his own candidate, Richard de Eccleshale,

---

[49] *Select Charters*, p. 166.

[50] Helmholz, *Oxford History of the Laws of England*, p. 487.

[51] CP 40/357, AALT 7468 (1349), http://aalt.law.uh.edu/E3/CP40no357/aCP40no357mm1toEnd/ IMG_7468.htm. 'Et episcopus per Bartholomeum Atte Mede attornatum suum venit et defendit vim et iniuriam quando etc. et dicit quod diu ante diem impetrationis brevis ipsius domini regis de *quare impedit* ecclesia predicta vacavit per mortem Johannis de Bradelegh tunc persone euisdem ecclesie, ita quod ecclesia illa sic vacante predictus Radulphus presentavit ei tanquam ordinario loci illius quendam clericum suum ad eandem ecclesiam et similiter quidam Johannes de Foreys de Westmyweton presentavit ei quendam clericum suum ad ecclesiam predictam per quas quidem presentationes et litigiositatem inter ipsos Radulpum et Johannem, idem episcopus impeditus extitit quod neutrum clericorum predictorum admittere potuit, per quod idem Radulphus quoddam breve regis de *quare impedit* versus predictum Johannem de Ferrers impetravit clamando advocacionem ecclesie predicte per narracionem suam tanquam ad manerium suum de Calyngton fore spectantem, ita quod pendente inter eos placito predicto tempus semestre transit.'

[52] CP 40/355, AALT 4070 (1348), http://aalt.law.uh.edu/E3/CP40no355/aCP40no355mm1toEnd/ IMG_4070.htm. 'Radulphus baron de Stafford summonitus fuit ad respondendum domino regi de placito quod permittat ipsum presentare idoneam personam ad ecclesiam de Suthull que vacat et ad suam spectat donacionem etc. et unde Johannes de Clone qui sequitur pro domino rege dicit quod quidam Thomas Corbet fuit seisitus de manerio de Calyngton cum pertinenciis ad quod advocatio ecclesie predicte pertinent tempore pacis tempore Henrici Regis proavi domini regis nunc. Et ad eandem ecclisiam presentavit quendam Johannem de Bradelegh clericum suum

whom Grandisson refused to admit, at which point Edward brought the writ of *quare non admisit* that culminated in the taking of the temporalities of the bishopric of Exeter into the king's hands.[53] As the advowson right to the church of Southill was part of the temporalities of the bishopric of Exeter, by taking those temporalities, the right to present to that benefice accrued to the king.

In a sister case brought the same year regarding the archdeaconry of Corn-

qui ad presentationem suam fuit admissus et institutus tempore pacis tempore eiusdem Domini Regis Henrici. Et de ipse Thoma descendit manerium predictum ad quod etc. cuidam Petro ut filio et heredi etc. qui quidem Petrus manerium predictum ad quod etc. dedit cuidam Roberto de Stafford in liberum maritagium cum Amicia sorore eiusdem Petri per quod donum iidem Robertus et Amicia fuerunt seisiti de manerio etc. ad quod etc. per formam etc. tempore pacis tempore Edwardi Regis avi domini regis nunc. Et de ipsis Roberto et Amicia descendit manerium ad quod etc. cuidam Nicholao ut filio et heredi etc. qui quidem Nicholaus tunc infra etatem fuit et quia predictus Robertus pater tenuit manerium de Stafford cum pertinenciis de ipso rege avo etc. per baroniam etc. Idem rex avus etc. post mortem predictorum Roberti et Amicie seisivit in manum suam predictum manerium de Stafford una cum advocatione predicta et aliis advocationibus etc. ratione minoris etatis eiusdem Nicholai una cum custodia eiusdem Nicholai post quam quidem seisinam ipso Nicholao filio Roberti infra etatem existente predicta ecclesia vacavit per mortem predicti Johannis de Bradelegh. Per quod ius presentandi accrevit ipsi rege avo etc. ut in iure ipsius Nicholai ratione minoris etatis eiusdem Nicholai. Etc. Et de ipso avo etc. descendit ius etc. cuidam Edwardo ut filio et heredi etc. et de ipso Edwardo ipsi domino regi nunc ut filio et heredi et ea ratione pertinent ad ipsum dominum regem nunc ad ecclesiam predictam ad presens presentare. Predictus Radulphus ipsum iniuste impedit ad dampnum ipsius Edwardi mille librarum.'

53   CP 40/357, AALT 7468 (1349), http://aalt.law.uh.edu/E3/CP40no357/aCP40no357mm1toEnd/ IMG_7468.htm. 'Johannes episcopus Exonie in misericordia pro pluribus defaltis etc. Idem episcopus attachiatus fuit ad respondendum domino regi de placito quare, cum idem dominus rex nuper in curia sua coram justiciariis suis hic recuperaverit versus Radulphum baronem de Stafford' presentationem suam ad ecclesiam de Suthull vacantem et ad regis donacionem spectantem per considerationem eiusdem curie sue propter quod mandavit idem rex eidem episcopo quod non obstante reclamatione predicti Radulphi ad presentationem Regis ad predictam ecclesiam idoneam personam admitteret. Idem episcopus Richardum de Eccleshale clericum regis ad dictam ecclesiam per regem presentatum ad eandem ecclesiam admittere recusavit in regis contemptum et preiudicium ac dampnum gravissimum.' KB 27/360, AALT 4856 (1350), http:// aalt.law.uh.edu/E3/KB27no360/bKB27no360dorses/IMG_4856.htm. 'Idem episcopus Richardum de Eccleshale clericum regis per ipsum regem ad ecclesiam predictam presentatum admittere recusavit, per quod dominus rex tulit breve suum de quare non admisit versus prefatum episcopum de contemptu predicto retornabile coram eiusdem justiciariis de banco a die Sancti Michaelis in XV dies anno superdicto, ita quod pendente placito predicto [melius: pependit placitum predictum] super predicto brevi de *quare non admisit* coram eiusdem justiciariis de banco apud Westmonasterium usque in Octabis Sancti Michaelis anno regni regis nunc vicesimo tercio, quo die idem episcopus erga dominum rege de contemptu predicto occasione predicta committus fuit, per quod coram prefatis Justiciariis ad tunc consideratum fuit quod temporalia episcopatus predicti in manum regis caperentur et seisientur, virtute cuius iudicii dominus rex incontinenti in iure fuit seisitus de temporalibus episcopatus predicti, ita quod extunc per legem terre accrevit domino regi ius presentandi ad omnia beneficia et dignitates episcopatus predicti quovismodo vacantur, et postmodum pro eo quod prefatus Johannes de Sancto Paulo electus fuit in archiepiscopum Dublini et consecrates, videlicet, die Dominica in prima septimana quadragesime tunc proximo sequens virtute cuius consecrationis prebenda illa vacavit temporalia episcopatus predicti in manu regis tunc et adhuc sit existentibus, et ea ratione quod temporalia episcopatus predicti adhuc in manu domini regis virtute iudicii predicti existunt et predicta prebenda modo vacat, pertinent ad presens domino regi nunc ad predictam prebendam presentare prefatus episcopus ipsum iniuste impedit ad dampnum ipsius domini regis viginti mille librarum.'

wall and the prebend connected with it, Grandisson again faced the worst penalties in the king's arsenal. The election and subsequent consecration of John of St Paul to the archbishopric of Dublin left the archdeaconry and its associated prebend vacant. This vacancy had fallen during the time that Edward III held the temporalities of the bishopric due to the Southill case, and thus it fell to him, by his reckoning, to present a suitable candidate to the benefice. Despite the accrual to the king of the temporalities of the bishopric of Exeter, which included the advowson right to the archdeaconry of Cornwall, Grandisson remained steadfast in his efforts to keep Edward's candidate, William Cusance, from entering the benefice.[54] Grandisson also stood as a defendant in five other cases concerning benefices, with three of them culminating in writs of *quare non admisit*.[55] Ultimately, the legal situation in the diocese of Exeter was not anomalous, and the evidence in the plea rolls indicates that the king was pursuing legal remedies in similar conflicts in many, if not all, dioceses in England. Edward III brought writs of *quare impedit* against a number of bishops in the years between 1342 and 1352, including those of Exeter, Lincoln, Ely, Norwich and York.[56] Of these, William Bateman, bishop of Norwich, was the only other bishop whose situation became so dire that he faced a writ of *quare non admisit* and had his temporalities taken. Their seizure drove him to barricade himself within his sanctuary in Norwich for six months.[57] Clearly, these bishops were caught in an extraordinarily difficult position, one that was exacerbated by the large numbers of provisions and presentations made in the wake of the Black Death.

Though the king and the pope, and to a lesser extent bishops, were the most powerful players in the contest for provisions, the influence and power of the provisors themselves should not be understated. While papal provisions often served to open doors for university scholars and new graduates – indeed it was customary for both Oxford and Cambridge to send lists of new graduates to the pope for consideration[58] – it can be certain that provisions were also made for those of wealth and influence. In contrast, Edward's presentations were more likely to be former royal clerks or people holding positions within his household or administration. Just as Edward III had favourites among the laity – his so-called New Men on whom he gifted lands and annuities[59] – so too did Edward have trusted men among ecclesiastics. John of St Paul, a clerk of the king whose election to the archbishopric of Dublin left the

[54] KB 27/360, AALT 4605 (1350), http://aalt.law.uh.edu/E3/KB27no360/aKB27no360fronts/IMG_4605.htm.

[55] Palmer, *English Law in the Age of the Black Death*, p. 47.

[56] Ibid., pp. 44–53.

[57] Ibid., p. 49.

[58] R. Swanson, 'Universities, Graduates and Benefices in Later Medieval England', *Past & Present* 106 (1985), 42.

[59] Bothwell, *Edward III and the English Peerage*, p. 58.

archdeaconry of Cornwall vacant along with a handful of other benefices, had originally held the prebend of Romsey and a canonry and prebend of Exeter.[60] He exchanged the prebendary of Romsey for prebendaries in York and Lichfield, which he then quickly exchanged for the provostry of Wells.[61] In 1347, he was installed into the archdeaconry of Cornwall, which he held along with the provostry of Wells and the prebend and canonry of Exeter.[62]

The aforementioned William Cusance, John of St Paul's successor, was presented to the archdeaconry of Cornwall in 1350 following the seizure of Exeter's temporalities, but his association with the crown reached further back than that. In 1320, Edward II had made him the Keeper of the Great Wardrobe, and after a short period away from service during the upheaval of the conflict between the Despensers and Edward II, he was reinstated as the keeper of Prince Edward's wardrobe in 1323.[63] By 1337, Cusance was a valued clerk of the king and had been entrusted with the safekeeping of the lands, goods and chattels of the king's late brother, John of Eltham, earl of Cornwall.[64] In 1342, although already the parson of the church of Wakefeld, Edward presented Cusance with the priory of Wangford (Suffolk) to administer during the war with France.[65] At the same time, he was a canon of St Paul's in London and acting as the king's treasurer. By 1349, Cusance was the Keeper of the Wardrobe and Edward presented him to the archdeaconry early the next year.[66]

The king rewarded John de Cloune, who acted as his advocate in the Southill case, with presentations to the chapel of Menacuddle (Cornwall) and the church of Bishopestrowe (Wiltshire).[67] John of St Paul, William Cusance and John de Cloune are illustrative of the men vying for benefices throughout England. In many cases, they were very powerful people in their own right, those who would go on to positions that held even more influence. Such people could put significant pressure on bishops like Grandisson, even indirectly, because of the influence they had with the king and in his administration. Their seemingly endless drive to acquire more and better benefices left them open to the accusations of greed and avarice so often levelled against pluralists.[68] Clearly, these clerics were both ambitious and greedy enough to feel no compunction about the penalties a bishop might face if he fought back against the king and his associates, particularly if that bishop did not owe his presentation to the episcopacy to the king.

[60] *CFR 1347–56*, pp. 19, 31, 339.
[61] *CFR 1347–56*, p. 97; *CPR 1348–50*, pp. 462, 587.
[62] *CPR 1345–48*, p. 364.
[63] W. Ormrod, 'Cusance, William (d. 1360)', *ODNB*, Oxford University Press, 2004 [http://www.oxforddnb.com/view/article/50142, accessed 12 April 2013]
[64] *CFR 1337–47*, p. 1.
[65] Ibid., p. 227.
[66] Ibid., p. 232; *CPR 1348–50*, p. 462.
[67] *CPR 1348–50*, pp. 356, 477.
[68] Waugh, *England in the Reign of Edward III*, p. 147.

Despite their generally less exalted station and influence, papal provisors challenged royal presentees and the king by using both physical and political means to secure these contested benefices. The most common and least dangerous method was for papal provisors to secure papal processes at the Roman court which stated that the pope had provided that cleric to the benefice. These processes were generally papers that indicated that the pope had provided the benefice to the bearer. Despite the fact that Edward and parliament had outlawed bringing papal processes into England in 1343, ecclesiastics continued to do so as a means of staking a claim.[69] John Wrey, an English chaplain in the diocese of Exeter, was involved in two major series of cases regarding illegal papal processes, and was associated with a third. In 1348, Edward summoned him to the King's Bench to answer for the carrying of illegal papal processes into England related to both the priory of Totnes (Exeter) and the vicarage of Brixham (Devon). In both cases, the king prosecuted jointly with Hugh de Askham, who especially argued that the bulls that Wrey had obtained undermined his presentation to the vicarage of Brixham.[70] Wrey was also named in the early documents of the case brought against John Crokhull, in which the evidence of Grandisson's excommunication is found.[71] Wrey spent a significant amount of time imprisoned in the Marshalsea for his crimes, as bringing such processes into the realm was grounds for immediate imprisonment.

This practice sometimes escalated on the relatively rare occasions when a cleric entered a benefice with force and arms. In the common law, reforms

---

[69] The Ordinance of Provisors was presented in parliament and approved by the king in 1343: see Barrel, 'Ordinance of Provisors', 264–77.

[70] KB 27/353, AALT 6447 (1348), http://aalt.law.uh.edu/E3/KB27no353/aKB27no353mm1toEnd/ IMG_6447.htm. 'Preceptum fuit vicecomiti quod venire faceret coram domino rege ad hunc die scilicet in Octabis Sancte Trinitatis ubicumque etc. proximo quarto tam milites etc. de visneto de Brixham per quos etc. Et qui Johannem Wrey capellanum nulla capabilis etc. ad recognoscendum etc. si predictus Johannes culpabilis sit de diversis impedimentis, notificationibus, citationes, appellacionibus, et aliis prejudiciis domino regi et Hugom de Askham cleric apud Brixham illatis super possest vicarie de Brixham etc. die Dominica proximo post Festum Omnium Sanctorum anno regni regis nunc Anglie vicesimo primo [4 November 1347], per quas bullas papales infra regni Anglie delatas et apud Brixham ostensas etc. notificatas in preiudicium legum et ipsum regem subversionem et corone sue exheredationis periculum manifestum contra pacem regis, sicut predictus Hugh qui tam pro domino rege quam pro se ipso sequitur dicit necne quia etc.'

[71] KB 27/349, AALT 2908 (1347), http://aalt.law.uh.edu/E3/KB27no349/aKB27no349fronts/IMG_ 2908.htm. 'Johannes Crokhull attachiatus fuit ad respondendum tam domino regi quam Johanni de Askham clerico de placito quare, cum dominus rex pluries ante hec tempora in singulis comitatibus regni sui Anglie proclamari et ex parte ipsius regis firmiter inhiberi fecerit ne quis indigena vel alienigena sub forisfactura omnium que eidem domino regi forisfacere posset bullas, litteras, seu alia eidem regi, magnatibus, aut populo ipsius regis preiudicialia infra domini regnum regis Anglie deferret seu deferri faceret, nec quicquam domino regi aut dicto populo suo preiudiciale attemptaret sub forisfactura predicta, predictus Johannes Crokhull simul cum Johanne Wrey et Phillipe de Tonsoure huiusmodi bullas, litteras, quamplura alia tam domino regi quam predicto Johanni de Askham valde preiudicialia infra domini regnum regis Anglie detulit in ipsius regis contemptum et preiudicium et legum et jurium regis subversionem et corone regie exheredationis periculum et ipsius Johannis de Askham dampnum gravissimum et contra proclamationem et inhibitionem regis predictas etc.'

made to the Assize of Novel Disseisin over the course of the late thirteenth
and early fourteenth century created a legal atmosphere in which potential
claimants began to enter tenements forcibly in order to start court proceedings.[72] This legal custom permeated society so thoroughly that papal provisors
may have taken their cue from the laity and begun to use similar practices in
claiming their benefices.[73] In 1346 Edward III brought a suit against Simon
Russel, a cleric in the diocese of Exeter, concerning the church of St Thomas
by Exeter, part of the temporalities of the priory of Colwyk.[74] These temporalities, like those of many other priories in England, were in the hands of
the king because they had been a part of the first reaping of alien priories
recovered under the 1337 Ordinance. Edward had recovered the presentation
to the church by this reason against the prior of Colwyk, but Simon Russel
forcibly entered the church and held it occupied. In addition to the occupation, Russel was in possession of provisions made to him at the Roman court
providing him to the benefice. Edward sued Russel for significant damages,
1,000 marks,[75] in litigation that lasted well into the 1350s. Meanwhile, in

---

[72] D. Sutherland, *The Assize of Novel Disseisin* (Oxford, 1973), p. 145. Sutherland detailed a
period of deliberate reform in the legal understanding of the writ of Novel Disseisin that led
to an expansion not only in the application of the writ itself, but also in the contemporary
conceptualization of what seisin was. The result was a legal atmosphere in which the relational
obligations had dropped away, leaving something very much like property right. Seisin became
something inherent, rather than something conferred. Where once a claimant would have had to
be on the land for a quarter year, a new process in the early fourteenth century suggested that
merely entering and completing a ritualized facsimile of fee administration before removal was
enough to be considered seisin. By the 1340s merely setting foot on the land could be considered
seisin, and claimants began to enter lands and tenements in order to initiate court proceedings.

[73] See the statute of forcible entry, *SR* 15 Richard II, st. 2, which prohibited this action due to the
increasing amounts of litigation generated by trespass to test seisin cases. Over the course of
the fourteenth century, trespass to test seisin cases grew significantly in number, perhaps not
least because of the confusion that ensued in the wake of the Black Death and its impact on the
English population. By the 1390s, the practice was so prevalent that it was necessary to curtail it
via statute.

[74] KB 27/343, AALT 8361 (1346), http://aalt.law.uh.edu/E3/KB27no343/bKB27no343dorses/
IMG_8361.htm. 'Jurata ad recognoscendum etc. cum temporalia prioratus de Colwyk ratione
guerre inter dominum regem et illos de Francie mote anno regni regis nunc Anglie undecimo in
manum domini regis seisita fuissent et idem rex postmodum presentationem suam ad vicariam
ecclesie Sancte Thome iuxta Exonie vacantem et ad regis donacionem spectantem ratione
temporalium predictorum in manum domini regis existencium coram justiciariis suis de banco
apud Westmonasterium versus priorem de Colwyk recuperavit rex, si Simon Russel die Lune
proximo post Festum Epiphanie Domini anno regni regis nunc Anglie quartodecimo [9 January
1341], virtute cuiusdam provisionis sibi ad Curiam Romanam facte vicariam predictam vi et armis
ingressus fuit et eam tenet occupatam in presenti in regis et iniurium corone sue preiudicium et
iudicii predicti enervationem manifestam et contra prohibitionem et contra pacem regis sicut
Johannes de Lincoln qui sequitur pro domino rege dicit vel non, sicut predictus Simon dicit necne
ponitur in respectum usque a die Pasche in XV dies ubicumque etc. pro defectu juratorum quia
nullus etc. Ideo vicecomes habeat corpora omnium juratorum coram domino rege ad prefatum
terminum etc. Et predictus Simon interim committitur marchalsie.'

[75] KB 27/343, AALT 8361 (1346), http://aalt.law.uh.edu/E3/KB27no343/bKB27no343dorses/IMG_
8361.htm. By contrast, Edward allowed his conflict with John Grandisson to be resolved by a fine
of a mere 200 pounds, *CPR 1350–54*, p. 312. This resolution was only offered in 1351, however,

1351, Russel was provided to another benefice by the pope for his efforts, perhaps because he had lost the vicarage at the church of Saint Thomas by Exeter.[76] A similar case began in 1345 that alleged that Robert Boner and Henry Gurdon had entered the church of Harpford (Devon) with force and arms, held it occupied, and brought various papal processes in contempt of the king.[77] Again, Edward had taken the temporalities of a priory into his hands as a result of the war between England and France, this time for the priory of Otterton (Devon). He had recovered the right to present to the vicarage of the church of Harpford and presented his clerk, John de Sibthorp, to the benefice.[78] Before Sibthorp could take possession, however, clerics Henry Gurdon and Robert Boner forcibly entered the benefice and Gurdon held it occupied. Together, Gurdon and Boner also produced claims, appeals, summonses and inhibitions in contempt of the king and in prejudice of his crown and the law of the realm. Though the text does not explicitly state that they had evidence of their provision to that benefice by the pope, as it does in the Russel case, the wording does make clear that they had brought diverse papal processes into the realm, contrary to the Ordinance of 1343.

Though uncommon, these cases allude to a larger domestic conflict between the church and the state. Thus far, five other cases of ecclesiastics forcibly occupying benefices have been found: one each in Berkshire, Kent, London, Suffolk and Leicestershire. Of these, three other clerics besides those in the diocese of Exeter forcibly entered churches with papal bulls

and perhaps illustrated Edward III's attempts to rebuild a collegial relationship with his bishops and maintain the existing social hierarchy in the wake of the Black Death.

[76] *CPL 1342–62*, p. 349.

[77] KB 27/342, AALT 0418 (1345), http://aalt.law.uh.edu/AALT1/E3/KB27no342/aKB27no342fronts/ IMG_0418.htm. 'Dominus rex per Johannem de Lincoln qui sequitur pro eo optulit se quarto die versus Henricum Gurdon et Robertum Boner de placito quare, cum dominus rex nuper in curia sua per considerationem eiusdem curie recuperasset versus priorum de Oteryton presentationem suam ad vicariam ecclesie de Harpford vacantem et ad regis donacionem spectantem ratione temporalium prioratus predicti in manu regis occasione guerre inter regem et ipsos de Francie mote existencium, et dilectum clericum regis Johannem de Sibthorp iure regis regio presentasset rex ad eandem, iidem Henricus et Robertus dictam vicariam ad donacionem regis sic spectantem vi et armis ingressi fuerunt dictusque Henricus eam sic tenet occupatam prefati, que Henricus et Robertus provocationes, appellaciones, citationes, inhibitiones, et alios processus diverses in hac parte fecerunt in regis contemptum et iuris sui et corone sue preiudicium ac iudicii pro rege in hac parte redditi enervacionem manifestam et predicti clerici regis grave dampnum et contra pacem regis.' See also: KB 27/344, AALT 9237; KB 27/346, AALT 9641; and KB 27/346, AALT 9682.

[78] The same church was the subject of another series of cases brought by the king against Hugh de Seton, who procured papal processes for the church of Harpford a mere two years later, before the litigation against Henry Gurdon and Robert Boner had even been completed. KB 27/349, AALT 3007 (1347), http://aalt.law.uh.edu/E3/KB27no349/aKB27no349fronts/IMG_3007.htm. That the king sued two papal provisors within such a short period suggests not only a lack of communication, but also a certain amount of chaos within the process of papal provision and royal presentation. Examination of the patent rolls shows Edward making presentations to various benefices repeatedly. Edward presented clerics to the vicarage of Barnstaple (Devon), a particularly embattled benefice, no fewer than five times between 1348 and 1351, only the last of whom seems to have actually taken possession.

supporting their claims.[79] Perhaps most interesting was a case in Suffolk, in which the cleric Robert Alred entered the church of St Peter at Stowmarket with papal support, but was then removed by the sheriff, who held the church until the true patron's choice could arrive to take control of the benefice.[80]

That there were physical conflicts over ecclesiastical benefices or between clerics is unsurprising, and indeed such conflicts happened with a modicum of regularity.[81] In Huntingdonshire in 1297, for example, the temporalities of the bishopric of Lincoln were in the hands of Edward I because of the vacancy left by the death of Oliver Sutton, the former bishop. The king presented John de Cadamo to the prebend of Leighton Manor and subsequently ordered the new bishop, John Dalderby, to admit his candidate. When de Cadamo travelled to the benefice, however, he found that three men (none of whom were ecclesiastics, but rather men of the surrounding area) defended the benefice against him.[82] Such incidents of protections against the entry of royal presentees were not uncommon; indeed, the case involving the church of St Peter at Stowmarket includes both forcible entry by a papal provisor and the subsequent defence and occupation of the benefice until the 'true' holder of the benefice could arrive.[83]

There is a distinction to be drawn between the defence of a church against a royal presentee and the forcible entry by a papal provisor into a benefice while holding documents of papal support. While it is true that a royal presentee may also be a papal provisor – as was the case in many episcopal and otherwise valuable provisions – the documents concerning these 1340s cases make clear that there was little, if any, compromise between papal and royal interests. Though each of the writs documenting these forcible occupations includes the phrase *vi et armis*, it is unlikely that any violence or armed aggression actually took place. Rather, its usage coupled with the distinct lack of any specific mention of weapons or assaults suggests that such incidents were largely non-violent, though physical, occupations.[84] Despite their

---

[79] For documents relating to the case against Robert de Thresk in Canterbury, see the following frames on the AALT: KB 27/335, AALT 0235 (1344), http://aalt.law.uh.edu/AALT1/E3/KB27no335/aKB27no335fronts/IMG_0235.htm; KB 7/344, AALT 8774; for Thomas de Abyngdon in Berkshire: KB 27/336, AALT 0218 (1344) http://aalt.law.uh.edu/AALT1/E3/KB27no336/aKB27no336fronts/IMG_0218.htm; see also KB 27/340, AALT 0053; KB 27/341, AALT 0061; KB 27/341, AALT 0230; KB 27/342, AALT 0275; KB 27/343, AALT 8272; KB 27/344, AALT 9100.

[80] KB 27/343, AALT 8319 (1347), http://aalt.law.uh.edu/E3/KB27no343/bKB27no343dorses/IMG_8319.htm. See also: KB 27/343, AALT 8333; KB 27/344, AALT 9148.

[81] Saunders, 'Royal Ecclesiastical Patronage in England', p. 332.

[82] KB 27/189, AALT 1493 (1297), http://aalt.law.uh.edu/AALT1/E1/KB27no189/aKB27no189fronts/IMG_1493.htm.

[83] KB 27/343, AALT 8319 (1346), http://aalt.law.uh.edu/E3/KB27no343/bKB27no343dorses/IMG_8319.htm.

[84] See n. 47 above, the assault cases on William Wyke, Robert Kirkham and Elias Wilde for the wording of a writ documenting the use of weapons and inflicted injuries. At this time it was common for legal writs handling trespasses to include *vi et armis*; its usage in these writs does not prove the use of violence, but it does suggest that some kind of force was involved. That

non-violent nature, these actions still represented direct opposition to the king's will and the common law process. Edward III took action against these provisors without reservation and penalized them harshly if they refused to submit, despite numerous pointed letters from Clement VI asking that he 'revoke novelties attempted against ecclesiastical liberty' delivered to Edward via numerous bishops, nuncios, and even his wife.[85] Yet despite the king's heavy-handed approach, clerics continued to enter and occupy benefices into the 1350s.

These seven cases of forcible entry (five with papal processes), while an admittedly small sample, suggest a number of things about the character of these provisors, the power they possessed, and the social and political under-currents that informed their actions. For these men, avarice had overcome ecclesiastic ideals of passivism and driven them to physical action, though there are no indications in the documents that injuries occurred during these forcible entries, and it is unlikely that there were weapons or true violence involved. Without a thorough investigation of the plea rolls, we cannot know whether these forcible entries were truly a new phenomenon, although preliminary examination of the evidence has uncovered no such forcible entries in the course of the 1330s.[86] Moreover, the 1340s were marked by both war and pestilence, providing unique opportunities of which the provisors could take advantage.

Regardless of the novelty of these acts, that several instances of forceful occupation occurred in a handful of years was alarming in itself. They are evidence of an upswing in the tension between the common law and the clergy within England but also in violence committed both by and against ecclesiastics. These were by no means isolated incidents, and court cases concerning warlike conduct against clerics and assaults and trespasses made by clerics were particularly prevalent from the late 1330s throughout the 1340s. Such cases suggest that tensions were high between the clergy and the laity, and could be indicative of an effort on the part of the lower clergy to subvert the will of the king in favour of the will of the pope.

It has been previously argued that the Ordinance of 1343 was created

said, the text of KB 27/343, AALT 8361 argued that actual weapons were used in Simon Russel's occupation of the Church of Saint Thomas by Exeter; however, only in the context of the king's testimony submitted via a writ close to the record.

[85]   *CPL 1342–62*, p. 31.

[86]   This issue is the subject of ongoing study into the reigns of Edward I, Edward II and Edward III. Though I have yet to find similar cases of forcible entry in the plea rolls prior to 1343, it is possible that this type of issue may previously have been handled in King's Council, for which there are no records. The cases of this sort that are evident in the plea rolls in the 1340s begin after the initial seizure of alien priories in 1337, though the first forcible entry was made in 1341, and it was not until 1343 that the first cases were prosecuted. Those cases continued for several years, most of them well into the 1350s, and thus it seems likely that evidence of earlier incidents would exist in the documents from the late 1330s or early 1340s. As it stands currently, forcible entries by clerics of this type seem to have been a hitherto unknown, and thus alarming, phenomenon.

with limited goals: to end the provision of aliens to English benefices, but more importantly, to do so only when it was considered in derogation of the king's right.[87] The evidence in this article supports that thesis, but also carries it one step further: Edward not only used the Ordinance to block those appointments that he did not support, but may also have done so as a way to suppress an increasingly agitated lower clergy. Plea rolls make it clear that many members of the clergy were compelled to circumvent the mandates of the king by seeking justice in the papal courts. Those with the power used excommunication to avoid the king's writs and judgments. Others resorted to criminality, either through the taking by force of benefices or in at least one case, outright banditry.[88] The conflict over advowsons and benefices provided an outlet for these growing tensions. It was an issue of both state and local importance, and one for which clerics were especially willing to fight. In an age where the prevailing theory held that the church in England was beholden to the king for its existence, Edward was unwilling to have members of that church work against him. As clerics became more aggressive in their efforts to secure benefices, Edward litigated against those in opposition to him that much harder. The plea rolls leading up to 1348 were increasingly filled with writs concerning the issue of benefices; after the plague, even though the overall caseload decreased dramatically, the number of cases concerning unruly clerical behaviour continued at a comparatively high rate.

Especially in the post-Black Death world in which these cases continued, it seems increasingly as if Edward's actions were largely directed towards those members of the English clergy he considered out of order. Moreover, documentary evidence shows a distinct shift in the focus of these cases after the Black Death. In the case of the archdeaconry of Cornwall and the prebend of John de Saint Paul discussed above, Bishop Grandisson was the main defendant from the start of the case through early 1351, and appeared as a named defendant in over half a dozen writs relating to the same case. He had, after all, refused to admit suitable candidates to those positions, and had wilfully disobeyed the king.[89] By Hilary Term 1351, however, Edward's agenda had changed, focusing instead on uniting the aristocracy against the lower classes.[90] The aristocracy included bishops, and thus Edward had begun working towards resolutions with Grandisson, Bateman and other troubled bishops in an effort to build a more collegial, conciliatory relationship with that section of the aristocracy. Edward's quarrels over the archdeaconry did

---

[87] See Barrel, 'Ordinance of Provisors', pp. 264–77.
[88] J. Aberth, *Criminal Churchmen in the Age of Edward III* (University Park, Pa., 1996), paints a vivid and detailed portrait of Bishop Thomas de Lisle of Ely, the bandit bishop, and his unruly, often criminal, behaviour.
[89] KB 27/360, AALT 4605 (1350), http://aalt.law.uh.edu/E3/KB27no360/aKB27no360fronts/IMG_4605.htm.
[90] Palmer, *English Law in the Age of the Black Death*, passim.

not end in 1351, but they probably did end with John Grandisson.[91] Starting in Hilary Term 1351, Grandisson's name drops almost completely from the records for this case; it is referenced only when stating that the temporalities of the bishopric had been taken into the hand of the king.[92] Instead, the litigation is redirected towards the cleric John Harewell, using verbiage nearly identical to that used in the mid-1340s when the 1343 Ordinance was being more heavily enforced. Rather than concentrating on the issue of Grandisson's refusal to admit a candidate, the suit now focused on the issue of the unlawful papal processes that Harewell had acquired.[93] This shift is evidence of Edward's changing attitude towards the English clergy: a reaffirmation of his intent to subdue a potentially defiant lower clergy and an attempt to settle peaceably with the upper clergy.

This period in 1351 was a turning point, one which hinged on the major statutory changes put into place after the Black Death. On paper, the Statute of Provisors of 1351 did much to put an end to the procurement of papal provisions; while this was a blow to England's clerics, the statute proved not without its benefits. The statute spoke at length against the clergy's 'grievances and mischief' that caused 'the greater damage and destruction of all', thus reading as an anticlerical statute.[94] In fact, this statute more clearly defined the steps by which the king would take control of the *ius presentandi* of a benefice. More importantly, at least for the clergy, it outlined the process by which the prosecution of violations of the statute would proceed. One distinct change, for example, was that violators would not be imprisoned prior to conviction.

---

[91] This was true of advowson cases, but Grandisson continued to be called before the king to answer for the unlawful excommunication of the king's messengers well into the late 1350s.

[92] KB 27/362, AALT 5721 (1351), http://aalt.law.uh.edu/E3/KB27no362/aKB27no362fronts/IMG_5721.htm. 'Dominus rex per Simonem de Kegworth qui sequitur pro eo optulit se quarto die versus Johannem de Harewell clericum de placito quare, cum dominus rex in curia sua coram rege per breve suum recuperavit dominus rex presentationem suam ad archidiactonatum Cornubie nuper vacantem et ad suam donationem spectantem rationem temporalium episcopatus Exonie in manu sua nuper existencium versus Johannem episcopum Exonie sicut per tenorem recordi et processus inde in cancellaria sua de mandato suo missum plenius apparet ac eidem Johanni de Harewell prohibiverimus ne quicquam quod in regis preiudicium vel iuris sui regii aut iudicii predicti enervationem cedere valeret attemptaret nec faceret aliqualiter attemptari idem Johannes de Harewell citationes, appellationes, inhibitiones, iudicationes, instrumenta, et quamplura alia domino regi et corone sue regie preiudicialia in hac parte faceat et fieri procuravit in domini regis contemptum et preiudicium et iuris sui regni ac iudicii predictorum enervationem manifestam et contra prohibitionem suam predictam ut dicitur.'

[93] KB 27/362, AALT 5976 (1351), http://aalt.law.uh.edu/E3/KB27no362/bKB27no362dorses/IMG_5976.htm. 'Dominus rex per Simonem de Kegworth qui sequitur pro eo optulit se quarto die versus Robertum Mounteyne de Exonie, Willelmum Pile capellanum, Robertum Pile capellanum, Johannem Harewell, et Johannem de Uphull de placito quare, cum dominus nuper in curia sua coram eo per diversa brevia sua recuperavitur idem rex presentationis domini regis ad archideaconatum Cornubie et ad prebendam illam quam Johannes de Sancto Paulo nuper tenuit in ecclesia Sancti Petri Exonie vacantes et ad regis donationem spectantes ratione temporalium episcopatus Exonie in manu ipsius Regis existencium versus Johannem episcopum Exonie prout preiudicia unde in dicta curia regis reddita.'

[94] *SR* 25 Edward III, st. 4.

John Wrey, previously discussed in regards to the Ordinance of Provisors of 1343, spent years in the Marshalsea between court appearances.[95] Other cases similarly show defending clerics being led to court from other prisons.[96] Under the guidelines charted in the new statute, this would no longer occur. Similarly, the statute decreed that clerics would only be outlawed if they refused to appear in court.[97] Again, this was a change in policy that worked in the favour of the clergy by allowing them the opportunity to appear in court before the king to defend any major actions made against them. Still, the Statute of Provisors was clearly intended to act in concert with other post-Black Death legislation by reinforcing Edward's authority and providing the king with the means by which to suppress a rebellious clergy.

The Statute *Pro Clero* of early 1352 provided clear evidence of the shift in Edward's policy.[98] Though it reaffirmed much of the 1351 statute, in fact it was a clear step towards a more collegial relationship with upper clergy. The statute confirmed the illegality of papal processes and the circumvention of the king's justice by the papal curia, but changes to the litigation process in these cases now allowed archbishops, bishops and ordinaries the ability to counter-plead against the king, in addition to offering specific, certain indictments. Thus the new statute not only let bishops know exactly how they would be charged, it also gave them the opportunity to defend themselves. As part of this new effort towards collegiality, Edward dropped the *quare non admisit* cases against Grandisson, Bateman and other unruly bishops, and settled these cases for much smaller fines than previously levied.[99] These modifications brought Edward's problem bishops back into the fold and ended the major cases against them, but for the lower clergy the litigation continued apace. While these new privileges were bestowed upon members of the upper clergy, the lower clergy was still subject to the original processes outlined in the Statute of 1351.

If Edward had used this type of litigation to subdue the clergy prior to the Black Death – and its calculated application against particularly subversive clerics is evidence that he did – the even more tumultuous socio-political

---

[95] KB 27/353, AALT 6447 (1348), http://aalt.law.uh.edu/E3/KB27no353/aKB27no353mm1toEnd/IMG_6447.htm. 'Et vicecomes non retornavit breve etc. Ideo sicut prius preceptus est vicecomiti quod venire faciat coram domino rege in Octabis Sancti Michaelis ubicumque etc. xxiiii tam milites etc. et quia etc. ad recognoscendum etc. et interim committitur Marschalsie etc.'

[96] KB27/350, AALT 3913 (1347), http://aalt.law.uh.edu/E3/KB27no350/aKB27no350fronts/IMG_3913.htm mentioned only that Hugh de Seton spent time in the 'prisona domini regis,' while John Crokhull spent time in both Fleet prison and Marshalsea: KB 27/349, AALT 2908 (1347), http://aalt.law.uh.edu/E3/KB27no349/aKB27no349fronts/IMG_2908.htm. 'Et Johannes de Crokhill per custodem regis gaole de Flete per preceptum regis ad barram dicitur.' In both cases, this was during the course of the case, rather than after conviction.

[97] *SR* 25 Edward III, st. 4.

[98] *SR* 25 Edward III, st. 6.

[99] *CPR 1350–54*, p. 312. The initial damages sought in this case were 20,000 pounds, a sum that had dropped to a mere 200 by the end of the case. For the initial fine levied, see KB 27/360, AALT 4605 (1350), http://aalt.law.uh.edu/E3/KB27no360/aKB27no360fronts/IMG_4605.htm.

atmosphere that arose in its wake removes any doubt of his intentions. The statutory changes wrought by Edward and his legal advisors in the aftermath of the plague, including the Statutes of Provisors (1351), Labourers (1351), Treasons (1351) and Praemunire (1353), show that Edward was willing to use litigation to quell potential unruliness. The Statute of Provisors in particular was not reactionary legislation. Rather, it was the implementation of a statute that made official and legally defined policies that had proven effective deterrents. The 1340s were the proving ground for such policies; Edward manipulated the law not only to consolidate royal authority, but to force the submission of those who attempted to challenge him.

The traditional narratives used to explain Edward's relationship with his clergy are incomplete. Although amplified in Exeter, events occurring in many of the dioceses across England mirrored the happenings in Devon and Cornwall; thus the conflict within the diocese of Exeter can stand as a microcosm for the larger conflict within the whole of the realm. The dichotomy of Edward's relationship with the clergy in that diocese – extremely generous to his trusted clerks and ecclesiastical administrators, while utterly ruthless in his prosecution of those working against him – suggests that Edward's anticlerical agenda was not directed towards papal authority or even the English clergy as a whole. Instead, these actions show a concerted effort in the 1340s to subdue those clerics acting against Edward's interests. The statutory confirmation of these policies in 1351, followed quickly by the Statute *Pro Clero*, reflected his larger post-Black Death domestic policies by conciliating the upper clergy, while reminding the lower clergy of both their place within the hierarchy and their duty to the king and his people. While further study is necessary, this article has sought to offer a new interpretation of Edward's inconsistent behaviour towards his clergy, one in which Edward employed both litigation and legislation to subdue an unruly and at times criminous lower clergy in a time of war and social unrest.

THE ARMOUR OF SIR ROBERT SALLE: AN INDICATION OF SOCIAL STATUS?*

Shelagh Mitchell

The chronicles of Jean Froissart state that during the Peasants' Revolt of 1381, Sir Robert Salle was in his native Norfolk; that the rebels reminded him he was the son of a villein, a mason; that they appealed to him to be their leader; that he refused, offering instead armed combat; that losing his footing in his stirrups he abandoned his horse and faced the large mob alone. Not surprisingly, he was hacked to pieces. According to Froissart, Salle was wearing his armour on that fateful day and while the vast numbers said to have been involved in the incident can be considered a little fanciful, the claim that Salle possessed armour is not. Contemporary documentary evidence confirms that he owned armour, or a harness, of excellent quality, even though there is no indication as to how he acquired it. Salle lived in an age when there were attempts to regulate a person's dress and accoutrements in accordance with their wealth and social status. Yet he was merely the son of a villein – a bondman – who by accepted norms should never have been wearing armour. In order to comprehend fully the significance of such a circumstance, this paper will examine the inventory of Salle's harness and his career in the royal household within the context of the fourteenth-century sumptuary legislation and the related parliamentary petitions, which sought to restrict the wearing of fine apparel. Sumptuary legislation of the following century, which cited specific exemptions and enhanced social status for members of the king's household, will then be considered. If Salle's possession of a fine harness can best be understood through the medium of his career at a time when the circumstance of war offered opportunities to a much wider social spectrum, it can also help us to comprehend the contemporary notion that 'service was ennobling'.[1] However, in this particular case, it is also possible to suggest

* A version of this paper was first read at the Late Medieval Seminar at the Institute of Historical Research. Viral encephalitis halted work in 2005. I am grateful to Dr Richard Nicholas, Consultant Neurologist, Charing Cross Hospital, for his initial and continuing care; to my husband Philip and family; to Elaine Cervantes-Watson and Gaenor Kyffin. Throughout these years, I have been sustained by the support of the historical fraternity and I thank them *all*. I am especially aware of the support received from Anita Hewerdine, Alison McHardy, Jim Bolton, Alasdair Hawkyard and (the late) Alf O'Brien. I thank Stephen O'Connor for his expert help and patience and Linda Clark for all her help with this and other papers and for her friendship and care over all these years; and my thanks also to Hannes Kleineke.

1   Maurice Keen, *Chivalry* (London, 2010) passim discusses the related themes of arms, knighthood,

that what we are presented with is an early instance of the concept articulated in the fifteenth century that *royal* service brought with it an even greater enhancement of social status.

In introducing his readers to Salle, Froissart immediately takes us into the area of social status. We are told that he was a knight and captain of the town of Norwich, but we are also told that he 'was not of gentle birth', and even more significantly that his father had been a villein; that he had not been born a free man.[2] We are informed that physical size had originally brought Salle to the attention of his superiors. In fact he was described by Froissart as 'the best-built and strongest man in all England'.[3] Physical size thus gave him his initial entrée into Edward III's fighting force and it is known that by 1360 he had already provided good service in France.[4] His innate military capabilities led not only to his knighthood, but also to his career as a household knight in the reigns of both Edward III and Richard II. Present research has not revealed the date or occasion of Salle's knighting, but it is known from letters patent that from November 1363 this *dilectus armiger noster Robertus Salle* was in receipt of an annuity of 10 marks from the exchequer while actively in the king's service, which was to be increased to £10 for life when he left such service with licence. Within three years he had risen in status to be a household knight, for in 1366 he was listed in the Wardrobe Book among the twenty-two of the king's bachelors (*bachelerii*) in receipt of Christmas robes. Further patent letters of 1372 granted him the larger annuity of 40 marks for life. In the following year Salle was authorized to arrest a ship to transport 'his victuals' and, of some significance for this paper, his 'harness' to the castle of Marck in the march of Calais, where he was to assume command of the garrison.[5] This was a meritorious rise not

chivalry, service; see also n. 53 below for examples of men rising through service, though there are no other examples of bondmen doing so; in this respect Salle seems to be unique.

2   'Point gentils homs n'estoit'. See J. Froissart, *Oeuvres complètes: Chroniques*, ed. J. M. B. C. Kervyn de Lettenhove, 25 vols (Brussels, 1867–77), ix, 407. The title 'captain of Norwich' has not appeared in any of the documents consulted. See also *The Peasants Revolt of 1381*, ed. R. B. Dobson (London, 1983), pp. 16, 237–8, 258, 261–4; *Knighton's Chronicle 1337–96*, ed. and trans. G. H. Martin (Oxford, 1995), pp. 224–5. For the social constraints attached to villeinage, see C. Dyer, *Standards of Living in the Middle Ages* (Cambridge, 1989), p. 11.

3   '... et l'avoit fait pour sa vaillance li rois Edouwars chevalier, et estoit li mieux tournés et li plus fors homs de toute Engletiere': Froissart, *Chroniques*, ix, 407; Froissart, *Chronicles*, trans. G. Brereton (Harmondsworth, 1978), pp. 222–4.

4   A patent letter of 6 June 1360 gives Salle a pardon for all felonies and trespasses of the king's suit because of his good service in the wars against France: C 66/259 m. 9.

5   The term 'suit of armour' does not appear until the seventeenth century; prior to that it was a 'harness' or 'an armour'. C 66/268 m. 5 for the 10 mark annuity; E 101/395/10 m. 1 for the Christmas robes; C 66/287 m. 24 for the 40 mark annuity; C 66/289 m. 21 for the power to arrest a ship. In the following reign, C 66/306 m. 6 and C 81/454/153 show him with the special style 'dilectus et fidelis miles noster/nostre chier et foial chivaler' reserved for household knights in the reign of Richard II (and beyond), for which argument, see Shelagh Mitchell, 'Some Aspects of the Knightly Household of Richard II', University of London PhD thesis (1998), chs 1–3, appendix I, pp. 236, 240, 249.

dependent upon social origins. However, his social origins were, according to Froissart, remembered by the peasants in 1381. The peasants accepted Salle as a knight, but they also reminded him, '... we know you well. You are not a gentleman, but the son of a villein and a mason, the same sort as us' (nous vous connissons bien. Vous n'estes mies gentils homs, mais fils d'un villain et d'un machon, sicom nous sommes). They then asked him to espouse their cause and be their leader, for which they promised to be in his obedience and to give him a 'fourth part of England'. Far from espousing their cause Salle, according to Froissart, began a single-handed attack on the peasants, having first addressed them as 'traitors' and 'dung'.[6] His sentiments were obviously not with the rebels. Froissart then tells us of Salle's skill in swordsmanship; that he used a long Bordeaux sword (une belle longhe espée de Bordiaux), and that he was dressed in his armour.[7]

Details of the armour worn by Salle are not provided by Froissart. Yet they are known to us because of a rather rash action undertaken by him not long before, in the first year of the reign of Richard II. Salle, then 'governor' of the castle of Marck, had decided to go absent without official leave and take a trip home to England, leaving others in charge. During his absence, the castle was taken by the French.[8] This action deprived the king of Marck and necessitated its recapture by the captain of the town of Calais.[9] For our purposes such a circumstance is fortunate, since it resulted in the confiscation of all the lands, goods and chattels Salle held in England, as well as all the movable possessions, including weapons, he had left behind in the castle. In May 1378, however, he received a pardon for his absence from his post and for all the forfeitures this had incurred. The warrant and the letter patent from the king both make specific mention of his harness: 'And concerning the harness and weapons which were the same Robert's in the said castle, of our grace, in as much as it is possible, we grant to the same Robert for his own person, one complete harness for war.'[10] There follows an exact description in

---

[6] 'Ariere, mescans gens, faus et mauvais traiteur que vous estes! Volés-vous que je relenquisse mon naturel signeur pour telle merdeille que vous estes et que je me déshonneure?': Froissart, *Chroniques*, ix, 408.

[7] Ibid., pp. 407–9; Froissart, *Chronicles*, pp. 222–4.

[8] The privy seal writ does not give an exact date for this absence, only saying that it happened while Salle was 'governor' of Marck with indentures in force from the feast of All Saints (1 November) 1377: C 81/456 no. 349. See also *The St Albans Chronicle: The 'Chronica Maiora' of Thomas Walsingham*, ed. J. Taylor, W. Childs and L. Watkiss, in progress (Oxford, 2003–), i, 172–3.

[9] At that time, the captaincy of the town was held by Sir Hugh Calveley: C 81/974 no. 15; C 76/61 m. 30; E 403/465 m. 5; and the captaincy of the castle by Sir Bernard Brocas: E 403/465 m. 21.

[10] My own translation of: 'et de hernesiis et armaturis que fuerunt ipsius Roberti in castro predicto de gracia nostra quantum in nobis est concessimus eidem Roberto pro proprio corpore suo unum hernesium integrum pro guerra': C 66/301 m. 5, dated 3 May 1378. It is made clear that Salle was entitled to the same armour he had left behind. See also E 403/468 m. 6; E 159/156, 'brevia directa baronibus', Trinity rot. 7 (26 May 1380). The former is a summons to Salle to attend the king and council and the latter is a discharge to him for the armaments and chapel goods remaining in the castle of Marck at the end of his keepership. The items included bows and quarrels, a set of vestments, a missal with musical notation, a towel and a corporal.

both Latin and French of the harness he had left behind at Marck and which was now returned to him. The Latin letter patent describes this as:

> unum hernesium integrum pro guerra videlicet unum par de braceys de ferro; unum par de sabatons de ferro; unum integrum hernesium de jambes de ferro cum poleyns quisseux et voideers; unam tunicam de ferro et unum par de plates panno aureo coop[er]t[um]; unum brest-eplate rubeam [*sic*]; unum jak de auro una cum bokles et pendentiis [*sic*] argenti de aurati; unum bacinetum cum uno aventallo de acere simul cum lestaples bacineti; unum chaplet argenti deauratum; unam galeam cum una cresta, unum par cerotecarum de plata; unum gladium et unum dagger [*sic*] de guerra; unum securum de Burdeux; unum scutum de cornu placatum de acere; unam lanceam rubeam cum capite de burdeux; et unum pavys album cum uno capite nigro de aquila racet …

The writ of privy seal, in French, reads:

> Un hernoys entire pur guerre, brays de fer, sabetons de fer, jambes de fer, poleyns, quisseux; voiders; une cote der fer; plates covertes de drap dor; un brestplate rouge; un jak dor ouvesquex les bocles et pendanatz dargent susorer; une bacynet ovesques un aventaill daster ovesques les estaples du bacynet; une chaplet dargent susorres; une heaume ovesques un crest une piere de grantz de plate; une espeye, un dagger de guerre, un hache de Burdeux; un escu de corn plates dasser; une lance rouge ove la teste de Bordeux; une payvs blanche ovesques une teste noir degle racer …

Both translate as:[11]

> One complete harness for war. Namely, one pair of iron vambraces (arm-defences); one pair of iron sabetons (foot-defences); one complete leg harness of iron greaves (lower leg-defences) with poleyns (knee-defences); cuisses (thigh-defences) and voiders (mail gusset at the back of the knee);[12] a complete mail habergeon; a pair of plates covered

---

11 This translation is not taken from the *CPR 1377–81*, p. 204, which gives, for example, 'pulley pieces' for 'poleyns' and 'coat of iron' for a complete mail habergeon. Instead, this translation is made with reference to both the warrant, C 81/456 no. 349, written in French, and the letter patent, C 66/301 m. 5, written in Latin, for which (the late) Claude Blair and Karen Watts provided the correct terminology. Thanks to Nicholas Karn, for deciphering the correct ending for 'de aurati'.

12 Mail gussets (later also articulated plate ones) that filled the gaps at the joints of the armour. At this date they were attached to the undergarment. There was such a gap at the back of the knees which is where these voiders would have fitted. No voiders would have been required elsewhere since a complete mail habergeon – here called 'tunicam de ferro (cote de fer)' – was still worn under the plate armour. This information, and that found in nn. 13, 14, 16 and 17, and at nn. 20, 22 and 47 below was kindly supplied by Claude Blair in a written communication of May 1999.

with cloth of gold (textile garment covered with riveted plates);[13] one red breastplate;[14] one jack (quilted surcoat) of gold with buckles and pendants of silver gilded with gold;[15] one basinet (light helmet) with an aventail of steel mail attached by the staples of the basinet; one silver gilt chaplet;[16] one helm with crest;[17] one pair of gauntlets of plate; one sword; one dagger of war; one 'Bordeaux' axe;[18] one shield of horn plated with steel; one red lance with a 'Bordeaux' head; one white pavise (shield) with a black head of an eagle, erased.[19]

The possession of armour immediately places Salle at a social station far removed from his origins. Indeed, the contemporary descriptions of his armour have led to expert opinion today assessing it as 'a very magnificent outfit of royal quality'.[20] The possession of armour of such quality also indicates that the owner was not only wealthy, but of a high social status.[21] Again, according to expert opinion, the cloth of gold would have formed part of the construction of the armour and such a circumstance indicates its very high quality; 'something more usually encountered in the royal wardrobe accounts'.[22] From the Great Wardrobe account of 1364–65, it is known that Edward III gave the king of Cyprus a complete harness of war, and although the account does not give itemized details, it does reveal the use of cloth of gold in the construction of this particular harness.[23] Salle's harness was also

Before I contacted him, he had not been aware of the inventory of Salle's harness and wanted me to make certain specific points in the event of any future publication and I here honour the undertaking I gave him. Nevertheless, the importance of reference to Claude Blair, *European Armour: circa 1066 to circa 1700* (New York, 1958), especially ch. 2, pp. 37 ff. must be stressed.

13 This was standard body armour of the period.

14 The colour being provided by the textile covering.

15 From all the documents researched for this paper the use of the word 'jak' has always been in the context of linen armour, either for war or for jousting. The use of a 'jak' as non-military attire for both men and women has not been encountered in the documents consulted. Thanks to Lisa Monnas for useful discussions on this subject.

16 It was not unusual for a knight to wear a chaplet or circle of precious metal round his mail hood or basinet.

17 At this date the visor of the basinet was commonly detached so that a much larger and all-enclosing 'helm' could be worn over it, and it was on this that the crest was normally worn.

18 In the fourteenth and fifteenth centuries Bordeaux steel had a high reputation. Froissart, amongst others, cites it as being sharp and well-tempered. Written information kindly supplied by Karen Watts, senior curator, Museum of the Royal Armouries, Leeds.

19 The Society of Antiquaries, *Dictionary of British Arms, Medieval Ordinary I*, p. 157 records the arms of a Sir Robert Salle from a later source as *gules, a lion ermine*; this is a topic of further research.

20 See n. 12 above.

21 I am grateful to Karen Watts for her opinion that 'This armour was extremely costly, indicating wealth and, by extrapolation, high social status'; written communication 1999.

22 See n. 12 above.

23 E 101/394/16 m. 2. The very high-quality cloth of gold baldekyn of Lucca was used, as was silk and also linen. Since we do not know the quality of the cloth of gold used in Salle's harness, an exact comparison cannot be made and it must here be stressed that while the king of Cyprus's harness of war was the gift of Edward III, we can make no such claim for Salle's. See also ibid. m. 1, for the same cloth of gold used in the making of jousting armour for the king of Cyprus.

constructed with cloth of gold and therefore it manifested high status, but no evidence has been found that he received this as a gift from Edward III or anyone else. Yet, despite his impressive appearance in his armour, his origins were not forgotten by the peasants in the summer of 1381. While accepting his new status as a knight, and promising to exalt it even further, they nevertheless still expected him to feel some solidarity with his equals by birth. This was rather simplistic, for as far as society, and indeed Salle himself, was concerned, the belt of knighthood had transformed him. His social status was proclaimed by what he wore and contemporary society was well versed in such signifiers. His origins could in no way be deduced from the visual message proclaimed by his armour. On the contrary, here was a mounted man of striking physique, wearing the accoutrements of a knight, and carrying a sword. If this was the same armour as that recorded in 1378 then we know, for example, that his jack was made of cloth of gold with buckles and pendants of silver gilded with gold: all signs which indicated that he was very definitely not the son of a bondman. His background had thus been obliterated through his right to wear such armour, and knighthood had given him that right. Moreover, the armour proclaimed him to belong to a further elite, for such was the transforming power of royal service that it contained cloth of gold.

Legislation of 1337 prohibited all, except the king, queen and their children, from wearing imported cloth.[24] This law may well have had its genesis in the spheres of trade and relations with France.[25] Yet banning cloth imports also impinged upon the area of apparel, since cloth of gold, in its many varieties, was an import. The 1337 legislation also prohibited the wearing of furs but the range of those exempted was much wider.[26] In 1363 there was further legislation 'for the outrageous and excessive apparel of diverse people against their estate and degree', and this ordinance set out detailed lists of the entitlement of each stratum of society. For our purposes, it stated that knights with land or rent of *less* than 200 marks per annum could not wear cloth of gold or cloaks furred with minever or ermine, but that knights and ladies with land or rents worth between 400 marks and £1,000 per annum might dress as they pleased.[27] The parliament of 1365 saw a commons' petition for the

---

So far, no other list of armour/harness has been found. The inventory of Salle's harness was made because it was the return of forfeited property; how he acquired it is not known and his armour is not specifically mentioned in his last will and testament.

24 *SR* i, 280.

25 Many thanks to Jennifer Ward for this suggestion.

26 In the matter of furs, exemptions included not only the royal family but also prelates, earls, barons, knights, ladies and churchmen with benefices of £100 p.a. The penalty laid down was forfeiture of the fur and further punishment at the king's will. See *SR* i, 280–1; also E. Veale, *The English Fur Trade in the Later Middle Ages*, 2nd edn (London Record Society, v. 2003), pp. 4–5 for a summary of the sumptuary laws relating to fur.

27 This legislation also forbade esquires without land or rent to the value of £100 p.a. from wearing cloth of gold, silk, silver, embroideries, rings, buttons or brooches of gold or any apparel of gold

repeal of the ordinance,[28] to which the king's response was that the people should be as free as they had been before, especially in the time of his grandfather and ancestors.[29] It is immediately noticeable that the king's response is somewhat vague, and this is especially worthy of comment: although the commons' petition of two years earlier had been couched in general terms, the resulting ordinance framed by the council was, in contrast, set out in strict hierarchical divisions.[30] The response does not make it clear whether any part of the ordinance still remained in force.[31] There were further commons' petitions for the regulation of dress: in 1379, 1402 and 1406.

It is of some importance that we should now look at the content of these petitions. That of 1379 asked that no one with less than £40 per annum be allowed to wear cloth of gold, ribbons of gold, silk, precious stones or furs. It also requested that knights and ladies be exempt. The thrust of this petition might thus be seen as a request that only those persons sharing the income level (or above) of those deemed worthy of knighthood might indulge in cloth of gold and other finery. The king's response was that he would consider this further before the next parliament.[32] There was, however, no resultant legislation. In the chronicle of Leicester Abbey, under the year 1388, Henry Knighton stated the necessity for sumptuary legislation since the 'lesser people' could not be distinguished in their apparel from their superiors nor a servant from his lord nor the clergy from others. The chronicler noted that the magnates' insistence upon a remedy led the king with the agreement of parliament to confirm 'the following statutes' and ordered them to be published and maintained in every county. The statutes of the Cambridge Parliament of 1388 are then set out but there is no mention of sumptuary legislation.[33] A further commons' petition of 1402 asked that no one under the rank of a banneret should use cloth of gold, velvet, crimson, velvet motley, or furs of ermine, lettice (the fur of a snow weasel) or marten; that no one with an income of less than £200 could use daggers or harness of silver. Exemptions were sought not only for the royal family but also for those of gentle birth when they were dressed in their armour, at which time they should have the liberty to wear what they pleased. In response the king commanded all to dress according to their station and stated that the council, by the authority of parliament, could make relevant ordinances, but there was no resultant legis-

---

or silver or pearl, and from wearing furs. For all the categorizations, see *SR* i, 378–83; also *Rotuli Parliamentorum*, ed. J. Strachey *et al.*, 6 vols (London, 1767–77), ii, 275–82; *PROME*, v, 158 ff., esp. 166–8.

[28] *Rot. Parl.*, ii, 286, item 2 for the petition and response; *PROME*, v, 182.

[29] *SR* i, 379 ff., items 8–14; ibid., i, 383 item 2 for the response.

[30] The resultant legislation was in the form of an Ordinance which the king could alter, whereas a statute would need parliamentary authority to repeal or alter.

[31] *Rot. Parl.*, ii, 286 for the response and *SR* i, 383. See also *PROME*, v, 165–7; 182 for the repeal.

[32] *Rot. Parl.*, iii, 66, item 55; *PROME*, vi, 134, no. 55, p. 135 for the response.

[33] *Knighton's Chronicle*, pp. 508–27. The roll for the Cambridge Parliament is missing.

lation.[34] Another, similar petition in 1406 elicited the response that the king would consider the matter further and make an ordinance as seemed appropriate to him, with the advice of the council.[35] Again, no legislation followed. It was not to be until the third year of Edward IV's reign that the ordinance of 1363 (issued a hundred years earlier), with its specific contents and categories of apparel, was expanded and written into statute.[36] Yet the commons' petitions and Knighton's chronicle reveal that there was indeed contemporary disquiet concerning people dressing above their station. What then are we to make of Robert Salle, the son of a bondman, owning a complete harness for war constructed with cloth of gold?

In assessing such ownership, several points should be remembered: that by 1366 Salle was one of Edward III's household knights or *bachelerii* in receipt of Christmas robes, on the same occasion as, for example, Lord Latimer;[37] that six years later he was in receipt of an annual fee for life from the exchequer of 40 marks (£26 13s 4d);[38] and that when he was appointed governor of the castle of Marck in 1373 he was given the authority to arrest a ship to take his 'harness' to Calais.[39] Therefore, by 1373 he was in possession of his costly armour, although we do not know how he had originally acquired it. In 1378 Salle was no longer governor of Marck, but despite this he had his harness returned to him by Richard II. Furthermore, in April 1380, styled as a household knight, he was retained for life by that king for his good services to Edward III, and his annuity of 40 marks was confirmed.[40] Meanwhile, as an indication of his standing in his native shire, in October 1378, some five months after receiving a pardon for leaving his post at the castle of Marck, he attended the Gloucester Parliament as a knight of the shire for Norfolk.[41] Salle thus continued to be a person of consequence. In trying to assess his income it might be recalled that in 1392 Richard II issued a proclamation for those with land worth £40 per annum to take up knighthood and it seems likely that Salle fell into this category.[42]

Yet, despite Salle's knighthood and possessions, his last will and testament make it clear that he had no pretensions concerning the social standing of his

---

[34] *Rot. Parl.*, iii, 306; *PROME*, viii, 205–6.
[35] *Rot. Parl.*, iii, 593; *PROME*, viii, 383–4.
[36] *SR* ii, p. 399 cap. 5; *Rot. Parl.*, v, 504; *PROME*, xiii, 108–11. I am grateful to Maureen Jurkowski for helpful discussions on the statutes; also to Philip Mitchell.
[37] E 101/395/10 m. 1: 'cest le roulle des seigneurs et autres gentz del hostel ...' (illegible/faded). Latimer, future steward and chamberlain of the household, was listed as a banneret.
[38] See C 66/306 m. 6 (7 April 1380) for a summary of Salle's fees from Edward III and Richard II, and for his changing designation from esquire to knight.
[39] C 66/289 m. 24 (22 March 1373).
[40] But now from the issues of Norfolk and Suffolk, C 66/306 m. 6; also n. 5 above. He was succeeded at Marck by Sir Edward Berkeley, a household knight: E 159/156, 'brevia directa baronibus'*, Easter rot. 13.
[41] *CCR 1377–81*, p. 221; with thanks to Hannes Kleineke.
[42] C 54/233 m. 14d. Although this was after Salle's death, it does suggest an accepted minimum figure in earlier years.

family. The high status proclaimed by the quality of his armour must therefore be seen entirely within the framework of the positions and property acquired through his service in the royal household – not as a signifier of family status. This last is clearly indicated by the contents of his will.[43] He left 40 shillings to the rector of the church of Oxnead for forgotten tithes; 100 shillings to John Haughayle, his chaplain; and a silver goblet with silver cover to John Tavener, a resident of Norwich. To his sister Margaret he left 40 shillings and to her son Nicholas also 40 shillings, so that he could be taught a craft (ad erudiend[um] unum artificium). To his niece Margaret, daughter of his sister, he left 5 marks of silver for her marriage, and to his servant Nicholas Grece he left a generous £20 for his good service. Salle's wife Frances (*Francisse*), and her heirs and assigns, were bequeathed his messuage called 'Godes- mannes' with all appurtenances in the city of Norwich, situated in the parish of St Michael Coslany near the tenement of a certain Richard Spynk, abutting on to the head of the king's highway and onto the water called the 'comon rever'. In addition his will mentioned all his other manors, messuages and lands – that is the manors of Oxnead near Aylsham, Bolewick in Aylsham, and Bromhall in South Walsham, and certain tenements known as 'Bryanes' in the town of Skeyton with the advowsons of churches. These were for Frances to hold for her life and then they were to be sold by his executors, or if they died in the meantime, by the hand of Frances's own executors, and the profits to be ordained for pious uses for their souls and for anyone to whom he was beholden. Also to be sold by his executors was the messuage and appurtenances he held in the town of 'Leystest' (perhaps Lowestoft), called 'Botildesplace', as well as his messuage across the Channel in Calais,[44] near the inn of the earl of Warwick, and the profits of these latter two were to be distributed by Frances, and if there was any residue after the sale of his goods and chattels and the payment of his debts and legacies this was left to her to dispose of as she saw fit.[45] Salle was obviously far from poor, but the small monetary bequests to his family and the intention that his nephew should learn a craft point to something of crucial importance that bears repeating: that the social status manifested by costly armour and cloth of gold, as well as the ability to acquire property, was an indicator of his service, and espe- cially his service within the royal household; it was not an indicator of his family status. That Salle apparently held no land in chief perhaps also makes the same point.[46]

Despite his original status, expert opinion today has judged Salle's armour to be of 'royal quality' and indicative of royal service, and evidence for this

---

[43] Norfolk Record Office, Norwich consistory court wills, Reg. Heydon, fol. 189. Many thanks to the Record Office, especially to Claire Bolster. The will was dated 8 September 1380 and proved on 3 July 1381, after his death on 17 June.

[44] The Calais property was worth 4 marks or £2 13s 4d per annum; C 66/312 m. 13.

[45] I am grateful to Maureen Jurkowski and Jonathan Mackman for their expert and invaluable help.

[46] No inquisition post mortem survives: *CIPM*, 1377–84, passim.

has already been cited.[47] Yet again, his connection with the king's household is made clear in his choice of executor: 'Lord William Danby called Lord Latimer'. Latimer was well known for his military service in France, including at Calais, but he also held household office, being steward – head of Edward III's *domus providencie* – from 1368 to 1370, and then chamberlain – head of the king's *domus magnificencie* – from 1371 to 1376, and had been in the same Wardrobe listing of Christmas robes for 1366 as Salle. Latimer was pivotal at court towards the end of Edward's reign, controlling access to the king, who named him as an executor.[48] Even after his impeachment in the Good Parliament he was readmitted to the king's council. Latimer's importance continued in the new reign, if to a lesser degree: he was named on Richard II's Regency Councils and acted as almoner at his coronation.[49] His link to Salle must have been sufficiently strong for him to have been named as one of his executors, and the fact that Edward III and Salle had an executor in common signifies just how far the latter, the son of a bondman, had risen.[50] We have seen that Salle's household service continued in the new reign and, indeed, that his costly harness was returned to him in 1378.[51] His possession of fine armour incorporating cloth of gold is thus a pointer to the fact that a man might transcend his original social status through the transforming belt of knighthood and that service in the king's household could raise him to an even higher degree;[52] and that the circumstance of war could, and did, facilitate such an elevation.[53]

While such an elevation is not found for another bondman, we can with profit look at the case of Sir Roger Acton. Acton became a household knight

---

[47] See n. 12 above.

[48] W. M. Ormrod, *The Reign of Edward III* (Stroud, 2000), pp. 112–14.

[49] *The Complete Peerage*, ed. G. E. Cockayne *et al.* (London, 1910–57), vii, 470–3 and notes therein; also *ODNB*, vol. 32, p. 643.

[50] The identification of 'Lord William Danby, called Lord Latimer' with the same Lord Latimer of Edward III's household is secure because Latimer had licence in 1365 as 'William Danby, Lord Latimer', to found a college of thirteen chaplains in the church of Helpringham: *GEC*, vii, 471. Latimer held Danby in Yorkshire of the king in chief: *CIPM*, 1377–84, p. 157, no. 381. It is perhaps of some relevance that Salle had letters to go to Marck, in the march of Calais, in 1373 – the same year as Latimer went as governor of Calais (where he too had property): ibid., no. 378. Latimer never acted as Salle's executor, for he died a few days before him, on 28 May 1381.

[51] C 66/306 m. 6, for his retention for life by Richard II with 40 marks a year. There is contemporary evidence that once Richard II used cloth of gold as livery for his household knights, see *St Albans Chronicle*, pp. 46–7. E 101/309/2 m. 7, privy seal dated May 1342, shows Edward III's gift of cloth of gold for the bed of a new knight (for his vigil); thanks to Lisa Monnas for the latter reference.

[52] See n. 57 below.

[53] For examples, see Michael Prestwich, *The Three Edwards* (London, 1980), pp. 265, 266, where Thomas Breadstone, James Audley, Robert Knolles and Hugh Calvely are cited but with the greatest accolade being reserved for Robert Salle, the bondman, who rose to knighthood and served in the royal household – all because of the increased opportunities offered by the circumstance of war. For examples of losses sustained because of war, see ibid., p. 265, and for a more general comment, pp. 190–1.

of Henry IV despite his humble origins as a Shropshire tiler's son – something made much of by the contemporary chronicler Adam of Usk. Despite his origins, there is evidence that he possessed a cloth of gold 'houppeland'. This was a very expensive fashion item, being a long loose gown with long loose sleeves, lined with silk or fur and most easily illustrated by reference to the dress of Richard II on the Wilton Diptych. Acton had not only been knighted by Henry IV himself but had been invested with the golden spurs by the king's eldest and second sons. In 1414, however, he was executed for his involvement with the Lollards, and following this event his cloth of gold houppeland was recycled within the king's knightly household.[54] Evidence from a privy seal writ shows that this same item was passed on to Sir Roger Leche, the treasurer of the king's household. That the houppeland was granted to the household treasurer gives some indication of the quality of the garment, for that official ranked second only to the steward, the head of the king's *domus providencie*.[55] If the harness of Robert Salle made plain the transforming power of knighthood and royal service, Roger Acton's possession of a cloth of gold houppeland is another example of such a transformation resulting from knightly service in the royal household. Thus the status and privileges conferred by royal service were made manifest through dress, through entitlement to cloth of gold. By the end of the fifteenth century an enhancement in the social status of the king's household was fully recognized and articulated. Advice in the *Babees' Book* states that each tier of the household should be treated as belonging to the social station above; so that knights of the household should be treated and seated as though they were barons. Significantly, the social enhancement of members of the royal household was to be sanctioned and codified in the sumptuary legislation of Edward IV passed in the parliament of 1463–65. This decreed that no one under the estate of a lord could wear the fur of sable, but that the steward, chamberlain, treasurer and controller of the king's household, together with the king's carvers and knights of the body as well as their wives, could wear both sable and ermine.[56] The king's knightly household was thus advanced socially. The knights were recognized as being the equal of lords. Indeed, the

---

[54] *The Chronicle of Adam of Usk 1377–1421*, ed. and trans. C. Given-Wilson (Oxford, 1997), pp. 246–7. See C 66/387 m. 7 for Acton's designation by the special style reserved for household knights.

[55] C 66/395 m. 20 (23 October 1414) for Acton's cloth of gold; C 81/660, no. 212 for its description as a 'hopelond de drap dor' first given to him by Henry IV, and for Henry V's grant of this same houppeland to Roger Leche, styled as 'nostre treschier et foial chivaler … Tresourer de nostre houstel'. E 101/406/21 states that Leche became *custos* of the king's household on 31 October 1413. Lisa Monnas has identified the dress worn by Richard II on the Wilton Diptych as a houppeland: see *The Regal Image of Richard II and the Wilton Diptych*, ed. Dillian Gordon, Lisa Monnas and Caroline Elam (London, 1998), p. 322 n. 4. For the hierarchy of the royal household, see A. R. Myers, *The Household of Edward IV: The Black Book and the Ordinance of 1478* (Manchester, 1959), pp. 104–8, 142–4.

[56] That carver knights were chamber knights, similarly with knights of the body, see Myers, *Household*, pp. 106, 240 n. 97.

Black Book states that the 'household steward and thesaurer in hys absence, within this court represent unto the astate of an erle'.[57] The inventory of Sir Robert Salle's harness has therefore alerted us to his membership of an elite group despite his low social origins. It has also provided us with a window from which to view those visual aspects and social signifiers of late medieval English society that might not be so obvious to us today.[58]

[57] Myers, *Household*, p. 144. For assigning the date of 1471–73 to the Black Book, see ibid., p. 31; for the 1463–65 legislation, see n. 36 above. That service in the royal household raised any member of it by one degree is shown in *The Babees' Book*, ed. F. J. Furnivall, EETS OS 32 (1868), p. 73. See also Veale, *English Fur Trade*, p. 7, which states that 'in the king's household, relatively humble forms of royal service carried with them the right to a furred livery'.

[58] I acknowledge my debt to David Starkey and his postgraduate seminars at the London School of Economics and Political Science, where household hierarchy and material artefacts of the Tudor court were used as one of several means of historical interpretation; I have applied these methods to an earlier period.

RICHARD II, THE MORTIMER INHERITANCE
AND THE MARCH OF WALES, 1381–84*

Mark King

Few things were as important to the late medieval nobility as the secure preservation of their estates and the right of their heirs to inherit unhindered. As Plucknett wrote, 'in a turbulent world, the idea of inheritance was one which all accepted without question as part of the natural order … the most telling charge which could be brought against a tyrant was to say that he had thrust men out of their inheritances.'[1] As a king who would ultimately be deposed for breaking this very principle, Richard II first gave his subjects cause for concern over this issue through his mishandling of the Mortimer inheritance after it fell into royal hands in late 1381.[2] The unexpected death in Ireland on 27 December that year of Edmund Mortimer, earl of March, not only removed one of the most promising members of the nobility from the domestic political scene, it also left his vast inheritance in the hands of his nine-year-old son and therefore subject to the royal prerogative of custody.[3] Edmund's wife had predeceased him in 1378 but his mother, the long-widowed Countess Philippa, was still alive at the time of his death and she held over a third of the family's estates either as dower or in jointure with her late husband. However, she too passed away shortly afterwards, dying on 5 January, and so by early 1382 the entire family inheritance had passed into royal hands for what looked likely to be a long minority.[4] Over the next two years Richard's treatment of these estates would prove sufficiently controversial to provoke a major clash between the king and certain of his nobility, to the extent that custody of the inheritance was eventually removed from his hands. The affair therefore stands as perhaps the earliest occasion in the reign that Richard's subjects took it upon themselves to resist him and

* I would like to thank all those who commented upon this paper at conferences and seminars, particularly David Carpenter, Chris Given-Wilson, Paul Cavill and David Green. Special thanks must go to Christine Carpenter and Andrew Spencer, who read the entire piece in draft form and whose comments were invaluable. Any remaining mistakes are mine alone.

1 T. Plucknett, *The Legislation of Edward I* (Oxford, 1941), p. 110.
2 For evidence that Richard did break this principle during his tyranny see C. Barron, 'The Tyranny of Richard II', *BIHR* 41 (1968), 1–18; C. Given-Wilson, 'Richard II, Edward II, and the Lancastrian Inheritance', *EHR* 109 (1994), 553–71.
3 *ODNB*, xxxix, 374; A. Dunn, 'Richard II and the Mortimer Inheritance', in *Fourteenth Century England II*, ed. C. Given-Wilson (Woodbridge, 2002), pp. 159–70.
4 *ODNB*, xxxix, 374; *CIPM 1377–84*, nos 562–6.

the first time that royal policy and the king's attitude towards his subjects' property became issues of contention.

What was it about Richard's handling of this minority that was so controversial? According to the chronicler Thomas Walsingham, it was the king's choice of custodians for the estates. Once the inheritance was in Richard's hands, says Walsingham, the king granted the petitions of numerous royal associates for custody of various parcels of it, breaking up this great collection of estates and granting their wardship to men whose status was thought to be insufficient and whose motives were distrusted.[5] This activity provoked the disapproval of the chancellor, Richard, Lord Scrope of Bolton, who refused to issue letters under the great seal authorizing the grants. In a fit of rage, the king then dismissed Scrope on 11 July 1382 and henceforth 'did as he pleased' until a coalition of magnates led by the earl of Arundel finally forced him to give way in December 1383 when they received custody of the entire inheritance for the remainder of the minority.[6]

Walsingham's account of the dispute portrays the young king as being misled by his chamber knights but it nevertheless apportions him a certain degree of personal responsibility, and the chronicler's emphasis upon the custodial grants has long influenced historians of the reign. The affair was first brought to scholarly attention in 1971 by Anthony Tuck, who found evidence to suggest that 'the keeping of the manors and lordships of the inheritance was granted piecemeal to more than a dozen individuals, many of whom were members of the royal household or close associates of the court, and none of whom was of greater rank than knight', and he cited several examples to demonstrate this.[7] Accordingly, Tuck argued that the affair should be seen as the first of the many clashes over the direction of royal patronage that he felt would characterize politics during the 1380s. He believed that the nobility were angry because they had been unable to obtain a share in the custody of these estates and that they were shocked at the king's refusal to heed their counsel and at his dismissal of the well-respected Scrope, who they thought had acted in good faith. Overall, Tuck concluded that the incident had raised questions that would remain central to politics for at least the next six years but he did not see Richard on this occasion as having pursued a particular policy, believing that at this date the king was still very much a pawn in the hands of his close associates.[8] It was not until a year or two later, Tuck argued, that Richard would begin his so-called 'system of patronage' as part of his wider attempts to endow his household knights and to exclude certain nobles from his favour, whereas this particular incident was simply a

---

5   *The Saint Albans Chronicle. The Chronicle Maijora of Thomas Walsingham: vol. i: 1376–94*, ed. J. Taylor, W. Childs and L. Watkiss (Oxford, 2002), pp. 621–3.

6   Quotation from *St Albans Chronicle*, i, p. 623. For the grant to Arundel and co. see *CFR 1383–91*, pp. 22–3.

7   A. Tuck, *Richard II and the English Nobility* (London, 1971), p. 88.

8   Ibid., pp. 88–9.

reflection of his 'youth and inexperience'.[9] The Mortimer inheritance might
have set the tone for domestic politics during the 1380s, therefore, but it was
not, according to Tuck, an early example of the policies the king was later
to pursue.

Over forty years later the central tenets of Tuck's interpretation of the
affair continue to be accepted by historians, especially his focus upon the
custodial grants, and it has not been felt necessary to pursue a more detailed
local investigation of Richard's treatment of these estates. Indeed, even
Alastair Dunn's excellent article on Ricardian policy towards the Mortimer
inheritance glosses over the events of 1382–84 since it is more concerned
with placing the king's treatment of these same estates in 1398 within the
new framework emerging from recent work on the final years of Richard's
reign.[10] However, since the publication of Tuck's account of the incident,
our understanding of politics during the early 1380s has undergone considerable revision. In particular, the date of the young king's political emergence
has been pushed further back and it is now accepted that he first sought
independence from tutelage in the months following the Peasants' Revolt,
only to be restrained by some of the nobility.[11] Indeed, certain case studies
have suggested that Richard might already have been developing his own
policies during these years. For example, Chris Given-Wilson's investigation of the king's seizure of the Leybourne inheritance and his repudiation
of Edward III's will has shown that Richard was personally helping to shape
royal policy by *c.* 1383 and that his treatment of these estates was designed
to achieve very clear objectives. Furthermore, this study has demonstrated
that, even at this early date, the king was already behaving with a startling
disregard for the law, established custom and his subjects' property rights and
demonstrating a willingness to override these similar to that which would
eventually result in his deposition.[12] This raises the question, therefore, of
whether the same might be true in the case of the Mortimer inheritance and
whether Richard's personal role in this dispute, and the extent to which he
had certain aims in mind in his treatment of these estates, have been significantly underestimated.

---

9   Ibid., p. 89; idem, 'Richard II's System of Patronage', in *The Reign of Richard II*, ed. C. Barron
     and F. du Boulay (London, 1971), pp. 1–20.
10 Dunn, 'Mortimer Inheritance', 160–1. For another example see C. Given-Wilson, 'Richard II
     and the Higher Nobility', in *Richard II: The Art of Kingship*, ed. A. Goodman and J. Gillespie
     (Oxford, 1999), pp. 107–28, at pp. 120–1. For important recent work on the 1390s see M. Bennett,
     Richard II and the Revolution of 1399 (Stroud, 1999), chs 5–8; A. Dunn, *The Politics of Magnate
     Power in England and Wales, 1389–1413* (Oxford, 2003), pp. 51–76; A. Gundy, 'The Earl of
     Warwick and the Royal Affinity in the Politics of the West Midlands, 1389–1399', in *Revolution
     and Consumption in Late Medieval England*, ed. M. Hicks (Woodbridge, 2001), pp. 57–70;
     C. Fletcher, *Richard II: Manhood, Youth, and Politics, 1377–99* (Oxford, 2008), chs 11–12.
11 See for example G. Dodd, 'Richard II and the Fiction of Majority Rule', in *The Royal Minorities
     of Medieval and Early Modern England*, ed. C. Beem (Basingstoke, 2008), pp. 103–60; Fletcher,
     Richard II, ch. 5, esp. pp. 84–90.
12 C. Given-Wilson, 'Richard II and his Grandfather's Will', *EHR* 93 (1978), 320–37.

Beyond this, wider developments in the historiography of the later Middle Ages also necessitate a reinterpretation of Tuck's account. In particular, historians now have a much better understanding of the conventions that governed a ruler's use of his prerogative of wardship and the expectations of his subjects as to the manner in which their lands should be treated.[13] Such work has contributed to a shift in the interpretative paradigm, whereby scholars have ceased to see wardships solely from the perspective of the king into whose hands the estates fell and the nobles who were eager to receive them, and more from that of the family subject to wardship and the aristocracy in general, who would have been aware that it could easily be their lands in the same position. This is itself one specific reflection of an attempt proposed by some historians to move away from the patronage-led approach of scholars such as Tuck and towards one that also considers the public responsibilities of the king, the unspoken rules that governed his position and the expectations his subjects had of him.[14] Such a methodology has already challenged conventional interpretations of Richard's retaining policy during the 1390s but it has yet to be applied to the 1380s and to the Mortimer inheritance.[15]

Finally, it is also clear that the incident must be viewed within the context of local geopolitics. In the years since Tuck wrote, a great deal of work has been produced on the interaction between private lordship and local government during the later Middle Ages, albeit mostly on the fifteenth century.[16] Such scholarship has provided countless examples of the impact minorities and custodies could have upon local structures of power and governance, and Richard's treatment of the Mortimer inheritance must be considered from this angle. This is all the more so, of course, because of the family's position as the premier dynasty of the Welsh March, which made them central to the region's government. By the late fourteenth century the Mortimers had amassed the second-largest noble estate in the realm, through the combination of their patrimonial inheritance with that of Philippa, daughter and heir of Lionel, duke of Clarence, who had brought the family her mother's

---

[13] See especially S. Waugh, *The Lordship of England: Royal Wardships and Marriages in English Society and Politics, 1217–1327* (Princeton, 1988). For an older work that drew similar conclusions see G. Holmes, *The Estates of the Higher Nobility in Fourteenth-Century England* (Cambridge, 1957), ch. 2.

[14] See in particular M. Carpenter, *Locality and Polity: A Study of Warwickshire Landed Society, 1401–1499* (Cambridge, 1992), pp. 2–9, 347–60; idem, 'Political and Constitutional History: Before and After McFarlane', in *The McFarlane Legacy: Studies in Late Medieval Politics and Society*, ed. R. Britnell and A. Pollard (Stroud, 1995), pp. 175–206; E. Powell, 'After "After McFarlane": The Poverty of Patronage and the Case for Constitutional History', in *Trade, Devotion and Governance: Papers in Later Medieval History*, ed. D. Clayton, R. Davies and P. McNiven (Stroud, 1994), pp. 1–16.

[15] H. Castor, *The King, the Crown and the Duchy of Lancaster: Public Authority and Private Power, 1399–1461* (Oxford, 2000), pp. 1–22; Gundy, 'The Earl of Warwick and the Royal Affinity'.

[16] There are far too many examples of such studies to list here, but for two surveys of this development see Carpenter, 'Before and After McFarlane'; G. Harriss, 'The Dimensions of Politics', in *The McFarlane Legacy*, pp. 1–20.

share of the de Clare estates, together with the de Burgh earldom of Ulster, when she had married the young Earl Edmund.[17] Despite these acquisitions, however, the heartland of the Mortimers' power remained in Wales, where they possessed the largest single collection of Marcher lordships held by any noble family and where the unique jurisdictional rights of these estates made them their most politically and financially valuable possessions. Within his domain a Marcher lord was sovereign. Judicially, he enjoyed the right to hear all pleas of the crown save treason in his own court, which was presided over by his steward and was therefore highly susceptible to pressure.[18] This judicial monopoly was one of the reasons Marcher lordship was so profitable, with a substantial proportion of the lord's income emanating from court issues, although the survival of many older extraordinary levies also played a part.[19] For example, the Mortimers' northern Welsh lordship of Denbigh alone had an annual income of approximately £1,100, almost a third of the family's entire estimated yearly revenue.[20] Perhaps still more significantly, Marcher lordship also retained an important military dimension that made these estates valuable in an entirely different way. As universal landlord within his domains, the Marcher lord held exclusive recruitment rights over his tenants, preserving the personal feudal bond of military service between lord and tenant that had effectively died out in the rest of the realm.[21] Within this dimension of Marcher lordship, castles were of great significance and very few were decayed by this period, in contrast to the situation in the rest of the realm. As 'a visible manifestation of lordship', a lordship's castles were its military and administrative backbone and control of them was essential to the lord's control of the surrounding region.[22] This Marcher perspective may therefore prove central to our understanding of the clash between Richard and his subjects, for we should have no doubt that the Mortimers' lordships constituted a very great politico-financial prize and would have conferred considerable private power upon whoever secured custody of them. Furthermore, since we now suspect that the king was already beginning to assert his rights aggressively by this date, it is highly possible that he saw these estates as a potential resource against his most powerful subjects. In 1397 Richard would infamously seek security in the landed power of the Marches; is it possible that he had already made a similar association by the early 1380s?[23]

---

17 Holmes, *Estates*, pp. 10–19.
18 R. Davies, *Lordship and Society in the March of Wales, 1282–1400* (Oxford, 1978), ch. 7.
19 Ibid., ch. 8. For examples see R. Davies, 'Baronial Accounts, Income and Arrears in the Later Middle Ages', *Economic History Review*, 2nd ser. 21 (1968), 211–29; L. Smith, 'Seignorial Income in the Fourteenth Century: The Arundels of Chirk', *Bulletin of the Board of Celtic Studies*, 28 (1980), 443–57.
20 Dunn, 'Mortimer Inheritance', 159. For the valuation, see SC 6/1185/4, m. 8.
21 Davies, *Lordship and Society*, ch. 4.
22 Ibid., pp. 70–6; quotation from p. 70.
23 R. Davies, 'Richard II and the Principality of Chester 1397–9', in *The Reign of Richard II*, ed. Barron and du Boulay, pp. 256–79; Dunn, *Politics of Magnate Power*, ch. 3.

To investigate these issues further and to reinterpret this crisis in the light of recent work on Richard's behaviour during the early 1380s, this article will look in greater detail at the king's treatment of the Mortimer estates in Wales during the two years that they were in royal hands. To this end we shall investigate what actually happened to these lordships during this time and consider what impact this might have had upon them, before contextualizing this within wider developments in the Marches taking place at the same time. The intention is to suggest a new interpretation of this affair and its significance within the political history of Richard's reign.

We shall begin by establishing a point of comparison for Richard's behaviour, since it was in fact less than ten years since the Mortimers had last suffered a minority. On that occasion, following the death of Roger Mortimer, second earl of March, in February 1360, and during the minority of Edmund Mortimer, which lasted until January 1373, there had been minimal royal intervention in the estates and their administration.[24] Many of the family's ancestral lands had been entrusted to a group of close associates by Earl Roger in August 1359 and these arrangements were respected by Edward III, who gave the feoffees livery of their share in June the following year.[25] Countess Philippa, the earl's widow, was then apportioned the customary third in dower and the few remaining estates were preserved in royal hands until February 1361, when the king granted them in custody to his eldest daughter, Isabella, at a token rent.[26] On 30 September 1364 Isabella leased all these estates back to Philippa Mortimer for an annual rent of 1,000 marks and over the following years the dowager countess was able to pass them on to her son as he awaited his majority.[27] Then, in late 1367 when the original enfeoffment was due to expire, Edward III himself stepped in to grant the feoffees' share to the young Edmund Mortimer to hold until he came of age and the minority was effectively over.[28] Overall, it is clear that it caused only minimal disruption, a result all landowners might hope for in similar circumstances. At every step in his treatment of these estates Edward III had taken care to respect the family's wishes and to protect their rights. Indeed, during the estates' time in royal hands, the family's chief officials, such as their main steward, John Gour, and their receiver general, Arnold de Pynkeny, were retained in office and allowed to go about their business unimpeded.[29] In his discussion of the case, George Holmes argued that this last step was particularly important to the successful handling of a wardship by the king and he suggested that by

[24]   This event is discussed in more detail in Holmes, *Estates*, pp. 45–7.
[25]   *CPR 1358–61*, pp. 266–7, 374; *CCR 1360–64*, pp. 113–14.
[26]   *CCR 1360–64*, pp. 46–7; *CPR 1358–61*, pp. 577–8.
[27]   *CPR 1364–67*, pp. 37–8.
[28]   *CFR 1356–68*, p. 356.
[29]   Both are named in the surviving account of 1359–60 and are still in office the following year according to the Pipe Roll account: BL, Egerton Rolls 8726; E 372/207, fols 41, 49.

the late fourteenth century such arrangements were 'probably an expansion of a well-established practice'.[30]

The only spanner in the works, and a significant one at that, was the Black Prince, who employed a questionable legal claim to challenge for custody of the lordships of Cedewain, Ceri, Denbigh and Montgomery.[31] In order to achieve this end the prince also ignored another uncompleted enfeoffment that had been made by Roger Mortimer to the same trustees, by which Denbigh would have been held in jointure by the earl and his wife.[32] The lordship was left untouched by the escheator, which suggests that the crown considered this settlement to be valid. However, the prince pushed ahead nevertheless, ordering his officials to seize Denbigh into his hands whilst the case was still being heard in chancery and before he had even been awarded a commission to investigate the matter or a writ of *venire facias* had been issued to summon a jury.[33] Worse was to follow. Once the prince had secured custody of these estates, he immediately took steps to incorporate them into his own neighbouring administration in Cheshire and north Wales. This is most evident in Denbigh, where the lordship's officials, even down to its parkers and foresters, were replaced by the prince's own men.[34] After this administrative takeover the new officers then tightened the screws of seigniorial exploitation to such an extent that they provoked widespread opposition, several of them were attacked, and the prince was petitioned by the commonalty of the lordship to reverse the changes he had made.[35]

The prince's divisive rule of Denbigh continued until *c.* 1371, when he was forced to hand the lordship back to Countess Philippa in a settlement brokered by Edward III.[36] However, according to the Mortimer Cartulary, he held on to Cedewain, Ceri and Montgomery until 1373, when he finally gave them up upon Edmund Mortimer's coming of age.[37] During this time he had demonstrated how the family's estates might be exploited during a minority and had set a precedent that the Mortimers would have hoped to avoid in the future. Indeed, the memory of this experience may have influenced Edmund Mortimer's decision to make his own enfeoffments as early as 1374, just a year after attaining his majority. In November that year he granted a collec-

---

[30] Holmes, *Estates*, pp. 46–7.

[31] Ibid., p. 46.

[32] *CPR 1358–61*, p. 267; BL, MS Harley 1240, fol. 36v. Mortimer had died before the lordship could be granted back to him and his wife.

[33] The prince's order to his officials is dated 9 May 1360; a commission and a writ of summons were not issued until mid-July: *BPR*, iii, 381; *CIPM 1352–60*, no. 640.

[34] This event is discussed in more detail in D. Owen, 'The Lordship of Denbigh, 1282–1425', University of Wales PhD thesis (1967), pp. 84–5, 124–5, 128–31. For a selection of the administrative appointments see *BPR*, iii, 381–93.

[35] For the exploitation see *BPR*, iii, 389–90, 440, 448–9, 461, 463, 467–8. For the assaults and other problems see 402–3, 405, 406–7. For the petition see 410–11.

[36] *CPR 1370–74*, p. 333.

[37] BL, MS Harley 1240, fol. 68.

tion of his family's oldest estates to some of his closest associates, including Sir Peter de la Mare, his famous steward, John de Bishopston, a leading servant of his father, Walter Compton, keeper of his wardrobe, and Hugh Boraston, a longstanding member of the family's Marcher administration.[38] Also employed in this capacity were William, Lord Latimer of Danby, Nicholas Carew, then keeper of the privy seal, and, significantly given his later opposition to Richard's treatment of these estates, Richard, Lord Scrope. The estates with which these men were charged focused upon a group of ancestral properties on the Welsh border, including the town of Ludlow and the lordships of Knucklas, Blaenllyfni, Radnor, Gwerthrynion, Comot Deuddwr and Ewyas Lacy. However, the urgency with which Edmund had initially acted to protect these lands did not last. In Michaelmas 1379 the feoffees were forced to bring a suit against the earl to secure their possession of these estates before they could grant them back to him and it was not until January the following year that the trust was completed formally.[39] These lands had therefore been safeguarded, but for whatever reason Edmund made no attempt to set up similar trusts for his other estates, even before he left for Ireland. Perhaps the headiness of youth had blinded the earl to the dangers of dying abroad, but it was a decision his family would come to regret.

Returning, then, to the events of 1382–83, it is clear that the differing policies of Edward III and the Black Prince had established two contradictory precedents for the treatment of the Mortimer estates whilst in wardship. The family would have hoped that the more laissez-faire of these would be adopted and initially there were indeed indications that Richard II's government was going to pursue a similarly non-interventionist policy to that of his grandfather. In January 1382, as news reached Westminster of the deaths of the earl and his mother, but before any inquisitions had been carried out, the council took steps to deal with the most pressing priority: the administration of the estates during the immediate future. On 16 January it authorized letters patent appointing stewards for the various collections of estates, in most cases it seems either confirming existing arrangements or appointing someone with close connections to the Mortimer family and a history of service in their administration. For example, the steward appointed to manage many of the Marcher estates formerly belonging to Countess Philippa was Philip Holgot, a Herefordshire lawyer who had spent much of his career as an attorney for the Mortimers and their associates.[40] Holgot had a particular connection to the countess, for whom he had been both a trustee and an executor, but most importantly he had also already served as steward of Denbigh and its associated Shropshire manors during the 1370s, to which office he was now

[38] Ibid., fols 46v–47; *CPR 1374–77*, pp. 33–4; Holmes, *Estates*, p. 51.
[39] BL, MS Harley 1240, fols 46v–47; CP 40/476, mm. 648–648d, 564; CP 40/477, m. 84d; C 206/93, fols 21–21h; Holmes, *Estates*, pp. 51–2.
[40] *CPR 1381–85*, p. 65. An incomplete biography of him is given in *HPC*, iv, 395–7.

reappointed.[41] In short, he was clearly the ideal choice to oversee his former employer's estates during the minority of her grandson and his appointment was mirrored elsewhere in the March. For the family's oldest properties, the lordships of Wigmore, Malmeshull, Nethewode and Clifton, the steward appointed was Hugh Boraston, Earl Edmund's feoffee and attorney and a beneficiary of the earl's will, who had been a Mortimer official in one capacity or another since at least 1358.[42] Elsewhere, Roger Partrich, the current steward of Clifford and Glasbury, was continued in this office and also appointed to the same position in the lordships of Usk and Caerleon.[43] This pattern was also matched by appointments outside the March. The stewardship of the great East Anglian lordship of Clare, for example, was entrusted to John Bataill, a longstanding tenant who had been an executor of the will of Elizabeth de Burgh, the Clare heiress who had brought this estate to Lionel, duke of Clarence.[44] Overall, therefore, these appointments showed no willingness on the part of the council to disrupt existing administrative patterns and continued the principle we encountered earlier that a deceased tenant-in-chief's own officials were those best suited to manage their estates during the minority of the heir.

However, these sensible appointments were short-lived. From late January 1382 we begin to see evidence of the sort of patronage that Walsingham says provoked disagreement between the king and his leading subjects, yet contrary to the usual interpretation of this chronicler's account there are very few examples of members of the royal household receiving custody of substantial portions of the Mortimer inheritance. Rather, royal associates appear to have been installed in important positions within the administration of these estates, while the estates themselves were kept almost entirely in the king's hands. This divergence of the evidence from the conventional interpretation is worthy of further comment. If the king's household men had been seeking to enrich themselves through access to the considerable revenues of the Mortimer inheritance, the most obvious way for them to have done so would have been to request custody of vast swathes of the estates themselves, rather than significant but not necessarily profitable positions within their administration. As we shall see, similar grants had occurred during Richard's minority, when the king's infamous under-chamberlain, Sir Simon Burley, and his half-brother, Sir John Holland, had taken the opportunity to secure Marcher lordships for themselves.[45] However, during the first six months of

---

[41] SC 6/1183/15; *CPR 1377–81*, pp. 391; J. Nichols, *A Collection of Wills Known to be Extant of the Kings and Queens of England* (New York, 1969), p. 102.

[42] *CPR 1381–85*, p. 65; Nichols, *Wills*, p. 115. Boraston first appears in 1358 as steward of Ludlow: *CIPM 1377–84*, no. 448.

[43] *CPR 1381–85*, p. 65. He was already steward of Clifford, Glasbury, Dynas and Ewyas by 1381: Bangor University Archives, Whitney and Clifford MS 315.

[44] *CPR 1381–85*, p. 65; *HPC*, ii, 144–5.

[45] See below, pp. 109–10.

1382, this pattern was not continued. It seems reasonable to conclude, therefore, that these grants were not the result of a series of opportunistic petitions to Richard from his chamber associates. On the contrary, they appear
to have been tailored specifically to give the royal household itself direct
control of the Mortimer estates. Indeed, an immediate priority seems to have
been to ensure that the inheritance's military power was in safe hands, for
the vast majority of the early grants concerned the Mortimers' castles and the
replacement of their constables. On 21 January, for example, Adam Ramsey,
a king's esquire, was made constable of Clare Castle for life, whilst on 27
January the chamber knight Baldwin de Raddington received the constableship of Bridgewater Castle and was made parker of the nearby park.[46] The
pattern was even more pronounced in the Marches, where control of the
castles of Builth, Caerleon, Clifford and Denbigh was given to members of
the royal household between 3 and 8 February.[47] According to a chancery
warrant that was never enrolled, the same was also to happen to Narberth
Castle, Pembrokeshire, on 11 February, but for whatever reason the letters
patent were never issued.[48]

More was to follow. On 4 February the stewards who had recently been
confirmed in office by the council were dismissed and the chamber knight
Sir Thomas Poitevin was appointed in their place as steward 'of all the lands
late the inheritance of Edmund de Mortuo Mari, both those which he held
and those held by Philippa his mother'.[49] The ramifications of this grant for
the administrative well-being of these estates is something we shall return to,
but for now it is sufficient to say that it installed a man with no prior connections to the Mortimers at the very head of their administration. Furthermore,
it seems likely that this office had never existed before and with good reason,
for Poitevin's vast jurisdiction was completely unfeasible. Being steward of
two neighbouring lordships was more than enough to occupy the earl of
Arundel's officers during the same period – how could Poitevin possibly be
expected to exercise the close management required by his office over a collection of estates that was spread across the entire realm, including Ireland?[50]
However, such considerations do not appear to have been taken into account
and, following Poitevin's appointment, the installation of chamber figures
continued unabated. On 17 March that year William Hart, a yeoman of the
chamber, was appointed master-sergeant of the lordship of Usk, whilst on 13

---

[46] *CPR 1381–85*, pp. 88, 92.
[47] Ibid., pp. 92, 96, 100, 104, 121.
[48] C 81/473, fol. 2073.
[49] *CPR 1381–85*, p. 96. For Poitevin see D. Green, 'The Household and Military Retinue of Edward
      the Black Prince', University of Nottingham PhD thesis, 2 vols (1998), ii, 117–18; R. Griffiths,
      *The Principality of Wales in the Later Middle Ages: The Structure and Personnel of Government.
      I: South Wales, 1277–1536* (Cardiff, 1972), pp. 231–2.
[50] For the Arundel administration at the same time see M. Rogers, 'The Welsh Marcher Lordship of
      Bromfield and Yale, 1282–1485', University of Wales PhD thesis (1992), ch. 4; L. Smith, 'The
      Lordships of Chirk and Oswestry, 1282–1415', University of London PhD thesis (1970), ch. 2.

May Thomas Ydfen, king's esquire, received the constableship of Cefnllys Castle, the *caput* of the lordship of Maelienydd.[51] Indeed, such was the extent of this official takeover that even many of the local parkers, foresters, bailiffs, beadles and ringilds were removed from office and replaced by minor household men, just as had happened in Denbigh under the Black Prince in the 1360s.[52] The same process also took place outside the March of Wales. In March that year, for example, Henry English, an associate of Robert de Vere, earl of Oxford, had been appointed steward of the lordship of Clare, and in May Thomas Shardlowe, a yeoman of the chamber, was made steward of all the king's lands in Kent, specifically including those lately of Edmund Mortimer.[53]

What was happening here and who was responsible for it? The contradiction between these appointments and those originally made by the council in January 1382 demonstrates clearly that there was a disagreement at the heart of the government over how these estates should be treated whilst in royal hands. On the one hand, following the precedent established by Edward III, the council evidently believed that these lands should continue to be administered by the Mortimers' own officials. On the other hand, however, someone, or some group of people close to the king, or perhaps even Richard himself, disagreed and wanted them to be run exclusively by the royal household, just as the Black Prince had attempted to do with his household in Denbigh during the 1360s. From whom this latter policy originated is more difficult to say, but the scale of the takeover and its thoroughness suggest a coherency of will emanating from the heart of the government and this can only mean that Richard himself was, at the very least, involved, if not the principal driving force behind the policy's implementation. The king's personal role in the dispute that developed over these estates is well known from Walsingham, and in the light of the aforementioned grants Richard's reaction to Scrope's attempted restraint looks all the more like that of a young man affronted by the criticism of a policy he himself had conceived, or had come to believe that he had conceived. This is not to suggest that the initiative was his alone, or that the king had a detailed knowledge of the Marches and the offices to which he appointed his associates, but he could easily have received encouragement and information from Simon Burley, whose Marcher background and service in Wales under the Black Prince would have given him such local expertise as well as an acute awareness of the power vested in Marcher lordship.[54] Indeed, it is more than possible that Burley was himself heavily involved in the development of this policy, just as it has been proposed

---

[51] *CPR 1381–85*, pp. 100, 117.
[52] Ibid., pp. 88, 90, 92, 93–4, 96, 98, 100, 102, 104, 105, 111, 112, 121, 131, 168, 178, 211, 213–14, 219, 268.
[53] Ibid., pp. 104, 118. For Henry English see Tuck, *Richard II*, p. 88.
[54] For biographies of Burley see Green, 'Household and Military Retinue', ii, 27; *ODNB*, viii, 869–70.

that he was the *éminence grise* behind so many of the young king's actions during these years.[55] The similarities between Richard's policy towards the Mortimer estates and the Black Prince's earlier treatment of Denbigh during the 1360s suggest the continued influence of the same advisor and it is highly significant that the placing of chamber figures within the inheritance only began after Burley's return in late January 1382 from Germany, where he had been negotiating the king's marriage.[56] As Given-Wilson has already shown in Kent, and as we shall see later in the Marches, Burley was busily constructing his own territorial powerbases during these years and his ambition was clearly the subject of much concern.[57] What is less clear, however, is the extent to which Burley remained the master in his relationship with Richard at this date. It may be the case that the young king had already become more than just an accomplice to his friend's schemes, but either way it is evident that we should look to the two of them if we are seeking to understand where this unorthodox treatment of a noble minority came from.

The suggestion that Richard and Burley were the driving force behind the crown's policy towards the Mortimer estates is reinforced by the events that took place following Scrope's dismissal from the chancery on 11 July 1382. Over the previous six months the king had not had everything his own way regarding the Mortimer inheritance. For example, on 16 May, perhaps as a last ditch attempt to safeguard the family's estates, the council had authorized further letters patent appointing receivers for the Welsh lordships, again observing the principle that these lands should be administered by the officials of their late owners.[58] Similarly, it had authorized the grant on 13 March of custody of all of the Mortimers' demesne lands in numerous counties and in the lordship of Usk to John Gilbert, bishop of Hereford, Peter de la Mare and Roger Nash, all of whom had been well connected with Edmund Mortimer.[59] It is also interesting to note that over this period the jurisdiction of Thomas Poitevin as steward had been given some degree of plausibility when it was reduced first to 'all lands beyond the Severne [sic]', before settling in April for the lordships of Denbigh, Usk and Caerleon, perhaps non-coincidentally the three most valuable and powerful of the entire estate.[60]

---

[55] This suggestion was first made in Tuck, *Richard II*, pp. 74–6.

[56] T. Tout, *Chapters in the Administrative History of Medieval England: The Wardrobe, the Chamber and the Small Seals*, 6 vols (Manchester, 1920–33), iii, 382–3.

[57] Given-Wilson, 'Richard II and his Grandfather's Will'.

[58] *CFR 1377–83*, pp. 292–4. For example, Countess Philippa's receiver, Geoffrey Buelt, was confirmed in office as receiver of Denbigh and her Shropshire estates: for his former service see SC 8/1183/20; 1184/13, 15. Owain ap Llewelyn ap Jon, the son of the former receiver, was appointed in the lordship of Buelt: BL, Egerton Rolls 8726; 8727, m. 2. Roger Partrich, one of the stewards formerly appointed by the council, was made receiver of the lordship of Wigmore: see above, p. 103.

[59] *CFR 1377–83*, p. 288. Gilbert was an executor of Earl Edmund's will, in which he was left two gifts: Nichols, *Wills*, pp. 114, 116. For Nash see Griffiths, *Principality of Wales*, p. 179.

[60] *CPR 1381–85*, pp. 100, 103.

However, the chancellor's removal in early July that year put an immediate halt to the council's attempts to subvert Richard's wishes and from then onward the government can be seen to have conformed to the policy apparently established by the young king and his tutor. For the first time Richard and his associates were now free to do as they pleased with the inheritance. If ever there was to be a sudden flurry of custodial grants to members of the royal household, therefore, this was the time during which it was most likely to take place. Indeed, in mid-June the foundations for this had perhaps been laid when William Ford, a former Mortimer clerk now retained by the king, was commissioned to survey the estates and to put them up for farm if he could find anyone willing to take them.[61] However, in the aftermath of this appointment almost no custodial grants were actually made. In fact, the only significant grant of this nature made around this time actually occurred on 25 September, after Bishop Braybrooke had been appointed as the new chancellor, when Simon Burley received custody of the Pembrokeshire lordship of Narberth at a highly favourable rent.[62] Otherwise, royal policy towards the estates continued primarily to target their administration, which further supports the suggestion that this was more about overall control, rather than the endowment of individual chamber knights. By mid-August a royal clerk, Walter Chippenham, had been appointed receiver general of all the Mortimer estates, and the few remaining Mortimer clerks had been granted royal retaining fees, bringing them directly into the king's employ, whilst Burley himself had been given an additional supervisory authority over all the family's estates in the March through his appointment as surveyor of all the Mortimer lands in Wales and the border counties.[63]

In late 1382 Richard did in fact finally make some custodial grants to certain members of his household, targeting certain regions within the Welsh Marches. However, if we investigate these grants in a little more detail they actually reinforce the argument that Richard and Burley were seeking to maintain the crown's close control over the Mortimer inheritance in Wales, for they only granted these estates away to reinforce the existing local power of certain important associates or to increase the local presence of the chamber in general in specific regions of the Marches. The example of the grant of custody of the lordship of Narberth to Burley has already been mentioned, and the separate case of Burley will be addressed later, but the other examples all relate to a particular section of the Herefordshire borders where a number of chamber figures already held lands. For example, on 10 November 1382, Thomas Poitevin, the king's steward of the Mortimer estates, was granted custody of the Herefordshire manors of Oreslone and

---

[61] *CFR 1377–83*, p. 296.
[62] Ibid., p. 320.
[63] Ibid., pp. 310, 315; *CPR 1381–85*, p. 164. For the retaining of Mortimer clerks by the king see SC 6/1293/4.

Winforton, which would have transformed his standing in this county.[64] Oreslone and Winforton were not manors in the traditional English sense; they
were commotes: Welsh knightly fees with extensive surroundings that were
held as semi-autonomous sub-lordships. Indeed, elsewhere in the chancery
rolls they are referred to as 'lordships'.[65] Together they comprised a considerable chunk of the hundred of Stretford, which, given their proximity to
Poitevin's existing manor of Twyford, would have increased Sir Thomas's
local power considerably and buttressed his authority as steward, something
that was very much in Richard's interests to do.[66] Similarly, on 5 November,
Simon Burley's relatives Richard and John Burley received custody of the
Herefordshire commotes of Marden and Orleton, which, combined with their
family holdings in the county, would also have made them prominent local
landholders, especially along Herefordshire's northern border with the March
proper.[67] They also received custody of the so-called 'manor' of Blaenllyfni,
which was in fact the *caput* of the Breconshire Marcher lordship of the same
name. Blaenllyfni itself was divided into three commotes and custody of its
principal demesne manor cannot have entailed anything less than the Burleys'
de facto control of at least one of these.[68] The benefits to the family and to
the overall power of the chamber in this region are therefore obvious but
the grant itself was in fact completely illegal. The entire lordship of Blaenllyfni had been among the lands enfeoffed by Edmund Mortimer in 1374, so
it should never have escheated and no part of it was in Richard's power to
grant away. Of course, it is highly possible that the king was unaware of this
until he was reminded by the late earl's feoffees, who procured a ratification
of their estate soon afterwards, perhaps partially in response to this grant, but
it is also equally possible that Richard simply did not care about the legal
protection these estates enjoyed.[69] During the following year the king would
ignore a number of enfeoffments made in his grandfather's will as part of
his attempt to give Simon Burley a comital endowment in Kent, so the case
of Blaenllyfni might stand as another early example of this same disregard
for the law.[70]

The king's policy towards the Mortimer estates was to continue to be
observed throughout the rest of the inheritance's time in royal hands, until
its grant to Arundel and his associates in December 1383. During this period
Richard not only re-extended Thomas Poitevin's unworkable jurisdiction

---

[64]   *CFR 1377–83*, pp. 331–2.
[65]   See for example ibid., pp. 293–4. For the tenurial composition of Marcher lordships and the
       nature of commotes see Davies, *Lordship and Society*, ch. 4.
[66]   For a map see W. Rees, *South Wales and the Border in the Fourteenth Century* (Southampton,
       1932).
[67]   *CFR 1377–83*, p. 333. For Richard Burley's Herefordshire estates see *CIPM 1384–92*, no. 515.
[68]   See Rees, *South Wales and the Border*.
[69]   *CPR 1381–85*, pp. 271–2.
[70]   Given-Wilson, 'Richard II and his Grandfather's Will'.

as steward to cover once more all the estates beyond the Severn but also secured several more of the inheritance's military fortresses for his household men.[71] However, these grants were little more than the finishing touches to a commanding position that had been largely completed during the first six months of 1382; hence the relatively few further grants after this date. By doing so, Richard and Burley had secured direct control of this powerful collection of lordships through the insertion of royal household men, to the almost complete exclusion of the Mortimers' own officials and of any other members of the nobility who might have taken an interest. Most significantly, however, they had done so whilst retaining the vast majority of these estates in royal hands, which suggests that their priorities went well beyond merely endowing their friends with valuable lands. Richard, like his father before him, clearly believed that it was his right to use these estates as if they were his own private lands during their time in his hands and it is notable that he pursued an almost identical policy to that which the Black Prince had employed in Denbigh during the 1360s, albeit on a much wider scale.

It is this comparison with the king's private estates and with the methods of rule previously employed by the Black Prince that is particularly significant here, for members of the royal household were not only being appointed to positions of local authority within the Mortimer inheritance during the early 1380s but also to similar offices elsewhere in Wales, particularly in the principality and the royal lordships, which might suggest that the treatment of the Mortimer estates was just one example of a greater policy that was already being employed by this date. Because many of the king's chamber knights had previously been members of the Black Prince's household, many of them had been appointed to offices in Wales during the prince's lifetime. After the prince's death, and again during Richard's minority, these were generally confirmed by the Gaunt-dominated government, almost certainly because John of Gaunt considered his late brother's retainers to be reliable allies in his attempts at this time to reassert royal authority.[72] Furthermore, the royal household's collective power in this region also increased during these years when several knights secured lucrative grants in the March proper. In some cases, such as that of Sir William Beauchamp's custody of the Hastings inheritance, which was awarded in March 1378, these were highly appropriate.[73] However, in other cases it seems more likely that the recipients had abused their proximity to the young king. For example, in June 1378

---

[71] *CPR 1381–85*, pp. 227, 309, 318.

[72] See for example *CPR 1377–81*, pp. 57, 223, 457, 613. Gundy has shown that Gaunt was also using members of the Lancastrian affinity in a similar capacity elsewhere at this time: A. Gundy, 'The Rule of Thomas Beauchamp, Earl of Warwick, in the West Midlands, 1369–1401', University of Cambridge PhD thesis (2000), pp. 94–109.

[73] *CFR 1377–83*, pp. 80–1, 91–2. Beauchamp was the cousin and preferred heir general of John Hastings senior: *ODNB*, iv, 607; I. Jack, 'Entail and Descent: the Hastings inheritance', *BIHR* 38 (1965), 1–19.

Simon Burley received a life grant of the lordship of Llanstephan in south-west Wales and in August 1380 John Holland was granted the lordship of Hopedale in Flintshire, both of which entailed the alienation of valuable royal patrimony during a time of war but do not appear to have been a response to a perceived governmental necessity.[74]

Given that Richard is now believed to have started to come into his own and to have taken an active interest in governmental matters for the first time from mid-1381, it would appear that, under the influence of men like Burley, he quickly adopted this policy as his own, for the king's emergence did nothing to stem the tide of grants flowing towards members of the royal household. On the contrary, their frequency only increased as Richard started to involve himself. However, it is notable that, with the important exception of Burley, the chamber knights involved were appointed to administrative positions in Wales, rather than receiving land grants, which again suggests that the policy was designed to increase the role of the household in local government in this region. On 5 May 1381, for example, the chamber knight Sir John Clanvowe was made steward of the royal lordship of Haverford, Pembrokeshire, and constable of the castle for life.[75] Then, in August that year, Sir John Holland's power in north Wales was increased by his appointment for life as chief justice of Chester, which office he would hold until his disgrace in 1385.[76] This is of course exactly the same policy that we have observed towards the Mortimer inheritance, and as Richard turned his attention to these estates during the following year, he expanded the policy in Wales in tandem. In March 1382, Gronov ap Tudor, a Welsh king's esquire, and Sir Baldwin Raddington, one of Richard's chamber knights and the nephew of Simon Burley, were appointed successive constables of Beaumaris Castle, Anglesey.[77] Then, on 29 October, another chamber knight, Sir Lewis Clifford, was confirmed by the king in his office of constable of Cardigan Castle, which he had held since 1378, and on 1 November Sir John Beauchamp of Holt, chamber knight and a future victim of the Merciless Parliament, replaced Edward St John, a retainer of the earl of Arundel, as constable of Conway Castle, north Wales.[78] If these appointments are considered along-side Thomas Poitevin's position as constable of Lampeter Castle, Aberystwyth, which he had held since 1370, and William Beauchamp's control of the Pembrokeshire castles of Cilgerran, Tenby and Pembroke itself as part of the Hastings estate, then it can hardly be denied that the chamber had been

---

[74] *CPR 1377–81*, pp. 256, 539.
[75] Ibid., p. 627.
[76] *CPR 1381–85*, p. 36.
[77] Ibid., p. 100. For Raddington see N. Lewis, 'Simon Burley and Baldwin of Raddington', *EHR* 52 (1937), 662–9.
[78] *CPR 1381–85*, pp. 183, 185.

transformed into a politico-military force in Wales over the space of just a few years.[79]

The exception to this rule was Simon Burley, who used Richard's favour to further his attempts to become a Marcher lord in his own right. Burley came from a Herefordshire family but he appears to have inherited no property in the region.[80] As mentioned above, he had been granted the lordship of Llanstephan by the king in 1378 and he had also been constable of Carmarthen Castle since September 1375, when he had been appointed by the Black Prince.[81] In 1382 this south Welsh power base was further enlarged through the grant of the lordship of Newcastle Emlyn, which both neighboured his current holdings and, like Llanstephan, had previously been attached to the Principality of Wales.[82] Furthermore, at the same time Burley also received a series of offices designed to expand his local authority even further. As noted earlier, on 4 August he was appointed surveyor of the former Mortimer estates in the Welsh borderlands and then on 19 August Burley was appointed chief justice of south Wales, giving him wide-ranging judicio-military authority over the region in which he had been given so many estates.[83] By the time of his aforementioned grant of the custody of the Mortimer lordship of Narberth in September that year, therefore, Burley had become one of the most powerful men in south Wales, particularly in the absence of the Hastings earls of Pembroke and the Mortimer earls of March; a remarkable transformation for a younger son of a minor Herefordshire gentry family with no proven administrative track record in offices of this magnitude. Moreover, his establishment in this region would also be matched elsewhere over the course of the following year, when Richard would begin to grant him lands and offices in Kent.[84] It therefore seems plausible to suggest that Richard and Burley's purpose was twofold. On the one hand they wanted Burley to receive an estate befitting a nobleman, almost certainly as a precursor to raising him into the ranks of the titled nobility, but on the other hand they were also trying to ensure that certain regions of the realm, such as the southern March of Wales, were put under his governance as an agent of the king's direct rule.

Burley, however, was the exception, not the rule and, as we have seen, the nature of the grants given to other members of the royal household during

---

[79] J. Rickard, *The Castle Community: The Personnel of English and Welsh Castles, 1272–1422* (Woodbridge, 2002), pp. 120, 390, 395, 397.

[80] *ODNB*, viii, p. 689.

[81] *CPR 1377–81*, p. 223.

[82] *CPR 1381–85*, pp. 107, 118, 206. For Newcastle Emlyn see G. Evans, 'The Story of Newcastle-Emlyn and Atpar to 1531, with Concluding Survey', *Transactions of the Honourable Society of Cymmrodorion* 32 (1922), 58–170.

[83] *CPR 1381–85*, p. 160.

[84] Given-Wilson, 'Richard II and his Grandfather's Will'; J. Gillespie, 'Dover Castle: Key to Richard II's Kingdom?', *Archaeologia Cantiana* 105 (1989 for 1988), 179–95; Tuck, *Richard II*, pp. 75–6.

these years strongly supports the suggestion that this was not about the endowment of individual chamber knights but an attempt to consolidate the crown's direct control of this region through a network of local agents. Taken as a whole, Richard's grants in 1381–83 suggest that he and Burley were already attempting to rule this region through the royal household, a policy usually associated with a much later date in the reign.[85] Crucially, however, the similarity between these grants and those through which chamber knights were inserted into the Mortimer inheritance makes it clear that the king and his chief advisor simply expanded their policy to encompass these estates as well after they fell into royal hands. Doubtless in 1381–82 Richard believed that this was sensible government. Given England's declining position in the Hundred Years War, the recent threat of a French invasion of Wales and, perhaps above all, the Peasants' Revolt, in which the young king had seen at first hand the failure of his minority government to resolve the problems afflicting the realm, it seems that Richard had come to the conclusion that decisive kingship was required and he turned naturally to the men he was closest to, his household knights, when he tried to put this into practice.[86] Furthermore, since Gaunt appears to have employed a similar policy in the late 1370s, the young king may simply have been following what he believed to be a sensible example.[87] However, when he started to apply this policy to the private estates of one of his greatest noble families, he quickly fell foul of his subjects' expectations concerning the treatment of an inheritance in wardship. There are several reasons for this.

On the one hand, there was the impact of Richard's policy upon the estates themselves. Unfortunately, because of the vicissitudes of document survival, it is difficult to determine how the value of the family's lordships changed during their time in royal hands, so we cannot know whether their new administrators wasted them in order to squeeze as much out of them as possible. However, one conclusion concerning their mismanagement can clearly be drawn from the evident failure of the chamber knight Thomas Poitevin as the inheritance's steward. It was suggested earlier that Poitevin's installation as steward of the entire inheritance was a recipe for the waste, local abuses and other kinds of depredation any landholder feared during a minority, because his jurisdiction was too extensive for him to be able to perform his role

---

[85] For the original study of Richard's use of the royal affinity in the localities see C. Given-Wilson, *The Royal Household and the King's Affinity: Service, Politics and Finance in England, 1360–1413* (London, 1986), pp. 203–26. For a more recent study that has also suggested that Richard was pursuing the same policy earlier in the reign see S. Mitchell, 'Some Aspects of the Knightly Household of Richard II', University of London PhD thesis (1998), chs 6–9.

[86] For the threat of a French invasion of Wales see R. R. Davies, *The Revolt of Owain Glyn Dŵr* (Oxford, 1995), pp. 86–7. For several accounts of Richard's role in the suppression of the Peasants' Revolt see *The Peasants' Revolt of 1381*, ed. R. B. Dobson, 2nd edn (Basingstoke, 1983), part iii.

[87] Gundy, 'Rule of Thomas Beauchamp', pp. 110–11. Similar conclusions are drawn in my forthcoming PhD thesis.

effectively. Accordingly, it is hardly surprising to find that Poitevin appears to have been completely incapable of carrying out even the most basic of his duties. For example, in later grants or inquisitions at which the steward would normally be present, Poitevin's place is always supplied by another.[88] Moreover, he seems to have been widely resented by the Mortimer tenants and, consequently, to have presided over at least one breakdown of order. This is suggested by a commission of inquiry issued centrally in August 1383, which records that the tenants of the Mortimer lordship of Halcester had abducted a resident of the neighbouring ecclesiastical lordship of Bishops Castle and imprisoned him in the Mortimers' own castle of Montgomery, presumably with the collusion of its constable, who was replaced shortly afterwards with another member of the royal household.[89] When Poitevin had approached the castle as the king's appointed steward and attempted to force them to release the man, they had driven him off and continued to ignore his authority.[90] Maladministration such as this would have provoked opposition to Richard's policy from a wide section of the nobility, for such incidents were worrying even to those who were not directly affected. This might help explain, therefore, why noblemen with no obvious links to the Mortimers, such as John, Lord Neville of Raby, were among the custodians to whom the estates were finally committed in December 1383. If it was the Mortimers' lands today it could easily be someone else's tomorrow and so it seems likely that the magnates' communal interests led many of them to unite in opposition to the king's policies.

Richard's continued employment of the methods of rule associated with his late father, rather than with his grandfather Edward III would also have concerned many of his subjects. During the Black Prince's lifetime his harsh lordship had provoked protest and criticism throughout his domains, culminating in a rebellion in Aquitaine.[91] In Wales the prince had so antagonized the Marcher lords that they had appealed to Edward III to strip him of his overlordship of their lands.[92] Clearly this type of governance would have had serious repercussions if applied to the realm at large. Furthermore, the Black Prince had never had to face the realities of ruling; he had never had to reconcile his private lordship with the public responsibilities of kingship, nor suffered the same awakening as that faced by Edward III in 1340–41. Now, already five years into his reign, Richard was showing no signs of understanding these issues either. What was different, however, was that the Black

---

[88] See for example *CPR 1381–85*, p. 261.

[89] For the replacement of the constable see ibid., p. 309.

[90] *CPR 1381–85*, pp. 351–2.

[91] For a discussion see R. Barber, *Edward, Prince of Wales and Aquitaine: A Biography of the Black Prince* (London, 1978), pp. 80–1, 155–6, 158–9, 181, 208–12, 216. His verdict on the prince's administrative record in general is that it varied 'from the competent to the disastrous': p. 239. Cf. Green, 'Household and Military Retinue', chs 4–5 for a less critical verdict.

[92] Davies, *Lordship and Society*, pp. 269–73.

Prince had only ever been just that, a prince. When he had seized Denbigh arbitrarily during the 1360s, replaced its officials and exploited its resources, Countess Philippa had been able to appeal to a higher authority, Edward III, who had eventually brokered a settlement. However, when Richard abused his prerogative and exploited the Mortimers' entire inheritance, he did so as the king and there was no higher power to petition. That is why it was left to noblemen like Scrope and Arundel to step in and try to bring the king to heel.

Beyond this, it is also worth considering how conventional or otherwise it was for a monarch to use his household in this way and whether Richard's direct control of the considerable politico-military resources vested in these estates would have worried his subjects, particularly the other Marcher lords, who knew better than anyone else just how much power they offered. After all, Edward III's policy had been very different, since he had used the established local nobility, such as the previous earl of Arundel (d. 1376), as the crown's agents in this region.[93] It may also have been alarming to see men like Burley, whose motives were clearly distrusted, being given such considerable local authority in this area. Furthermore, as the relationship between Richard and certain of his leading subjects became increasingly strained during the early 1380s, the king's eagerness to secure direct control of the resources of these lordships and his associated unwillingness to involve the other Marcher lords in their custody may well have led many of the local nobility to question Richard's intentions. If by 1384–85 it was possible to believe that the king was involved in a plot to kill the duke of Lancaster it was surely possible to think that Richard might eventually try to use the power vested in these lands against those members of the nobility who had begun to criticize him.[94]

It is also clear that the decision of the king's critics to voice their concerns only caused the dispute to escalate further. From the unprecedented grant of the stewardship of the entire inheritance to Sir Thomas Poitevin, which is surely an indication of Richard's determination to have his own way at any cost, to the illegal grant of custody of Blaenllyfni to Simon Burley's relatives, which speaks of a similar disregard for protocol, it is evident that the king's behaviour became more extreme as the disagreement spiralled, contributing considerably to the growing political tension that would have such an impact upon the events of the 1380s. One telling example of this, which demonstrates just how much the relationship between Richard and his subjects had already broken down over this affair, comes from the parliament of October 1382, when the king's handling of the Mortimer inheritance was clearly called into question. At this assembly, which is usually thought to have been concerned with little more than the Way of Flanders/Way of Castile

---

[93] For Arundel's service in Wales see *ODNB*, xix, 768.
[94] For the rumours of plots against Gaunt by *c.* 1384 see *St Albans Chronicle*, i, 723–5, 751.

debate, Richard faced renewed scrutiny of his household and a commons petition calling for his use of the royal prerogative of wardship to be better regulated.[95] Almost certainly in response to the king's recent dismissal of Scrope, whom the commons were known to favour, Richard was petitioned that 'good governance be set in place around your honourable person so that you may live honestly and regally within the revenues of your kingdom, and that all kinds of wardships, marriages, reliefs, escheats, forfeitures and all other resources *be kept for your wars, and for the defence of your kingdom, and not used elsewhere* [my emphasis]'.[96] According to the parliament rolls, his response at the time was simply that he would do 'whatsoever shall seem best to him in terms of his honour and benefit', but after the assembly had been dissolved a fuller statement of the king's personal intent was enrolled upon the patent rolls.[97] On 14 November that year, in open defiance of his subjects' wishes, they record an order from Richard and his council that all issues from all the lands in royal hands by the deaths of Edmund Mortimer and his mother, Philippa, should, in fact, 'be applied entirely to the expenses of the household'.[98] This remarkable declaration, a veritable two-fingered salute to the commons' wishes, demonstrates the extent to which Richard and his subjects were clearly at loggerheads over the question of the Mortimer inheritance and gives us an important insight into the tense political atmosphere which had developed as this dispute progressed.

It seems likely, therefore, that the dispute over the Mortimer inheritance and Richard's reaction to his subjects' criticism had a significant impact upon the king's relationship with several members of the nobility. One obvious example is the former chancellor, Richard Scrope, who, according to Walsingham, was so disgusted with the king's behaviour that he vowed never again to hold public office under Richard.[99] Arguably even more important, however, especially given his subsequent role in the politics of the 1380s, is the earl of Arundel, who moved into outspoken opposition to the king in early 1384, immediately after the resolution of this dispute. Up until his outburst at the Salisbury Parliament of April that year, there is no evidence whatsoever to suggest that Arundel had been a critic of the king. On the contrary, it is known that he was present in the Tower with Richard during the Peasants' Revolt and that, following Sudbury's murder, he was even temporarily entrusted with custody of the great seal.[100] His appointment by the Commons in 1381 to reside in the royal household and to advise the king may in fact denote, therefore, not that he was already seen as someone who would stand

---

95 *PROME*, vi, 277–8.
96 Ibid., vi, 295.
97 Ibid.
98 *CPR 1381–85*, p. 184.
99 *St Albans Chronicle*, i, 623.
100 A. Goodman, *The Loyal Conspiracy: The Lords Appellant under Richard II* (London, 1971), p. 8.

up to Richard but that he had developed some sort of a rapport with the young king during his early years and was thought to be someone who could have a positive influence upon him.[101] By early 1384, however, Arundel had clearly seen enough to convince him that something was wrong and he chose the next parliament to launch a public attack upon the government and, by implication, upon Richard himself.

Arundel's outburst is usually explained as a reaction to the discussion in this assembly of a draft treaty with France. The earl is believed to have been among the hawks in the nobility and to have disapproved strongly of the foreign policy advocated by those close to the king. It is also often suggested that he was concerned about the growing cost of Richard's household and that he was angered at his own loss of influence to the king's associates.[102] All of this may well be true. However, Arundel's tirade has never yet been viewed in the light of recent developments within the Marches and, in particular, of his struggle for custody of the Mortimer inheritance, which he had secured as recently as December 1383. The parliament was possibly the first time that the king and the earl had been in each other's presence since this settlement and certainly the first time they would have had such an audience. As the principal Marcher lord in Mortimer's absence, it seems that Arundel somewhat characteristically took it upon himself to let the king know what the Marchers thought of his government. However, given Arundel's position in the household since November 1381, from which he would have had a bird's-eye view of its operation and of the influence of the chamber knights and other royal associates upon the young king, it is interesting to note that when the earl chose to make his criticisms in April 1384 he launched his attack on the entire government, thereby implicitly including the king. Whilst his tirade, as recorded by the Westminster Chronicler, refrained from explicitly naming Richard himself as personally responsible for the 'state of decay' of the realm, this was nevertheless the first time that any criticism of the government had not been directed exclusively at those around the king.[103] In the previous parliament, for example, the commons had continued to complain about the influence of Richard's associates and had asked that he take full personal responsibility for government henceforth.[104] That Arundel's diatribe did not continue this line of attack suggests that he at least was by now fully aware of who was really responsible for the royal policy he found so undesirable and, having finally secured control of the Mortimer inherit-

---

[101]   *PROME*, vi, 226.

[102]   See for example C. Given-Wilson, 'The Earl of Arundel, the War with France, and the Anger of King Richard II', in *The Medieval Python: The Purposive and Provocative Work of Terry Jones*, ed. R. Yeager and T. Takamiya (Basingstoke, 2012), pp. 27–38, at pp. 28–9; N. Saul, *Richard II* (New Haven and London, 1997), pp. 130–1; Tuck, *Richard II*, p. 92.

[103]   *The Westminster Chronicle 1381–94*, ed. L. C. Hector and B. F. Harvey (Oxford, 1982), pp. 68–9.

[104]   Ibid., p. 55; Tuck, *Richard II*, p. 91.

ance, he was prepared to let his thoughts be known, even if he could not quite directly accuse the king. Richard certainly understood the implications of the earl's criticism, growing white with anger and responding that 'if it is to my charge ... that you would lay this, and if it is supposed to be my fault that there is misgovernment in the kingdom, you lie in your teeth. You can go to the Devil!'[105] Apparently it was only following Gaunt's 'explanation' of what Arundel really meant that the king was placated.

To sum up, it seems that the significance of Richard's treatment of the Mortimer inheritance in 1382–83 has been significantly underestimated. Despite the king's youth, the incident does appear to have been one of the earliest occasions upon which Richard attempted to play a personal role in shaping governmental policy and one of the first times that he clashed publicly with certain of his subjects over the form this policy should take. Contrary to what has previously been proposed, however, this dispute was not the result of the king's willingness to accept his chamber knights' petitions for custody of the inheritance. Rather, it was precipitated by Richard's attempt to secure personal control of these estates through the insertion of his household men into their administration and his dismissal of the Mortimers' own officials. By this date the king can already be seen to have started to use his chamber knights in a similar way in the neighbouring Principality of Wales, probably due to the influence of men such as Burley and perhaps initially as a response to the political turmoil of the late 1370s and early 1380s, and once the Mortimer inheritance fell into his hands in early 1382 he appears simply to have expanded this policy to encompass these estates as well. However, this unorthodox behaviour soon provoked opposition from many of Richard's greater subjects, who felt that this was not how a monarch was supposed to handle a noble estate in wardship. Simply put, their grievances were that the king's treatment of the inheritance not only threatened its administrative well-being but also raised significant questions concerning his intentions, the style of rule he was attempting and the reasons why he thought it was necessary to secure direct control of the military and financial resources of these lordships. Accordingly, they took it upon themselves to challenge Richard's freedom of action for perhaps the first time in the reign and were eventually able to force him to hand over custody of these estates, thereby inflicting upon him his first significant political defeat.

The incident also seems to have been a turning point in the relationship between Richard and several of the men who opposed him, most notably the earl of Arundel, from which it never recovered. Arundel would never return to the king's side after this confrontation but would go on to become one of the most prominent and vocal of Richard's critics during the 1380s and one of the leading figures in the coalition of noblemen who challenged the king in

---

[105] *Westminster Chronicle*, pp. 68–9.

1386–88. Richard, for his part, would harbour an enmity towards the earl that would only be increased by the events of this decade and would ultimately result in Arundel's execution for treason in 1397.

Over the intervening years the king would experiment with a number of other controversial policies, such as his unprecedented use of the royal affinity during the 1390s and his eventual creation of the Principality of Chester, which gave Richard the greatest private powerbase held by any medieval English monarch to this date. In the light of the evidence outlined above, such behaviour does not appear to have been an aberration from the style of rule that the king had pursued earlier in his reign; on the contrary it seems to have been the logical extreme of a policy that Richard had first begun to experiment with from his earliest participation in politics. The similarities between the king's behaviour during the early 1380s and the late 1390s have often been recognized but it is rarer for historians to argue that he can be seen to have pursued a coherent policy throughout his entire reign – yet that is exactly what the affair of the Mortimer inheritance in 1382–84 appears to suggest.[106] It is quite clear from the evidence disclosed here that by 1382 Richard was already attempting to rule certain regions of the realm through his household and that an important aspect of this policy was the exclusion of certain members of the established nobility. As further studies of the deployment of the royal affinity increasingly demonstrate that it was designed to achieve exactly the same ends during the 1390s, and since it has long been apparent that this is what the king was trying to do in 1397–99, it rapidly becomes clear that this may have been the goal that Richard sought throughout his entire reign and that so many of the political crises of the period may have been provoked by this antagonistic policy. Furthermore, it is also evident from the affair of the Mortimer inheritance that the clear association in Richard's mind between private landed power and his own personal safety was an integral part of his kingship from very early in his reign and that this was not caused by the events of 1386–88. It was this obsession that was to determine politics for much of the rest of his reign, as Richard strove increasingly to be not just king of England but also the greatest landed magnate in the realm, and which would result ultimately in the seizure of the Lancastrian inheritance and the king's deposition. By 1399, as Davies so succinctly put it, 'Richard II was still acceptable as prince of Chester but no longer as king of England'.[107] Clearly, even as early as 1382, Richard was already thinking and behaving as a prince and showing few signs of thinking like a king.

---

[106] For an earlier comparison between the king's policies during the 1380s and late 1390s see Tuck, *Richard II*, pp. 203–4, 225.
[107] Davies, 'Principality of Chester', p. 279.

WAR, CHIVALRY AND REGIONAL SOCIETY: EAST ANGLIA'S WARRIOR GENTRY BEFORE THE COURT OF CHIVALRY

Philip Caudrey

In recent decades the surviving late medieval records of the Court of Chivalry have received considerable scholarly attention.[1] Presided over by the constable and earl marshal of England, the Court was in all likelihood extremely active during the age of the Hundred Years War.[2] Its registers are now lost and only sporadic cases have survived, often in miscellaneous collections, or in later copies.[3] The Court was usually the first port-of-call for military men who possessed unresolved grievances relating to campaigns on which they had served, and its jurisdiction principally covered matters relating to treason, ransoms, rights to prisoners, and rights to armorial bearings.[4] The last of these types of disputes has been extensively treated,[5] largely because testimony from three prominent armorial cases – *Scrope v. Grosvenor* (1385–90), *Lovel v. Morley* (1386–87) and *Grey v. Hastings* (1407–10) – survive in bulk and indirectly reveal a great deal about the military careers and martial outlook of those gentry who gave evidence.[6]

The first of these disputes pitted the Lancastrian retainer, Sir Richard Scrope, against the Cheshire knight, Sir Robert Grosvenor, with each man

---

[1]   For a general survey of the Court of Chivalry, see G. D. Squibb, *The High Court of Chivalry: A Study of the Civil Law of England* (Oxford, 1959).

[2]   M. Keen, 'The Jurisdiction and Origins of the Constable's Court', in *Nobles, Knights and Men-At-Arms in the Middle Ages*, ed. M. Keen (London, 1996), pp. 135–48.

[3]   Ibid., pp. 137, 139–42.

[4]   Ibid., pp. 141–2.

[5]   M. Keen, 'English Military Experience and the Court of Chivalry: The Case of Grey v. Hastings', in *Nobles, Knights and Men-At-Arms*, ed. Keen, pp. 167–85; A. Ayton, 'Knights, Esquires and Military Service: The Evidence of the Armorial Cases before the Court of Chivalry', in *The Medieval Military Revolution: State, Society and Military Change in Medieval and Early Modern Europe*, ed. A. Ayton and J. Price (London, 1998), pp. 81–104; M. Keen, *Origins of the English Gentleman: Heraldry, Chivalry and Gentility in Medieval England, c.1300–c.1500* (Stroud, 2002), pp. 25–70; J. Rosenthal, *Telling Tales: Sources and Narration in Late Medieval England* (Philadelphia, 2003), pp. 63–94; A. Bell, *War and the Soldier in the Fourteenth Century* (Woodbridge, 2004), pp. 140–50; J. Sumption, *The Hundred Years War III: Divided Houses* (London, 2009), pp. 735–7; A. Ayton, 'Military Service and the Dynamics of Recruitment in Fourteenth-Century England', in *The Soldier Experience in the Fourteenth Century*, ed. A. Bell and A. Curry (Woodbridge, 2011), pp. 45–59; A. Bell, 'The Soldier, "hadde he riden, no man ferre"', in *The Soldier Experience in the Fourteenth Century*, ed. A. Bell and A. Curry (Woodbridge, 2011), pp. 209–18; A. Bell, A. Curry, A. King and D. Simpkin, *The Soldier in Later Medieval England* (Oxford, 2013), pp. 117–22.

[6]   *Scrope v. Grosvenor*; C 47/6/1 (Morley); PRO 30/26/69 (Lovel); *PCM*.

claiming the right to Scrope's arms, *azure a bend or*.[7] *Lovel v. Morley* and
Grey v. Hastings were centred in East Anglia and revolved around the claims
of John Lord Lovel of Oxfordshire and Wiltshire and Reginald Lord Grey
of Ruthin to the respective arms of Thomas Lord Morley and Sir Edward
Hastings, both of Norfolk.[8] The *Lovel v. Morley* case was strongly linked
to an earlier dispute in 1346–47, during which Nicholas Lord Burnell had
unsuccessfully challenged Morley's grandfather, Robert, for the same arms,
while both cases were also indirectly related to wider land disputes between
the protagonists.[9]

Morley and Hastings were the defendants in their cases and Scrope was
the plaintiff in his. All three required witnesses who could attest to having
seen them, or their ancestors, bearing the disputed arms. Their witnesses thus
comprised, on the one hand, an assortment of locals from their native regions
who could point to public spaces, such as parish churches or manor houses,
where their arms were displayed, and, on the other, militarily active men
(often very active) who could attest that they, or their ancestors, had borne the
arms on campaign. Most of their deponents were consequently middle-aged
or elderly soldiers, who fitted the latter bill, supplemented by churchmen
and non-military gentry, who could, in the words of Andrew Ayton, 'speak
convincingly about the legitimacy of [the protagonists'] heraldic identity'.[10]

A small number of the many gentry who spoke for Scrope were East
Anglian,[11] while Morley and Hastings, as the heads of distinguished Norfolk
families, relied extensively upon supporters from the eastern counties.[12]

---

7   M. Bennett, *Community, Class and Careerism: Cheshire and Lancashire Society in the Age of Sir
     Gawain and the Green Knight* (Cambridge, 1983), pp. 82–3, 166. For the Scropes, see B. Vale,
     'The Scropes of Bolton and Masham, *c.* 1300–1450', University of York PhD thesis (1987).
     For Grosvenor, see R. Stewart-Brown, 'The Scrope and Grosvenor Controversy, 1385–1391',
     Transactions of the Historic Society of Lancashire and Cheshire 89 (1938 for 1937), 1–22.

8   Ayton, 'Knights, Esquires and Military Service', pp. 84–5; Keen, 'Grey v. Hastings', pp. 172–6.
     For Lovel, see *CP*, viii, 219–21. For Morley, see *CP*, ix, 216–17. For Grey and Hastings, see
     R. I. Jack, 'Entail and Descent: The Hastings Inheritance, 1370 to 1436', *BIHR* 38 (1965), 1–19.

9   Lovel's goal appears to have been to acquire a stake in the lucrative Burnell-Haudlo inheritance.
     Hastings and Grey each considered themselves heir to their kin, the recently extinct Hastings
     earls of Pembroke. Ayton, 'Knights, Esquires and Military Service', 89–90, 84; Keen, 'Grey v.
     Hastings', pp. 172–5.

10   Keen, *Origins of the English Gentleman*, pp. 25–70; Ayton, 'Military Service and the Dynamics
     of Recruitment', p. 46.

11   *Scrope v. Grosvenor*. Fourteen were prominent knights or esquires from Norfolk or Suffolk. Sir
     John Brewes (i, 63; ii, 208–10); Sir Thomas Erpingham (i, 59; ii, 194–6); Robert Fitzrauf (i, 52;
     ii, 172–3); Sir Thomas Geney (i, 67; ii, 220); Sir Stephen Hales (i, 163; ii, 369–70); Sir Hugh
     Hastings III (i, 51; ii, 168–9); Sir John Loudham (i, 150–1; ii, 175–6); Sir Thomas Morieux (i,
     56; ii, 183–7); Sir Robert Morley (i, 60; ii, 202–3); Roger Lord Scales (i, 67; ii, 219–20); Sir
     Richard Waldegrave (i, 165; ii, 377–8); Sir John White (i, 59; ii, 196–7); Sir John Wilton (i, 71;
     ii, 231–2); Sir William Wingfield (i, 173–4; ii, 396–7). Additionally, Sir Miles Boys, the third son
     of a Yorkshire gentry family, had married into East Anglian society and had settled in Norfolk. (i,
     68; ii, 220–1).

12   For the Morleys' lands, see *CIPM*, 1353–60, no. 634; 1361–4, no. 365; 1377–84, nos 124–9. For
     the Hastings' lands and the disputes surrounding them, see Jack, 'Entail and Descent', 1–19.

East Anglian knights and esquires thus testified in all three of these cases and comprised the most prominent cohort amongst Morley's and Hastings' deponents.[13] Despite this, the East Anglian dimension in these disputes has remained a side-issue within the existing scholarship, which has predominantly focused upon the bigger picture of what the testimony reveals about fourteenth-century English military society in general, in particular investigating the military records of the deponents, their patterns of magnate service, and the role of chivalric culture at a national level.[14] *Scrope v. Grosvenor*, however, has been utilized in a regional context in studies of the military communities of north-western England[15] and, along similar lines, this essay will use all three Court of Chivalry disputes to explore the character of military society in East Anglia[16] – a region, unlike the north-west, that has been little studied from a military perspective and whose reputation for home-grown lawyers and bureaucrats seemingly far outweighed its military contribution to the wars of the fourteenth century.[17]

---

[13] The regional element is equally clear amongst Lovel's and Grosvenor's witnesses. Lovel's witnesses hailed primarily from his strongholds in Oxfordshire, Wiltshire and Berkshire, with further connections in the Somerset–Dorset area, while Grosvenor acquired the support of large sections of Cheshire's gentry military community. Ayton, 'Knights, Esquires and Military Service', pp. 85, 99 (n. 28); Bennett, *Community, Class and Careerism*, pp. 82–3, 166; P. Morgan, *War and Society in Medieval Cheshire, 1277–1403*, Chetham Society 3rd ser. 34 (Manchester, 1987), pp. 128–30.

[14] See n. 5.

[15] Bennett, *Community, Class and Careerism*, pp. 82–3, 166; Morgan, *War and Society in Medieval Cheshire*, pp. 128–30.

[16] In the context of what follows, East Anglia is taken to mean only Norfolk and Suffolk. These counties shared a single shrievalty, their greater gentry were heavily intermarried, and most of the county elite maintained estates and political interests on both sides of the Norfolk–Suffolk border. This was naturally, to some degree, true of their relations with the gentry of nearby Cambridgeshire, Huntingdonshire and Essex, but the Norfolk–Suffolk connection was particularly strong, as a number of distinguished scholars of the region have demonstrated: R. Virgoe, 'The Crown and Local Government: East Anglia under Richard II', in *The Reign of Richard II*, ed. F. du Boulay and C. Barron (London, 1971), pp. 218–41; R. Virgoe, 'The Crown, Magnates and Local Government in Fifteenth-Century East Anglia', in *The Crown and Local Communities*, ed. J. Highfield and R. Jeffs (Stroud, 1981), pp. 72–87; R. Virgoe, 'Aspects of the County Community in the Fifteenth Century', in *Profit, Piety and the Professions in Late Medieval England*, ed. M. Hicks (Stroud, 1990), pp. 1–13; C. Richmond, *The Paston Family in the Fifteenth Century: The First Phase* (Cambridge, 1990); H. Castor, *The King, the Crown, and the Duchy of Lancaster: Public Authority and Private Power, 1399–1461* (Oxford, 2000), pp. 53–189.

[17] Contemporaries and their descendants certainly peddled this stereotype. In the late fourteenth century, Geoffrey Chaucer made his rapacious reeve in *The Canterbury Tales* a Norfolk man; in the early sixteenth century, monks of Bury St Edmunds prayed 'That it may please Thee to preserve us from all Norfolk barrators [sic]'; and, in 1589, a bill was introduced in parliament designed to limit the number of Norfolk's attorneys to fourteen. Additionally, East Anglia's most famous medieval family, the Pastons, had made their fortune through the legal profession, while the Paston Letters themselves have done nothing to dampen the perception of East Anglia as a highly litigious region. Geoffrey Chaucer, *The Canterbury Tales*, intro. D. Wright (Oxford, 1998), p. 16; *The Chronicle of Jocelin of Brakelond*, ed. H. Butler (London, 1949), p. 12; A. Smith, *County and Court: Government and Politics in Norfolk, 1558–1603* (Oxford, 1974), p. 3; H. Castor, *Blood and Roses: The Paston Family in the Fifteenth Century* (London, 2004), pp. 9–24; *Paston Letters and Papers of the Fifteenth Century*, ed. N. Davis, 2 vols (Oxford,

East Anglia in many ways deserved its subsequent non-military reputation. It was one of the more prosperous and stable parts of England during the period when these disputes arose. It was remote from the warfare of the Scottish and Welsh Marches, and its military contact with the French was limited to very occasional and small-scale raids upon its coastal towns.[18] Numerous magnates maintained a landed interest in the area, but most were absentees and none sought to dominate it. East Anglia's wealthiest landowner until 1399 was Margaret of Brotherton, countess of Norfolk, who naturally, as a woman, did not seek to establish a strong military retinue.[19] After Henry IV's usurpation of the throne, the Lancastrian knight Sir Thomas Erpingham headed a gentry clique that effectively governed the region in the absence of its traditional magnate powerbrokers, who had either been destroyed in the tumults of the 1390s, or else were enduring minority crises.[20] Those East Anglian deponents who spoke in defence of Scrope, Morley and Hastings provide us with only a small sample of the strength of East Anglia's gentry military community, but, as we shall see, the lack of resident magnates left the region's greater gentry as the foremost military recruiters in their native shires, often on behalf of great lords who rarely if ever visited the eastern counties. One is therefore dealing with a military community that was rather different in its structure and composition from the military communities of the north-west, and whose gentry acquired an impressive degree of autonomy from outside interference when mobilizing their localities for war.

Finally, before proceeding any further, a word must be said about the limitations of the source materials, for the patchiness of the surviving testimony and the obscurity of many of the deponents naturally have a bearing upon the ways in which the evidence may be interpreted. In no instance is the testimony complete, though far more depositions survive for Morley and Hastings than for Lovel and Grey.[21] In all, 239 depositions survive from *Lovel*

1971–76); *Paston Letters and Papers of the Fifteenth Century (Part III)*, ed. R. Beadle and C. Richmond, EETS supplementary series 22 (2005).

18 A. Saul, 'Great Yarmouth and the Hundred Years War in the Fourteenth Century', *BIHR* 52 (1979), 105–15; J. Alban, 'English Coastal Defence: Some Fourteenth-Century Modifications within the System', in *Patronage, the Crown and the Provinces in Later Medieval England*, ed. R. A. Griffiths (Stroud, 1981), pp. 57–78.

19 Those magnates with a significant territorial stake in East Anglia during the 1380s and 1390s were: John of Gaunt, duke of Lancaster; Margaret of Brotherton, countess of Norfolk; Thomas Mowbray, earl of Nottingham (heir to the elderly Margaret); the de la Pole earls of Suffolk; the Fitzalan earls of Arundel; the Mortimer earls of March; the de Vere earls of Oxford. For analyses of magnate–gentry relations in late fourteenth-century East Anglia, see Virgoe, 'The Crown and Local Government', pp. 218–41; R. Archer, 'The Estates and Finances of Margaret of Brotherton, *c.* 1320–1399', *BIHR* 60 (1987), 264–80; S. Walker, *The Lancastrian Affinity, 1361–1399* (Oxford, 1990), pp. 182–209.

20 Castor, *The King, the Crown, and the Duchy of Lancaster*, pp. 53–81.

21 The bulk of the testimony from *Lovel v. Morley* is housed in The National Archive, Kew. Details from several of these depositions, including a few additional ones, are to be found in the topographical history of the Norfolk antiquarian Rev. Francis Blomefield, *An Essay towards a Topographical History of the County of Norfolk*, 2nd edn, 11 vols (London, 1805–11), ii, 437–9.

v. Morley, of which 177 are from Morley's supporters; 102 laymen spoke for Morley, of whom 84 mention their participation on at least one military expedition.[22] In *Grey v. Hastings*, thirty-eight testators spoke for Grey, while nearly a hundred supported Hastings, forty-two of whom touched upon their own military careers.[23] In *Scrope v. Grosvenor*, military matters came to the fore to a much greater extent and all of Scrope's East Anglian deponents described their careers in arms to varying degrees.[24]

The incompleteness of the surviving testimony foreshadows equally thorny issues that arise when attempting to precisely quantify the extent of Morley's, Hastings' and Scrope's East Anglian support bases. For Scrope, it is a relatively straightforward matter. His witnesses included magnates and barons, and the majority of his gentry testators were knights and wealthy esquires, easily identifiable. His East Anglian supporters may therefore be definitively numbered at fourteen.[25] For Morley's and Hastings' witnesses, matters are less clear-cut. Virtually all of Morley's knightly deponents can be identified as having hailed either from Norfolk, Suffolk or Essex. A handful came from Cambridgeshire, Huntingdonshire or Lincolnshire, and one from as far away as Northumberland.[26] Morley's militarily active esquires repre-sent more of a challenge. A number of the better off among them were clearly from the eastern counties, including a few relatively high-profile Norfolk and Suffolk men.[27] Several, though, were rather obscure individuals whose regional origins remain unclear.[28] Many were probably from Morley's Norfolk–Suffolk–Essex nexus, however, since the barons and bannerets under whom they saw military service were generally well-connected figures in the eastern counties.[29] As for Hastings, twenty of his forty-two militarily active witnesses can be identified as Norfolk or Suffolk men, almost all from distinguished knightly families.[30] Most of Hastings' esquires appear to have

---

The surviving records for *Grey v. Hastings* are more or less complete, running to over 700 pages. They survive only as a seventeenth-century transcript of the now lost original proceedings and are housed in the College of Arms, London.

22 PRO 30/26/69; PRO, C 47/6/1. Figures for Lovel's and Morley's deponents are corroborated in Ayton, 'Knights, Esquires and Military Service', p. 86.

23 *PCM.* Figures for Grey's and Hastings' deponents are corroborated in Keen, 'Grey v. Hastings', pp. 178–9.

24 On the chivalric evidence in *Scrope v. Grosvenor*, see Rosenthal, *Telling Tales*, pp. 63–94.

25 See n. 11.

26 C 47/6/1. For example, Sir William Papeworth from Cambridgeshire and Huntingdonshire (no. 28); Sir Nicholas Goushill from Lincolnshire (no. 29); Sir Alan Heton from Northumberland (no. 97). For their landed wealth, see *CIPM*, 1392–9, no. 1265 (Papeworth); *CIPM*, 1399–1405 no. 908 (Goushill); *CIPM*, 1384–92, no. 592 (Heton).

27 e.g. the Norfolk esquire, Hugh Curson. C 47/6/1, no. 99. For the Curson family, see *HPC*, ii, 719.

28 Ayton, 'Knights, Esquires and Military Service', pp. 90, 94–6.

29 See below, pp. 128–9.

30 *PCM*, i: Edmund Barry (393); Sir William Berdewell (390); Sir Robert Berney (474); Sir William Calthorpe (457); Sir Thomas Erpingham (439); Sir Simon Felbrigg (443); Sir John Geney (425); Sir Thomas Gerbergh (496); David Hemenhale (458); Thomas Hengrave (492); Sir Leonard Kerdiston (456); Sir Robert Morley (421); Thomas Lord Morley (435); Constantine Mortimer

been men who had served extensively in the military retinues of his banneret ancestors.[31]

Thus, while it is not possible to precisely count the number of Norfolk and Suffolk gentry who spoke for Morley and Hastings, it is clear that the majority of their witnesses were men from these counties or those surrounding them.[32] Precision in this regard, moreover, is not necessarily as helpful as it may first appear. The political and social connections amongst the gentry of Norfolk and Suffolk were powerful and complex, as Colin Richmond, Roger Virgoe, Helen Castor and others have shown.[33] However, the political division of England into shires rarely reflected military realities. From a military and chivalric perspective, county boundaries did not greatly matter, since patterns of military recruitment amongst the gentry and with the nobility were generally predicated upon landed wealth, social influence and local contacts, which cut across the shire system with impunity.[34] On the other hand, since the heartland of the Morleys' and Hastings' estates was indisputably focused in central and southern Norfolk, it was in Norfolk and Suffolk that their reach was strongest,[35] and it is these East Anglian networks, as well as Sir Richard Scrope's connections with the region, that will comprise the focal point for what follows. This essay, then, will reconsider why these numerous East Anglian knights and esquires spoke before the Court of Chivalry; it will outline the types of networks that prevailed amongst the upper echelons of East Anglia's military community; and it will show how East Anglia's warrior gentry fitted into the national military community cultivated by Edward III and his war captains.

From their testimony before the Court, it is clear that East Anglian knights and esquires were significant contributors to the military enterprises of the

---

(509); John Payn (502); John Reymes (444); Sir Ralph Shelton (423); Sir Miles Stapleton (442); Sir John Wilton (497); Sir John Wiltshire (401).

31   The survival of twenty-four of Sir Edward's father's subcontracts from the Brittany expedition of 1380 reveal the ways in which he utilized his local standing in East Anglia, but also sought recruits from further afield. A. Goodman, 'The Military Subcontracts of Sir Hugh Hastings, 1380', *EHR* 95 (1980), 114–20.

32   Knightly testators in particular often held land in various locations throughout the eastern counties. For example, the Essex knight Sir Richard Sutton was also an influential landholder in Norfolk. C 47/6/1, no. 38; *CIPM*, 1384–92, nos 383, 389, 392, 674, 821.

33   See n. 16.

34   For the concept of 'military communities', as distinct from 'county communities', see A. Ayton, 'Armies and Military Communities in Fourteenth-Century England', in *Soldiers, Nobles and Gentlemen: Essays in Honour of Maurice Keen*, ed. P. Coss and C. Tyerman (Woodbridge, 2009), pp. 215–39. For a deeply critical survey of the 'county communities' model, see C. Carpenter, 'Gentry and Community in Medieval England', *JBS* 33 (1994), 340–80. More sympathetic views of the model can be found in M. J. Bennett, 'A County Community: Social Cohesion amongst the Cheshire Gentry, 1400–1425', *Northern History* 8 (1973), 24–44; N. Saul, *Knights and Esquires: The Gloucestershire Gentry in the Fourteenth Century* (Oxford, 1981); S. Payling, *Political Society in Lancastrian England: The Greater Gentry of Nottinghamshire* (Oxford, 1991).

35   For the Morleys' and Hastings' landed wealth, see n. 12.

Hundred Years War.[36] From Thomas Lord Morley's witnesses, out of eighty-four self-proclaimed militarily active deponents, predominantly from East Anglia and surrounding counties, fifteen men claimed service at the sea battle of Sluys in 1340; twenty-three on the Crécy campaign in 1346; thirty-one at the siege of Calais in 1347; twenty at the sea battle of Winchelsea in 1350; and forty-one on the Rheims expedition in 1359–60.[37] A few men also described their participation in smaller ventures, including three who served in Brittany in 1342–43, and one who was at the battle of Auberoche in 1345,[38] while five of Morley's oldest testators claimed service in Scotland in the 1330s.[39]

Those Norfolk and Suffolk gentry who spoke for Sir Richard Scrope in his dispute the previous year were largely describing the same era and revealed martial records of similar ilk. For example, Sir John Wilton described his service in Scotland and would later see action in Castile and probably Ireland.[40] Sir Stephen Hales attested to having been present on the Rheims expedition in 1359–60, at the battle of Nájera in 1367, and in Scotland in 1385,[41] while Sir Thomas Morieux claimed military service in France, Gascony, Brittany, Spain and Scotland.[42] In both cases, the majority of witnesses only touched upon campaigns on which the protagonists or their ancestors were present. So, for instance, Sir John Brewes, who gave evidence in both disputes, described in *Scrope v. Grosvenor* his participation at the battle of Mauron in 1352, because a Scrope was in attendance, but did not bother mentioning this engagement when he spoke for Lord Morley the following year.[43]

Those who testified for Sir Edward Hastings in 1407–10, although fewer in number than Morley's testators, primarily focused upon the slightly later campaigns of the 1370s and 1380s, when Sir Edward's father, Sir Hugh III, was at the peak of his career. According to their testimony, three men fought on Gaunt's French *chevauchée* in 1373,[44] eight recalled their service at St Malo in 1378,[45] twelve were on the earl of Buckingham's expedition

---

[36] For an overview of the testimony for all three disputes, see Keen, *Origins of the English Gentleman*, pp. 43–70. Much of the Morley testimony focused upon the 1330s through 1360s, although fifty-two deponents made some mention of their military careers during the second phase of the Hundred Years War from 1369. Ayton, 'Military Service and the Dynamics of Recruitment', p. 46.

[37] Ayton, 'Knights, Esquires and Military Service', pp. 91–2.

[38] C 47/6/1, nos 20, 27, 29, 99.

[39] Ibid., nos 10, 29, 92, 97, 106.

[40] *Scrope v. Grosvenor*, i, 71; ii, 232.

[41] Ibid., i, 163; ii, 369.

[42] Ibid., i, 56; ii, 186.

[43] *Scrope v. Grosvenor*, i, 63; ii, 208–9; PRO, C 47/6/1, no. 102. Dr Ayton has made the same point using this very example. Ayton, 'Knights, Esquires and Military Service', p. 91.

[44] *PCM*, i, 413, 495, 529.

[45] Ibid., i, 329, 390, 405, 423, 435, 458, 478, 492.

to Brittany in 1380,[46] eighteen served in Scotland in 1385,[47] and the same
number followed Gaunt to Castile in 1386.[48] Again, some overlap with the
previous generation is apparent, with one of Hastings' witnesses present on
the Crécy expedition in 1346, one at the siege of Rennes in 1356–57, and one
at the battle of Nájera in 1367.[49]

These three disputes, then, collectively provide us with a glimpse of the
careers-in-arms of some of East Anglia's most militarily active knights and
esquires over the better part of half a century, between the 1330s and the
1380s. Many were very young (sometimes adolescents) when first armed,
and were well into middle age when they retired.[50] Fifteen of Sir Edward
Hastings' witnesses, for instance, described themselves as being younger
than sixteen when they first saw action and four claimed to have been less
than twelve.[51] At the other end of the scale, thirty of Morley's deponents had
been in arms for more than twenty years, and several of Hastings' witnesses
re-enlisted in middle age for the Agincourt campaign in 1415.[52] In this
context the overlap in personnel from one campaign to the next was only
natural and resulted in a consistent blend of youth and experience amongst
gentry combatants throughout the period.

These factors – the length and intensity of the deponents' military careers
– have been thoroughly treated in the existing scholarship, though not in a
specifically East Anglian context.[53] It should be borne in mind, however,
that these were essentially legal cases over heraldic rights. None of the militarily active deponents who gave evidence were doing so in order to reveal
anything about their personal military careers. Indeed, as has been touched
upon, it is clear that a great many witnesses described only portions of their
war records, not bothering to mention expeditions in which the defendant/
plaintiff, or his ancestors, had not participated.[54] There is, consequently, the
danger of reading rather too much into their depositions, which were limited
in scope and aimed at the specific purpose of assisting the defendant/plaintiff

[46] Ibid., i, 329, 404, 405, 413, 427, 435, 458, 478, 486, 496, 497, 500.
[47] Ibid., i, 329, 401, 405, 413, 421, 423, 425, 439, 444, 451, 456, 458, 464, 474, 495, 496, 519, 533.
[48] Ibid., i, 393, 397, 399, 401, 421, 423, 425, 439, 443, 444, 445, 474, 478, 495, 500, 502, 509, 513.
[49] Ibid., i, 544, 426, 496.
[50] Keen, 'Grey v. Hastings', pp. 179–80; Ayton, 'Knights, Esquires and Military Service', p. 92.
[51] The four men who claimed to have been less than twelve when first armed were Sir William
      Berdewell, Sir Robert Morley, Thomas Hengrave and Thomas Clifford. *PCM*, i, 390, 421, 492,
      500, 456.
[52] Ayton, 'Knights, Esquires and Military Service', p. 92; A. Curry, *Agincourt: A New History*
      (Stroud, 2005), pp. 282–6.
[53] Keen, 'Grey v. Hastings', pp. 179–80; Ayton, 'Knights, Esquires and Military Service', pp. 88–92;
      Ayton, 'Military Service and the Dynamics of Recruitment', pp. 45–59.
[54] Ayton, 'Knights, Esquires and Military Service', pp. 90–1; Ayton, 'Military Service and the
      Dynamics of Recruitment', pp. 46–9. The military careers of many of Morley's and Hastings'
      witnesses, beyond the campaigns they described before the Court of Chivalry, can be fleshed out
      using the online database of 'The Soldier in Late Medieval England' project. This issue has been
      considered recently by Dr Ayton. Ayton, 'Military Service and the Dynamics of Recruitment', pp.
      45–59. For the website, see http://www.medievalsoldier.org.

in winning his case. Yet, whether intentionally or not, the knights and esquires who spoke on behalf of Scrope, Morley and Hastings have provided us with a glimpse of England's genteel military community at its core – amongst its most militarily active members. Due to the regional origins of many of those who spoke, their depositions also provide us with an insight into the world of East Anglia's military community at its upper reaches.

Perhaps more importantly, the comparative neglect of the East Anglian dimension in these disputes has coloured our understanding of the support networks that came to the aid of Scrope, Morley and Hastings. These support networks reveal the ways in which horizontal and vertical ties within county society interacted with the parallel military and chivalric connections that developed between East Anglia's warrior gentry. For *Scrope v. Grosvenor*, it has long been understood that John of Gaunt brought the full weight of his Lancastrian affinity to bear in Scrope's favour, while Grosvenor, as an obscure knight from England's north-west, was forced to rely upon testimony garnered from his fellow Cheshire gentry.[55] The Lancastrian connection has been perceived as equally central to the *Grey v. Hastings* case, since Sir Edward Hastings' father, grandfather and great-grandfather had been prominent Lancastrian bannerets for many years,[56] and consequently the majority of his militarily active witnesses had seen most, if not all, of their war service in the Lancastrian military retinue.[57] In *Lovel v. Morley*, the picture is more complex, firstly because only a handful of Morley's deponents declared that they were his kinsmen, retainers or servants, and secondly because the Morleys were not officially aligned with any particular magnate affinity.[58] Nonetheless, given that the Morleys were one of only three major baronial families in the Norfolk–Suffolk region,[59] networks of lordship, patronage and association were bound to have played their part, even if only indirectly. Amongst Scrope's East Anglian witnesses, the wider connections of the region's knightly class were laid bare, reminding one that the horizons of such men were not limited by county borders.

In all three of these cases, an intricate web, combining vertical ties of lordship and affinity with horizontal ties of intra-gentry solidarity, appears to have been at work. Few of Thomas Lord Morley's testators claimed any official connection with his family. Three stated that they were his kinsmen,[60] two declared that they were his servants,[61] one described himself as 'de

---

[55] Bennett, *Community, Class and Careerism*, pp. 82–3, 166; Morgan, *War and Society in Medieval Cheshire*, pp. 128–30.

[56] Walker, *The Lancastrian Affinity*, pp. 271, 294–5; Jack, 'Entail and Descent', 1–19.

[57] See below, pp. 141–2.

[58] See below, Ibid.

[59] The others were the Lords Bardolf and Scales. *CP*, i, 417–21; *CP*, xi, 503–6. The Lords Fitzwalter of Essex and Willoughby of Lincolnshire also held significant estates in Norfolk and Suffolk. *CP*, v, 472–85; *CP*, xii (ii), 658–66.

[60] C 47/6/1, nos 28, 30, 41.

[61] Ibid., nos 26, 100.

l'alliance' with Lord Morley,[62] three knights and six esquires declared that they had fought regularly under the Morley banner,[63] and a few men, some quite prominent, were his tenants.[64] These official and semi-official associations, however, did not lie at the heart of Morley's recruitment policy as he set about gathering support. The true extent of his reach amongst the East Anglian gentry, and particularly amongst its militarily active members, becomes apparent only when one considers some of the indirect channels through which local men came to speak on his behalf.

In particular, Morley utilized his family's longstanding relationships with other members of East Anglia's county elite. His more prestigious testators included Sir Leonard Kerdiston, Sir John Brewes and Sir Robert Ufford,[65] each of whose families had been active alongside Morley's ancestors on military campaigns, in shire office, and in land transactions, since the reign of Edward I.[66] Each of these families in turn, so it appears, encouraged their own current and former military followers to contribute to the Morleys' defence, with several lesser gentry witnesses revealing war records forged primarily under Ufford or Kerdiston banners, or beneath the banner of the Uffords' late cousin, Sir John Norwich.[67] Moreover, through the Morleys' indirect associations with Edward the Black Prince, and the Kerdistons' and Uffords' more formal ties with the prince's affinity, one likewise finds that a few of the prince's longest-serving East Anglian retainers also appeared before the Court.[68] The Ufford–Kerdiston–Brewes connection, too, was not the only one Thomas Lord Morley exploited, for other greater gentry who spoke for him included his distant kinsmen Sir William Elmham and Sir Robert Marney, as well as followers of Sir Hugh Hastings, to whose family the Elmhams, Marneys and Morleys were all related by marriage.[69]

These interlocking associations starkly reinforce the extent to which Morley relied upon his noble, baronial and greater knightly friends, kinsmen

---

[62] Ibid., no. 46.

[63] Ibid., nos 31, 40, 64, 5, 10, 11, 20, 26, 59.

[64] e.g. Sir Thomas Gerbergh and Hugh Curson. C 47/6/1, nos 40, 99; *HPC*, iii, 178–80; *HPC*, ii, 719. Morley also utilized his ties of lordship and patronage within East Anglian ecclesiastical circles. The long list of non-military witnesses who spoke for him included numerous clergymen with surnames matching lands either held by the Morleys or adjacent to their estates, while several friars with whose houses the Morleys were associated also spoke on Lord Thomas's behalf: e.g. C 47/6/1, nos 138–44.

[65] C 47/6/1, nos 64, 102, 48.

[66] P. J. Caudrey, 'War and Society in Medieval Norfolk, c. 1350–c. 1430', PhD thesis, University of Tasmania (2010), pp. 80–3, 87–92.

[67] e.g. C 47/6/1, nos 13, 39, 42, 12, 92, 99.

[68] e.g. C 47/6/1, nos 8, 104. For the Black Prince's East Anglian connections, see D. S. Green, 'Edward the Black Prince and East Anglia: An Unlikely Association', in *Fourteenth Century England III*, ed. W. M. Ormrod (Woodbridge, 2004), pp. 83–98.

[69] C 47/6/1, nos 62, 27, 53. Illustrative of the interwoven character of these relationships is the fact that Elmham was also part of the Kerdiston–Ufford–Brewes connection through his long-term role in the Black Prince's military retinue. *HPC*, iii, 13–17; *CP*, ix, 217; Green, 'Edward the Black Prince and East Anglia', pp. 83–98.

and contacts to come to his aid. These men did not always speak for him personally, but the underlying importance of military ties of affinity is clear. Even when the lord in question was dead and his military retinue had long since disbanded, a few highly militarily active knights and esquires from his affinity nonetheless appeared before the Court. Only a minority of gentry from each shire were long-serving military participants and the Morleys appear to have been well aware of which old soldiers were still around. Some of the men who spoke for them had evidently seen action under any lord who would take them.[70] A few had been tied to a particular affinity.[71] For the most part, though, the Morleys' more militarily active testators appear to have made the most of local opportunities within their own regional military community, serving under East Anglian captains, or in the larger retinues of magnates who held a landed stake, or actively recruited, in the area.[72]

The previous year, Sir Richard Scrope had acquired the support of fourteen East Anglians in his dispute with Sir Robert Grosvenor. Given that his witnesses included men of the highest profile, including his lord, John of Gaunt, and the latter's son, Henry of Bolingbroke, as well as a plethora of well-regarded barons, bannerets and knights from across the realm, it is clear that his testators represented a solid spread of martial talent.[73] Despite the overt Lancastrian element involved, Scrope's East Anglian deponents did not simply represent the East Anglian contingent within John of Gaunt's affinity. A few of them certainly fitted this bill. Sir Hugh Hastings III – Sir Edward Hastings' father – was a third-generation Lancastrian, who fought for Gaunt in France, Scotland and Spain.[74] Sir Thomas Morieux was married to Gaunt's bastard daughter, Blanche, and was soon to be named marshal of the Lancastrian army for the Castilian expedition.[75] Sir John White had served Gaunt in Scotland and later became feodary of his East Anglian estates.[76] Best known is Sir Thomas Erpingham, who, by the Revolution of 1399, had risen to national prominence on the back of two decades of loyal Lancastrian service

---

[70] e.g. Sir William Berdewell, one of Morley's younger deponents, who also spoke for Hastings, outlined his participation in seven campaigns in nine years between 1378 and 1387. The captains under whom he served included Lord Willoughby (St Malo – 1378), Lord Clifton (Bishop Despenser's crusade to Flanders – 1383) and Lord Camoys (the earl of Arundel's naval expedition – 1387). C 47/6/1, no. 93; *PCM*, i, 390–2. Berdewell was a 'landless' cadet during his militarily active youth. However, a number of unexpected deaths saw him inherit his family's fortune in the late 1380s, just as the second phase of the Hundred Years War was drawing to a close. *HPC*, ii, 125–6.

[71] See nn. 68, 69.

[72] e.g. John Loudham served under Lord Scales, Sir Robert Ufford and the Earl of Hereford (who recruited widely amongst the gentry of the eastern counties). C 47/6/1, no. 52.

[73] *Scrope v. Grosvenor*, ii, 163–6 (Gaunt and Bolingbroke); Rosenthal, *Telling Tales*, pp. 63–94.

[74] *Scrope v. Grosvenor*, i, 51; ii, 168–9.

[75] C. Given-Wilson, *The Royal Household and the King's Affinity: Service, Politics and Finance in England, c.1360–1413* (New Haven, 1986), pp. 13, 203, 275; *Scrope v. Grosvenor*, i, 56; ii, 183–7.

[76] *Scrope v. Grosvenor*, i, 59; ii, 196–7; R. Somerville, *History of the Duchy of Lancaster*, 2 vols (London, 1953–70), i, 378.

in peace and war, first to Gaunt and then to Henry of Bolingbroke.[77] The presence of these men reinforced Gaunt's influence on Scrope's behalf. Yet Scrope's small East Anglian support base stretched beyond long-time Lancastrians. The Norfolk baron Robert Lord Scales merely maintained an informal relationship with Gaunt, rather similar to that between Robert Ufford, earl of Suffolk, and the Lords Morley.[78] The cadet Sir Robert Morley also spoke for Scrope, despite no overt Lancastrian connections.[79] Sir John Brewes, as an Ufford kinsman, had closer ties to Edward the Black Prince's affinity than to Gaunt's[80] – ties that were even more pronounced in the case of Sir Stephen Hales and Sir William Wingfield, whose military careers had been carved out almost exclusively under the late prince.[81] The presence of these distinguished non-Lancastrian warriors is unsurprising. While Sir Richard Scrope was a committed Lancastrian, his ancestors included famous knights attached to the royal court, and others who had established their reputations under a variety of commanders during the military campaigns of the high Edwardian age.[82]

Sir Edward Hastings, in similar vein, was able to call upon the support of his ancestors' old Lancastrian companions. Sir Edward, though, did not possess a reputation comparable to Sir Richard Scrope, and he also did not receive direct assistance from the Lancastrian affinity, since by 1407 Gaunt was dead and Henry of Bolingbroke was otherwise preoccupied with the burdens of kingship.[83] Notwithstanding this, some of Hastings' testators were current and active Lancastrians, most prominently Sir Thomas Erpingham, Sir Robert Berney, John Reymes and Edmund Barry, who were all members of Norfolk's pro-Lancastrian governing elite at the time when the case came before the Court.[84] Yet, a clear distinction should be drawn between these men and their fellow testators who were veterans of Gaunt's wars. The latter had been regular wartime followers of the extremely militarily active Gaunt, but they had little or no relationship to the Lancastrian affinity in peacetime. Such men included Sir Thomas Gerbergh – a Morley military follower and steward of the duke of York – who recalled his service alongside Sir Hugh Hastings II and Sir Hugh Hastings III at Nájera in 1367,

---

[77] Castor, *The King, the Crown, and the Duchy of Lancaster*, pp. 59–73; A. Curry, 'Sir Thomas Erpingham', in *Agincourt 1415: Henry V, Sir Thomas Erpingham and the Triumph of the English Archers*, ed. A. Curry (Stroud, 2000), pp. 53–70. For Erpingham's military career, see *Scrope v. Grosvenor*, i, 59; ii, 194–6; *PCM*, i, 439–42.

[78] Walker, *The Lancastrian Affinity*, pp. 204–5; Caudrey, 'War and Society in Medieval Norfolk', pp. 80–3, 87–92.

[79] *Scrope v. Grosvenor*, i, 60; ii, 202–3.

[80] Ibid., i, 63; ii, 208–10.

[81] *HPC*, iii, 268–9; Green, 'Edward the Black Prince and East Anglia', p. 90; *Scrope v. Grosvenor*, i, 163, 173–4; ii, 369–70, 396–7.

[82] Keen, 'Grey v. Hastings', pp. 177–8; Rosenthal, *Telling Tales*, pp. 63–94.

[83] Castor, *The King, the Crown, and the Duchy of Lancaster*, pp. 25–31.

[84] *PCM*, i, 439–42, 474–6, 392–5; Castor, *The King, the Crown, and the Duchy of Lancaster*, pp. 59–81.

in Guienne in 1370, on the earl of Buckingham's expedition in 1380, and on Richard II's Scottish campaign in 1385;[85] Sir Ralph Shelton, son of a follower of Edward the Black Prince, who described his presence at St Malo in 1378, in Scotland in 1385, and on Gaunt's Spanish venture in 1386;[86] and Sir Simon Felbrigg, a long-time friend of Sir Thomas Erpingham, who began his career in Lancastrian military service in Castile, before achieving greater heights as chamber knight and standard-bearer to Richard II.[87] Thomas Lord Morley – Sir Edward Hastings' stepfather – who had been active alongside Sir Hugh III on the campaigns of the 1370s and 1380s, also gave evidence.[88] Indeed, Morley's marriage to Sir Hugh's widow was not unusual, for this was a relatively common practice amongst long-serving East Anglian knights.[89] It is noteworthy too that, although lacking the direct support of King Henry, Hastings nonetheless had the countesses of Norfolk and Pembroke in his corner,[90] while his family's standing in Norfolk was such that it provided a rare instance of a county in which inquisitions post mortem had adjudged Hastings, and not Lord Grey, as heir to the earl of Pembroke.[91]

Morley, Scrope and Hastings undoubtedly sought assistance from individuals and families with whom they had strong connections, but, beyond politicking and social ties, the types of evidence provided by their deponents strongly suggest that the martial reputations of these three families was a vital factor in enabling them to accrue such widespread support. Armorial bearings stood at the very heart of the medieval knight's sense of identity.[92] Such insignia embellished family crypts, memorial brasses, church windows, and even personal items, from weaponry to kitchenware to wall hangings.[93] Moreover, when the knight bore his arms on the field of battle, he was placing his family's name and reputation on the line, for his arms had been those of his ancestors and thus, when he entered the fray, he was representing not just himself, but also his lineage.[94] Every armigerous knight or esquire contributed to the collective war record of his family and, should he have

---

85 *PCM*, i, 498–500; *HPC*, iii, 179.
86 *PCM*, i, 423–4; *HPC*, iv, 356.
87 *PCM*, i, 443; J. Milner, 'Sir Simon Felbrigg KG: The Lancastrian Revolution and Personal Fortune', *Norfolk Archaeology* 37 (1978), 84–6.
88 *Calendar of Papal Registers, Papal Letters* (London, 1893–1998), iv, 375; *PCM*, i, 435–9.
89 Caudrey, 'War and Society in Medieval Norfolk', pp. 76–80.
90 According to several witnesses, the countesses begged Sir Hugh III to bear the Pembroke arms on Gaunt's Castilian venture in 1386 in order to do honour to the arms, while the teenage earl was still too young to fight. *PCM*, i, 418, 475, 509. The story is recounted in C. Young, *Reginald Lord Grey and Sir Edward Hastings* (London, 1841), p. xv.
91 Keen, *Origins of the English Gentleman*, pp. 51, 56–7; *CP*, vi, 155–6, 357.
92 M. H. Keen, *Chivalry* (New Haven, 1984), pp. 125–42; R. W. Jones, *Bloodied Banners: Martial Display on the Medieval Battlefield* (Woodbridge, 2010).
93 For East Anglian examples of heraldic display, see *List of Rubbings of Brasses: Classified and Arranged in Chronological Order*, ed. H. W. Prior (London, 1915), pp. 1–4; *William Worcestre: Itineraries*, ed. J. H. Harvey (Oxford, 1969); Blomefield, *History of the County of Norfolk*, 11 vols.
94 Jones, *Bloodied Banners*, pp. 20–1; Keen, *Origins of the English Gentleman*, pp. 9–16.

performed valiant deeds, his memory would have been fondly recalled by
his descendants.[95] The Morleys, Scropes and Hastings were all families of
significant military prowess and this appears to have lain at the heart of why
so many distinguished and long-serving soldiers spoke in their defence, for
many had been present when these families had performed their most memorable feats of arms. This type of heroic behaviour, to a class for whom birth,
lineage and deed were tightly interwoven, emphasized the genteel status of
the protagonists' families and demonstrated not only that they had borne the
disputed arms in war, but that they had honoured them as well through their
performances in the field.

Indeed, the depositions of the militarily active witnesses in all three cases,
as a number of scholars have noted, contain a powerful chivalric flavour
that supports this contention.[96] In *Lovel v. Morley*, one old soldier recalled
a tournament held at Smithfield in June 1343 when Robert Lord Morley
had participated dressed as the pope, accompanied by twelve companions
dressed as Cardinals;[97] another described Sir William Morley's gift of his
coat armour to the parish church at Somerton;[98] others referred to a statuette
in Reydon church, celebrating the spot where the heart of a thirteenth-century
crusader Morley was buried;[99] numerous witnesses focused upon the earlier
Burnell–Morley dispute of 1346–47, describing how Robert Lord Morley's
possession of his arms had been upheld;[100] and several witnesses recalled that
Thomas Bolyngton had erected banners in various churches to commemorate
this same Lord Robert after the latter's death on the Rheims campaign in
1360.[101]

The Hastings family was remembered in similar fashion. Witnesses
recalled Sir Hugh III's participation on crusades to the East and his presentation of an escutcheon of his arms to the Knights Hospitaller at Rhodes,
and in other places in the eastern Mediterranean;[102] Sir Thomas Erpingham
described having seen the Hastings arms displayed in the church window
of Marienburg Cathedral;[103] a number of witnesses made great play of Sir
Hugh III's bravery in the skirmishing at Brest on the way to Castile, where
he subsequently met his death;[104] Nicholas Braynton described this same Sir

---

95   Several fifteenth-century East Anglian knightly families, for example, maintained genealogies
     celebrating their families' ancient lineages and military prowess. Some of their family trees were
     more imaginative than others. Norwich, Norwich Public Library, MS 7197, fols 307–11.
96   Keen, 'Grey v. Hastings', pp. 177, 180–2; Ayton, 'Knights, Esquires and Military Service',
     p. 187; Keen, *Origins of the English Gentleman*, pp. 48–54; Rosenthal, *Telling Tales*, pp. 63–94.
97   C 47/6/1, no. 7.
98   Ibid., no. 82.
99   Ibid., nos 151–7.
100 e.g. William Kyng recalled the judgment being pronounced in English by Henry of Grosmont,
     duke of Lancaster. Ibid., no. 96.
101 Ibid., nos 158–64.
102 *PCM*, i, 429, 533, 453.
103 Ibid., i, 441.
104 Ibid., i, 402–3, 440, 446.

Hugh being knighted on the field during the *chevauchée* of 1373;[105] and, perhaps most evocatively, David Hemenhale recounted how Sir Hugh III had led the assault on St Malo by ladder, whereupon Lord Fitzwalter reportedly said, 'Here's one of the finest knights of the kingdom.'[106] Moreover, the case was even adjourned at one point, in order to allow the judges to examine the famous Hastings memorial brass in St Mary's church at Elsing, where Sir Hugh Hastings I (d. 1347) was interred in an elaborate tomb that commemorated his family ties and military connections with a dozen royal and noble families, including that of Edward III.[107] In both of these cases, one gains a sense of the witnesses' admiration for the military deeds and chivalric reputations of the Morleys and Hastings, and many, when questioned, were quick to claim variously that the disputed arms had belonged to the defendants' family since time out of mind, or by popular repute.[108]

Such sentiments were in some ways even more prominent amongst Sir Richard Scrope's East Anglian supporters. The Scropes possessed a particularly grand reputation in the world of English chivalry, having, across the generations, borne arms in such varied locations as Scotland, France, Spain, Eastern Europe and Turkey.[109] Their standing is confirmed in the testimony provided on their behalf by regular references to popular knowledge of their deeds in arms. Some deponents referred not only to personal experience, but also to the hearsay of their ancestors. Sir Hugh Hastings III and Sir Robert Morley attested that their fathers and grandfathers had made mention to them of the Scropes' possession of the disputed arms.[110] Sir John White suggested that by public report the arms had belonged to the Scropes since time immemorial.[111] Sir Richard Waldegrave declared that the Scropes were of ancient lineage and that, since the dispute had begun, he had been told that their family dated back to the Norman Conquest.[112] Sir John Brewes provided a mildly more colourful version of essentially the same claim, stating that he had seen the Scropes bearing the arms since the battle of Mauron in 1352, and that, when the Scropes had had their arms challenged during the siege of Calais, Brewes's uncle, Robert Ufford, earl of Suffolk, had expressed his amazement that a family of such ancient gentility should have been so challenged.[113] Sir Stephen Hales provided perhaps the most interesting description of why the Scropes deserved to keep their arms. He said that he had seen the

---

[105]   Ibid., i, 529.
[106]   Ibid., i, 458–9.
[107]   *PCM*, i, 348–54. More generally, see L. Dennison and N. Rogers, 'The Elsing Brass and its East Anglian Connections', in *Fourteenth Century England I*, ed. N. Saul (Woodbridge, 2000), pp. 167–93.
[108]   See below, pp. 133–4.
[109]   Keen, 'Grey v. Hastings', pp. 177–8.
[110]   *Scrope v. Grosvenor*, i, 51, 60; ii, 168–9, 202–3.
[111]   Ibid., i, 59; ii, 196–7.
[112]   Ibid., i, 173–4; ii, 396–7.
[113]   Ibid., i, 63; ii, 208–10.

Scropes bearing the arms at Rheims and Najéra, but also that, in his youth, he had heard an old Yorkshireman assert that the ancestors of Sir Richard and Sir Henry Scrope were the finest tourneyers in northern England. By contrast, he added that while he had served many times with the Scropes in the Black Prince's retinue, he could never recall any of the prince's many Cheshire followers bearing the disputed arms, and furthermore he had never heard of Sir Robert Grosvenor until the dispute in question had commenced.[114]

The Scropes' regular service over several decades in both John of Gaunt's and the Black Prince's affinities evidently shaped their military connections to a significant degree, at least as regards their East Anglian support base. Those who had served longest with them on the fields of France were men who were likewise established military followers of the two princes. As such, Lancastrians from East Anglia, like Sir Thomas Erpingham, Sir John White, Sir Thomas Morieux and Sir Hugh Hastings III, appeared before the Court to speak for the Scropes, alongside the Black Prince's old soldiers, like Sir Stephen Hales and Sir William Wingfield, as well as members of militarily active comital families like Sir John Brewes, Sir Robert Morley and Roger Lord Scales, who were less directly associated with the two princes. The presence of this small number of prominent East Anglian barons and knights from different affinities firstly underscores the importance of noble retinues as a framework in which a sense of comradeship could develop and, secondly, reminds one that the Scropes were highly regarded by their fellow soldiers of all noble allegiances, regardless of which military retinue the latter served. By contrast, Grosvenor was a rather obscure figure from the north-west, for whom these well-known East Anglian knights had little regard.

The testimony in defence of the Morleys the following year fleshes out this snapshot of military connections in a more specifically East Anglian context. Lord Thomas's grandfather, Lord Robert, as a long-serving soldier at the lower end of the peerage, appeared to have surrounded himself with a small core of regular military followers, who would naturally have seen plenty of action in each other's direct company.[115] Alongside these loyal few were to be found other middling and lesser gentry who, as their depositions reveal, could quite easily move from the Morleys' retinue to those of the Uffords, Scaleses, Norwiches, Hastingses or Kerdistons.[116] Regular military service under the command of close-knit war captains, which these families appear to have been, would surely have allowed groups of East Anglian soldiers to become familiar with one another through joint participation in the same companies on multiple expeditions. From these connections, an element of *esprit de corps* may very well have developed within their ranks, although such ties would not necessarily have reflected long-term loyalty to the lord

[114]   Ibid., i, 163; ii, 369–70.
[115]   See nn. 61–5.
[116]   See nn. 68–9.

in charge.[117] Rather, their relationships may perhaps be better understood as a bond of circumstance, in which men who had been thrust together in a war zone in years past developed a series of shared war memories, and, in certain instances, would have actively fought side by side, developing their trust at the strategy table, around the campfire, and in the heat of battle.

Such a scenario is particularly evident in the composition of Sir Edward Hastings' East Anglian witnesses. As we have seen, they revealed in their depositions that their military records had been made almost exclusively in John of Gaunt's service and in the specific company of Sir Hugh Hastings II and Sir Hugh Hastings III. Several had been recruited during the early 1380s prior to Gaunt undertaking the 'way of Spain', and the expeditions to St Malo, Scotland, Brest and Castile, in particular, featured heavily in their testimony.[118] The Lancastrian affinity, however, had not been mobilized on Sir Edward's behalf, as John of Gaunt had done for Sir Richard Scrope a generation earlier. Some testators, as we have seen, were committed members of Gaunt's affinity. Others had merely been semi-regular members of the Lancastrian military retinue, in all probability because Gaunt was the most active and influential captain of the 1370s and 1380s. The motives for many of Sir Edward's knightly witnesses in testifying before the Court, then, may largely have derived from their fond memories of his father and grandfather, who had been important bannerets on the campaigns of their youth in the 1360s through 1380s. They, along with Sir Hugh II and Sir Hugh III, would have been among Gaunt's captains and lieutenants, essentially part of his officer corps. As such, they would have dined together in camp; they would have organized and executed their lord's strategies; and they would have faced the fortunes of war in each other's immediate company.[119] Moreover, among Gaunt's core of regular captains – those who served with him on three, four or more occasions – the number of familiar East Anglian faces would have been fewer still.[120]

The same may be said for those East Anglian knights and esquires who fought regularly beneath the banners of Edward the Black Prince, Robert Ufford, earl of Suffolk, or even under the leadership of lesser peers and bannerets, like the Lords Morley and Scales, Sir John Norwich or Sir William Kerdiston.[121] Extensive military participation in royal and ducal expeditions, broadly overlapping service records, and a common regional background in the eastern counties, were all things that the majority of Hastings' and

---

[117] e.g. Sir Ralph Shelton served regularly in the Lancastrian military retinue during the 1370s and 1380s, but possessed few ties to the Lancastrian affinity in peacetime. *PCM*, i, 423–4; *HPC*, iv, 356.

[118] Keen, 'Grey v. Hastings', p. 182.

[119] For a detailed study of the Lancastrian military retinue, including the development of a sense of *esprit de corps* amongst its gentry officers, see Walker, *The Lancastrian Affinity*, pp. 39–116.

[120] Ibid., pp. 50–3.

[121] See nn. 68–9.

Morley's militarily active supporters had in common. Judging from these three disputes, therefore, one may say that a certain measure of camaraderie appears to have existed between long-serving East Anglian knights and esquires, which in all likelihood reflected a combination of retinue-based and regional solidarities, for many of these gentry – drawn from the same part of the realm – would have been familiar with one another, at least as acquaintances, long before they ever set off on campaign.[122]

So what do these social ties and military connections reveal about East Anglian martial culture in the second half of the fourteenth century? One point of note is that those who spoke before the Court often focused upon specific military actions, whose worth seemingly outstripped the wider outcome of the expedition. The classic example is the way in which Lord Morley's deponents invariably described the Rheims campaign of 1359–60 as the occasion when the royal army had stood before the gates of Paris.[123] Here we see a fine instance of oral traditions at work. It was this single chivalrous moment, in which the English army had made their stand before the French capital, which was evidently the most memorable event of the campaign as far as Morley's testators were concerned.[124] It had been the high point of a large-scale expedition that had witnessed no set-piece battle and which, as we now know, largely failed to achieve its broader objectives.[125]

This tendency to focus upon specific actions is even more apparent amongst Sir Edward Hastings' deponents. They were describing the twenty years between the Black Prince's final triumph at the battle of Nájera in 1367 and Gaunt's failed bid for the Castilian throne from 1386. This depressing period witnessed the loss of conquered territory, a terrible naval disaster, a

---

[122]　The issue of whether or not knightly associations were created, or merely reinforced, by joint military service is an important one, though often difficult to prove either way. It seems likely, for example, that the Morley deponent, Sir William Elmham, and Sir Nicholas Dagworth, who established their military reputations with the Black Prince in the 1350s, before consolidating their standing by leading their own freelance companies to Spain in the following decade, developed their lifelong friendship on campaign. By contrast, the Hastings' deponents, Sir Thomas Erpingham and Sir Simon Felbrigg, who participated together on John of Gaunt's Castilian venture in 1386, had been childhood friends and neighbours. *HPC*, iii, 13–17; *HPC*, ii, 733–5; *PCM*, i, 439–42, 443–4; Castor, *The King, the Crown, and the Duchy of Lancaster*, pp. 67–8.

[123]　C 47/6/1. Dr Ayton has also drawn attention to this point. A. Ayton, 'English Armies in the Fourteenth Century', in *The Wars of Edward III: Sources and Interpretations*, ed. C. J. Rogers (Woodbridge, 1999), pp. 303–4.

[124]　This moment had also captured the attention of several contemporary chroniclers. Thomas Walsingham, *Historia Anglicana*, ed. H. T. Riley, 2 vols, Rolls Ser. (London, 1863), i, 288; Jean Froissart, *Oeuvres*, ed. K. de Letttenhove, 26 vols (Brussels, 1870–), vi, 256, 265–6; Henry Knighton, *Chronicon*, ed. J. R. Lumby, 2 vols, Rolls Ser. (London, 1895), ii, 111; *The Brut or the Chronicle of England*, ed. F. W. Brie, 2 vols, EETS OS 131, 136 (1906–8), i, 310; John of Reading, *Chronica Johannis de Reading et anonymi Catuariensis, 1346–1367*, ed. J. Tait (Manchester, 1914), pp. 135–6.

[125]　J. Sumption, *The Hundred Years War II: Trial By Fire* (London, 1999), pp. 405–54; C. J. Rogers, *War Cruel and Sharp: English Strategy Under Edward III, 1327–1360* (Woodbridge, 2000), pp. 385–422.

series of expensive *chevauchées*, a heavy death toll exacted by disease, and considerable political strife on the domestic scene.[126] Yet, the tone of the depositions was little different from those of Morley's or Scrope's testators a generation earlier.[127] It was the high points, like the crusading pedigree of the Hastings family, the courage of Sir Hugh III in skirmishing off Brest, and his death on campaign in Spain, that merited the greatest attention. Sir Hugh III was undeniably perceived as following successfully in the footsteps of his father and grandfather, whose own military careers had spanned the earlier, much more triumphant period, of Edward III's halcyon days.

In all three cases, Scrope's, Morley's and Hastings' testators would obviously have wanted to portray them in the best possible light, in order to prove that they were worthy bearers of the disputed arms. Highlighting their chivalrous deeds would have been a natural means of accomplishing this. Their focus upon individual acts of bravery, moreover, mirrored the style of war chronicling pioneered by Jean Froissart, and, in fragmented, oral form, was not entirely dissimilar to the glowing catalogues of feats of arms expounded in medieval knightly biographies.[128] In the context of the court cases themselves, such testimony served a dual purpose. On the one hand, it represented a matter-of-fact statement of occasions when the deponent had seen the defendant or plaintiff (or his ancestors) bearing the disputed arms. However, it is surely not coincidental that the moments selected were quite often ones when these families had distinguished themselves militarily. Martial prowess, after all, traditionally legitimized genteel status and armigerous rank, demonstrating, in this instance, that Scrope, Morley and Hastings possessed ancestors who had not only borne the disputed arms, but had honoured them through their deeds with the sword.[129]

Oral traditions, too, were not limited to campaigning memories. The assertions made by East Anglian witnesses about the Scropes' good name, and the insinuations in all three cases that their deeds in arms were common knowledge, illustrate the extent to which chivalric culture – as expressed in tales of martial prowess – was disseminated locally. In the case of *Scrope v. Grosvenor*, we can see that tales of the Scropes' deeds in arms had evidently

---

[126]   C. T. Allmand, *The Hundred Years War* (Liverpool, 1988), pp. 20–6; G. L. Harriss, *Shaping the Nation: England 1360–1461* (Oxford, 2005), pp. 411–19, 437–44.

[127]   Dr Keen has suggested that the testimony provided by the *Grey v. Hastings* witnesses lacked the overt chivalric flavour found in *Scrope v. Grosvenor* and *Lovel v. Morley*. Keen, 'Grey v. Hastings', pp. 182–5. Yet, given that the English were, by and large, losing more than they won in the 1370s and 1380s, Hastings' testators certainly appeared proud of what they and their comrades had achieved, individually and collectively, although they would undoubtedly have been aware that they had experienced no cherished victories of the stamp of the battles of Crécy or Poitiers.

[128]   Froissart, *Oeuvres*; for English knightly biographies, see especially, *L'Histoire de Guillaume le Maréchal*, ed. P. Meyer, 2 vols (Paris, 1891); Chandos Herald, *The Life of the Black Prince*, ed. and trans. E. Lodge and M. K. Pope (Oxford, 1910).

[129]   Jones, *Bloodied Banners*, pp. 20–1; Keen, *Origins of the English Gentleman*, p. 51.

reached the eastern counties, perhaps through the storytelling of their East Anglian comrades. Similarly, in the recollections of the Burnell–Morley dispute of 1346–47, as described by Morley's witnesses, one gains a further glimpse of collective memory in action. There were descriptions of Henry of Grosmont, duke of Lancaster, announcing the judgment in St Peter's church outside Calais, at which large crowds had gathered together to hear the verdict pronounced, with several witnesses attesting that they were present.[130] There was to be found a strong degree of chauvinism in their recollections, however, since Lord Lovel had been able to conjure up a handful of witnesses who could recall the same dispute but with the opposite, or an unclear, verdict.[131] The Morleys were one of East Anglia's most powerful families and the Burnell–Morley dispute had clearly been a matter of considerable interest to the East Anglian gentry at the time. It was a dispute that numerous East Anglian knights and esquires could still recall forty years on.

Although the recollections of old soldiers in many ways represented the centrepiece of Scrope's, Morley's and Hastings' defence, the heraldic evidence central to the testimony of their civilian witnesses – and largely garnered from the surrounding localities – was also of vital importance.[132] Through such evidence, one may gauge the social significance of heraldic display at the local level, in which prominent regional families advertised their rank, lineage, family achievements and the extent of their personal authority, through the erection of their armorial bearings in public spaces. Several witnesses recalled places across East Anglia in which the defendants' arms were displayed.[133] The cellarer at Norwich Cathedral described how the Morleys' arms were hung there, and similar testimony was imparted by an Austin Friar at Lynn, by members of the Church of Canons at Walsingham, and by monks at St Benet's Holm.[134] A number of deponents recalled Thomas Bolyngton's erection of banners to commemorate the death of Robert Lord Morley on the Rheims campaign in 1360.[135] Perhaps most evocatively, at the request of Sir Edward Hastings, the judges in his dispute, as we have seen, visited St Mary's church at Elsing, in order to view Sir Hugh Hastings I's splendid memorial brass. With the judges present, Sir Edward personally pointed out iconographic details in the church that he believed supported his case. This monument, in short, was clearly something of a local landmark by the first decade of the fifteenth century, emphasizing the martial accom-

---

[130] C 47/6/1, nos 96, 103.
[131] PRO 30/26/69, nos 167, 175, 176.
[132] Scrope's witnesses largely focused upon the localities of northern England. From an East Anglian perspective, the testimony in favour of Morley and Hastings is of more immediate relevance.
[133] A few civilian witnesses (and some soldiers) also described their presence at domestic tournaments, reminding one of the grey area between military and civilian experiences. C 47/6/1, nos 2, 7, 14, 15, 19, 71–3, 92.
[134] Ibid., nos 113, 138, 141–3, 144–7.
[135] Ibid., nos 158–64.

plishments and the social connections of the Hastings family, and important enough for the judges to adjourn their sitting to examine it.[136]

It is apparent from these three Court of Chivalry cases that the successful military careers of the Morleys and Hastings, and even of a distinguished knightly family from beyond the region, the Scropes, were well known amongst East Anglia's more militarily active gentry. For Morley and Hastings, there clearly existed a stock of accepted stories about their families' deeds in arms. The Morleys' crusading achievements were commemorated in the statuette in Reydon church; their martial prowess was celebrated through Robert Lord Morley's leadership at Sluys, his tourneying dressed as the pope, his victory in the Burnell–Morley dispute, and his death on the Rheims expedition. Sir Hugh Hastings II and Sir Hugh Hastings III were remembered as crusaders to the East, as active warriors in three European theatres, for Sir Hugh III's courage at Brest and leadership at the siege of St Malo, and for his death on campaign in Spain.

Finally, the words of the protagonists themselves make plain the extent to which their personal and family honour was tied to the rightful possession of their coats-of-arms. During the Burnell–Morley dispute, Robert Lord Morley reportedly swore that, should he lose the case, 'he would never again be armed against Christians or in the war of his liege lord'. Sir Edward Hastings, who did lose his case, subsequently found himself in the Marshalsea Prison. In 1420, from this abode, he prepared to appeal against the judgment yet again, stating that his quest for a favourable verdict should be pursued by his family notwithstanding his death, rather dramatically declaring that 'for which descent, right, claim and inheritance ... God's curse and mine have all mine heirs that will not sue after me'. In a more temperate frame of mind, Sir Richard Scrope succinctly explained that 'the highest and most sovereign things a knight ought to guard in defence of his estate are his troth and his arms'.[137] These emotive responses reinforce just how important an event these disputes were, not only for the protagonists, but also for their friends, relatives and admirers.

So what can we learn about the character, function and mentalities of East Anglia's military community from the scattered testimony provided by the region's gentry before the Court of Chivalry? In general terms, these disputes highlight the extent to which the mid-fourteenth-century East Anglian gentry became militarized under the leadership of Edward III and his war captains;[138] they demonstrate how widespread were the opportunities for military service,

---

136 *PCM*, i, 348–54; Keen, *Origins of the English Gentleman*, p. 52.
137 As cited in Keen, *Origins of the English Gentleman*, p. 58.
138 For a more general discussion of this process, see A. Ayton, 'Sir Thomas Ughtred and the Edwardian Military Revolution', in *The Age of Edward III*, ed. J. S. Bothwell (York, 2001), pp. 110–14.

with East Anglians fighting everywhere from Scotland and France, to Spain, Prussia, Turkey and the Eastern Mediterranean; and through the chivalric iconography they describe, one gains a sense of the ways in which the East Anglian knightly class sought to commemorate their lineage and personal achievements and to shape the ways in which they wished to be recalled in popular memory. All of this, though, merely reveals that the East Anglian gentry, like their contemporaries all over the realm, contributed to the military campaigns of the Edwardian age and found themselves influenced by the chivalric culture of the time. They were, quite simply, following the national trend.[139]

Such conclusions to some extent rely upon viewing East Anglia's military community from above. From such a perspective, the East Anglian gentry represented a fertile source of recruits for the numerous magnates and barons who possessed a territorial stake in the eastern counties. It is this top-down approach that has previously (and quite understandably) been adopted when analysing the surviving testimony of Scrope's, Morley's and Hastings' deponents. Viewed from the perspective of those East Anglian gentry who gave evidence in these disputes, however, East Anglia's military community may be perceived – like all military communities – as unique unto itself in the face of local circumstances.[140] In particular, their testimony enables one to broadly gauge the dynamics of military recruitment amongst the gentry at the local level and to perceive the interplay between military and political society.

First of all, when selecting their deponents, neither Morley nor Hastings was mobilizing the support of East Anglia's military community in any general sense as a regional entity. The composition of Morley's witnesses reflected in large measure the East Anglian social networks at his disposal. True, few of his witnesses were officially tied to him as tenants, kinsmen or military retainers, but his use of indirect relationships was wide-ranging. He was supported by a number of bannerets and knights whose families had long been associated with his own, either in public office, in the prosecution of the king's wars, or in their private business within the world of the shire, often as far back as the 1340s or earlier. Amongst his militarily active middling and lesser gentry testators, those who described the captains under whom they had served revealed that their military careers had been largely undertaken under the command of prominent East Anglian war captains – like the Ufford

---

[139] On national developments, see J. Barnie, *War in Medieval English Society: Social Values and the Hundred Years War, 1337–99* (New York, 1974), pp. 56–96; J. Vale, *Edward III and Chivalry: Chivalric Society and Its Context 1270–1350* (Woodbridge, 1983); M. Prestwich, *Armies and Warfare in the Middle Ages: The English Experience* (London, 1996), pp. 219–44; Keen, *Origins of the English Gentleman*; D. S. Green, *Edward the Black Prince: Power in Medieval Europe* (New York, 2007), pp. 73–105; Sumption, *Divided Houses*, pp. 723–73; Jones, *Bloodied Banners*; W. M. Ormrod, *Edward III* (New Haven, 2011), pp. 299–321; N. Saul, *For Honour and Shame: Chivalry in England, 1066–1500* (London, 2011), pp. 93–134, 283–324.

[140] In general, see Ayton, 'Armies and Military Communities', pp. 215–39.

earls of Suffolk and their cadets, the Lords Scales and Willoughby, Sir John Norwich, Sir William Kerdiston, Sir Hugh Hastings, and the Morleys themselves – or under the command of the region's absentee territorial magnates – like the dukes of Lancaster, the Black Prince, and the de Bohun earls of Northampton and Hereford.

These patterns of military recruitment amongst Morley's witnesses underscore the centrality of locally powerful barons, bannerets and greater knights to the militarization of East Anglian gentry society in the mid-fourteenth century. The estates of Morley, Hastings, and their fellow East Anglian war captains were sufficiently localized that they sought to construct their retinues, at least initially, from within the web of contacts they possessed in the eastern counties. Their retinues would certainly not have been wholly regional in composition, but their first port of call would undoubtedly have been those knights, esquires and lesser men living in their immediate vicinity. Moreover, although only hinted at in the surviving testimony, it does appear that the militarily active lesser knights and esquires who served in the retinues of East Anglia's barons and bannerets were able to move quite freely between them, facilitated, in part, by the close ties enjoyed by many of the region's leading families. These recruitment dynamics were abetted by the general absenteeism of East Anglia's magnates, which left the Ufford earls of Suffolk as the only resident magnate family playing a regular and active role in the wars with France. This would have placed an even greater responsibility upon the region's barons and bannerets, who were often the eyes and ears of their absentee magnate employers in their native shires.[141]

Through Sir Edward Hastings' witnesses (and a significant proportion of Morley's),[142] one may view the same military community in a slightly later period and from a slightly different angle. These men undertook most of their military service in the 1370s and 1380s, at a time when large-scale, mixed retinues were becoming the norm, placing increasing authority in the hands of fewer magnates, whose 'super-sized' retinues were considerably larger than those of their mid-century forebears.[143] Most of Hastings' testators had been members of the Lancastrian military retinue and had campaigned in an era when John of Gaunt had been the most militarily active magnate in the realm and the largest-scale recruiter of knights and esquires for purely military purposes. Gaunt, indeed, as we have seen, had recruited extensively

---

[141] Edward the Black Prince, for instance, acquired the services of the veteran banneret Sir William Kerdiston as he sought to consolidate his East Anglian military retinue in the 1340s, while Sir Hugh Hastings II became the very first East Anglian officially retained by John of Gaunt after he succeeded his father-in-law, Henry of Grosmont, as head of the Lancastrian affinity. Green, 'Edward the Black Prince and East Anglia', p. 88; Walker, *The Lancastrian Affinity*, pp. 294–5.

[142] Fifty-two of Morley's witnesses testified that they had campaigned at least once between 1369 and 1385. C 47/6/1. See also, Ayton, 'Military Service and the Dynamics of Recruitment', pp. 46–55.

[143] J. W. Sherborne, 'Indentured Retinues and English Expeditions to France, 1369–1380', *EHR* 79 (1964), 718–46; Ayton, 'Armies and Military Communities', pp. 218–19.

amongst the East Anglian gentry prior to undertaking his 'way of Spain' in the mid-1380s. Yet, before the Court of Chivalry, and despite the overt Lancastrian connections of most of his deponents, Sir Edward Hastings was certainly not being supported by the Lancastrian affinity in any formal sense. His militarily active witnesses largely hailed from Norfolk, Suffolk or surrounding counties, and had served on multiple campaigns alongside his father and grandfather, Sir Hugh II and Sir Hugh III, but relatively few maintained any official paid position within the Lancastrian affinity and several had no peacetime Lancastrian connections at all.[144] It appears that it was their longstanding associations with the Hastings family, initiated or consolidated whilst campaigning in John of Gaunt's military retinue, that they had in common. Their recollections of Sir Hugh II's and Sir Hugh III's martial prowess suggest that the Hastings family was held in high esteem in East Anglian military circles and certainly that their finest feats of arms were common knowledge amongst the more militarily active sections of East Anglian gentry society. The same conclusion may be drawn from the Morley depositions, which were particularly fulsome in their praise of Lord Thomas's grandfather, Lord Robert, who, as we have seen, had been a hero of Sluys and a veteran of Crécy.

A great many men spoke for Morley and Hastings because of their personal connections, either vertical or horizontal, with the defendants' families. All, however, would have been imbued with the chivalric values common to genteel military society in the fourteenth century. Most possessed a heraldic identity of their own, pivotal to their good name and honourable standing, and many, as they themselves revealed, had developed war records that justified the possession of their arms and doubtless represented a source of personal and familial pride. At one level, therefore, the depositions in favour of Morley and Hastings reveal how well connected these families were amongst the gentry of the eastern counties. At another level, in a broad, chivalric context, it does appear that these two families may have been upheld as fine exemplars of East Anglian knighthood.[145] A combination, therefore, of ties of professional association in wartime and/ or social connections in peacetime, together with a general admiration for the chivalric reputations of the defendants' families, were the twin factors

---

[144] For a list of John of Gaunt's retainers and annuitants, see Walker, *The Lancastrian Affinity*, pp. 262–84.

[145] There certainly appears to have been an awareness in some quarters of the region's martial prowess. There survives, for instance, a Norfolk and Suffolk Roll of Arms, compiled *c.* 1400, containing the heraldic devices of 150 fourteenth-century Norfolk and Suffolk knights. Oxford, Queen's College MS 158, fols 295–304. Later, in the mid-fifteenth century, Sir John Fastolf's secretary, William Worcester, took a keen interest in the achievements of bygone generations of East Anglian knights. P. J. Caudrey, 'William Worcester, *The Boke of Noblesse*, and Military Society in East Anglia', *Nottingham Medieval Studies* 52 (2008), 206–7.

that enabled Morley and Hastings to accrue the support of so many veteran East Anglian soldiers.

These conclusions raise a number of broader questions about the character of fourteenth-century regional military communities.[146] The military community has been aptly defined by Andrew Ayton as 'first and foremost a community of the mind and of function, of shared mentality, skills and perhaps focus: of shared identity'.[147] From the crown's perspective, England comprised a raft of different military communities into which they needed to tap in order to construct their armies. Regional origins represented only one type of military community (albeit a very important one). On the one hand, therefore, one can describe those East Anglians who spoke for Scrope, Morley and Hastings as being part of East Anglia's regional military community, especially since most of the barons, bannerets and knights in question would have been familiar with one another from their prior public and/or private interactions within the world of the shire. Indeed, we have seen that Morley and Hastings were supported by several families with whom they had shared long-term associations. On the other hand, other factors undoubtedly outweighed regional origins. For example, some of the East Anglian gentry who spoke in these disputes were career soldiers – often self-made men – seeking to live from the profits of war. Their priorities would have been rather different from men of established stock, whose families had been prominent landowners and semi-regular participants in the king's wars since at least the reign of Edward I. Likewise those lesser gentry who spoke for Morley were a rung or two down the social ladder. Their status within East Anglia's military community derived from their reputations as experienced soldiers, but they were of little account within the political world of the shire. Some were very obscure figures and, almost without exception, these types of men never held county office or possessed much of a landed stake in their native locality.

In short, East Anglia's militarily active gentry maintained multiple military identities and were members of multiple military communities. Sir William Elmham, who testified for Lord Morley, provides a case in point. He began his military career in the service of Edward the Black Prince; led his own company to Spain in 1365; became a noted garrison commander in occupied France during the 1370s; and, by his old age, had entrenched himself as a

---

[146] For an overview, see Ayton, 'Armies and Military Communities', pp. 215–39. For regional studies, see Morgan, *War and Society in Medieval Cheshire*; Bennett, *Community, Class and Careerism*, pp. 162–91; Saul, *Knights and Esquires*, pp. 36–59; A. King, '"Pur salvation du Roiaume": Military Service and Obligation in Fourteenth Century Northumberland', in *Fourteenth Century England II*, ed. C. Given-Wilson (Woodbridge, 2002), pp. 13–31. For the fifteenth century, see A. J. Pollard, *North-Eastern England during the Wars of the Roses: Lay Society, War and Politics, 1450–1500* (Oxford, 1990); J. Ross, 'Essex County Society and the French War in the Fifteenth Century', in *The Fifteenth Century VII: Conflicts, Consequences and the Crown in the Late Middle Ages*, ed. L. Clark (Woodbridge, 2007), pp. 53–80.

[147] Ayton, 'Armies and Military Communities', p. 216.

Ricardian diplomat and courtier.[148] In 1383, he was entrusted by his friend, Henry Despenser, bishop of Norwich, to construct an army for the bishop's Flemish crusade, and in so doing his multiple military identities came to the fore.[149] He turned, on the one hand, to friends and associates amongst the East Anglian knightly class, who assisted him in galvanizing local support.[150] At the same time, however, Elmham also reached out to a number of his old wartime companions – fellow career soldiers, like Sir Hugh Calveley of Cheshire and Sir Thomas Trivet of Somerset – whose status in the world of chivalry provided new and wide-ranging avenues for recruitment and made the impending crusade appear far more of a professional enterprise than it otherwise might have done.[151] We thus may perceive, in the context of this single, locally organized expedition, Sir William Elmham's dual identity as respectable East Anglian landowner and self-made soldier of fortune. Those militarily active lesser gentry we have encountered before the Court of Chivalry may have leaned even further towards the latter group. They were of little consequence in East Anglian political society, yet had fought in many a military retinue, in some cases acquiring steady employment in garrison service.[152] The Norfolk esquire William Thweyt, for example, whose career has been painstakingly reconstructed by Andrew Ayton, was simultaneously part of East Anglia's military community (by virtue of birthplace and land-ownership); of the Ufford/Norwich military retinue (under whom he served regularly); and a member of the Corfe Castle garrison in Dorset (where he acted as deputy constable).[153]

Through Morley's, Hastings' and Scrope's militarily active witnesses, one may perceive some of the ways in which these various military communities overlapped. Barons, bannerets and the knightly elite recruited soldiers, above all, in those areas where their lordship was strongest and their influence greatest.[154] These areas may well have spread across several counties and

---

[148] *HPC*, iii, 13–17.

[149] J. Magee, 'Sir William Elmham and the Recruitment for Henry Despenser's Crusade of 1383', *Medieval Prosopography* 20 (1999), 181–90.

[150] These included Sir Ralph Shelton (who testified for Hastings), Sir Thomas Gerbergh (who testified for Morley) and Sir John Brewes (who testified for both Morley and Scrope). Magee, 'Sir William Elmham', 187–8.

[151] Magee, 'Sir William Elmham', 183–6.

[152] Garrisons, as much as regions, provided important centres in which a sense of military community could develop. D. J. Cornell, 'Northern Castles and Garrisons in the Later Middle Ages', PhD thesis, University of Durham (2006); D. Grummitt, *The Calais Garrison: War and Military Service in England, 1436–1558* (Woodbridge, 2008).

[153] A. Ayton, 'William de Thweyt, Esquire: Deputy Constable of Corfe Castle in the 1340s', *Somerset and Dorset Notes and Queries* 32 (1989), 731–8.

[154] The fortuitous survival of a small number of military subcontracts enables the historian to glean how this might have been accomplished. Morgan, *War and Society in Medieval Cheshire*, pp. 150–4 (for Sir Ralph Mobberley of Cheshire); S. K. Walker, 'Profit and Loss in the Hundred Years War: The Subcontracts of Sir John Strother, 1374', *BIHR* 58 (1985), 100–6 (for Sir John Strother of Northumberland); and especially, Goodman, 'The Military Subcontracts of Sir Hugh Hastings', 114–20 (for Sir Hugh Hastings III).

may have been relatively fragmented. Yet, even for the greater gentry, landed wealth was generally located primarily in a particular part of the realm and the authority of such families was naturally most ingrained in their county of residence. Hence, the composition of Morley's and Hastings' witnesses reflected their local influence in Norfolk and Suffolk, and more broadly in the eastern counties as a whole. A certain element of regional patriotism may have played its part as well, but Morley's and Hastings' relations with their deponents were firmly grounded in the practical world of local connections at the level of shire and hundred. Likewise, vertical ties of lordship, drawing the greater gentry into the sphere of particular magnate affinities, overlaid these types of local connections, since most bannerets and knights tended to hitch their star to one or two larger magnate military retinues over the course of their careers. This is clear in the case of Hastings' and Scrope's witnesses, for the former's connections were heavily coloured by his family's military ties with the house of Lancaster, while the latter's East Anglian deponents were largely drawn from the affinities of John of Gaunt and Edward the Black Prince.

Through the testimony provided in these three Court of Chivalry disputes, therefore, one may perceive East Anglia's military community as only one of many military communities to which the region's militarily active gentry belonged. East Anglia's military community, in short, represented a complex web of loyalties, some vertical, some horizontal; some long-term, some limited only to the duration of individual military expeditions; some purely military, and some extending into peacetime. The military community at its upper reaches – amongst the militarily active gentry – to a significant degree shaded into the political and social world of the shire and into the world of the magnate affinity: a situation that Thomas Lord Morley, Sir Edward Hastings and Sir Richard Scrope each, in their own way, utilized to their advantage before the Court of Chivalry.

A 'STERRE OF ÞE SEE TO 3YUE LY3T TO MEN' AND 'MYRROURE TO ALLE SINFUL': A COMPARATIVE ANALYSIS OF BIBLICAL WOMEN IN THE *ENGLISH WYCLIFFITE SERMONS* WITH JOHN MIRK'S *FESTIAL*

Beth Allison Barr

A late medieval English sermon penned during the last two decades of the fourteenth century describes Mary Magdalene as preaching. Her sermon was inspired after she witnessed a local lord in Marseilles offering sacrifices in a pagan temple.

> Whan see Magdaleyn grete pepul comyng towarde þis tempul and þe lorde of þe cuntre to hau done offering and sac*ri*fice to here mawmentis, but Mag// daleyne was so ful of grace of þe holy goste . þt scheo be hur gracious wordys turned hem alle a3eyne hom. And for þis lorde sethe hyr ful of alle swet//nesse and gentryes. He had grete luste to heren hyr spekyn and sayde thus to hur. If thi God þt þai prechyst of is so grete of mythe as þu sayste pray to hym þt I may haue a chyles be my wyf þt is bareyne. And I will leven on hym.

Mary Magdalene acquiesced to the pagan lord's request and his barren wife conceived a child, which Mary Magdalene – through another miracle – saved along with his newly delivered mother. The sermon concludes this story with a description of Mary Magdalene as a dynamic and persuasive preacher whose prayers not only produced miracles but whose words helped convert France to Christianity.

> and whan þei [the lord and his newly saved wife and child] comyn hom . þei foundon Magdaleyne p*r*echyng þe pepul and þan a none þei felon donn to hur fette . and thanked hyr wt alle here mythe and prayd hur to telle hem whatte þei schulde done and þei wolde wt glade herte. Þan Magda//leyn bad hem distroy þe tempulles of þt londe. And make þhe schyrches and revon fonts þt þe pepul myghte be c*ri*stened. And so in schorte tyme alle þe londe was turnyd to C*ri*sten feyth þan for Magdaleyne.[1]

This account of Mary Magdalene's preaching is often associated with Lollardy, the English heresy conceived in the aftermath of John Wyclif's

---

[1] BL, MS Cotton Claudius A. II, fols 92v–93r.

reform movement.[2] Indeed, the Lollard William Brut used Mary Magdalene as evidence of female preaching in his late fourteenth-century heresy trial.[3] The connection between Lollardy and Mary Magdalene has become such accepted currency that Katherine Jansen has simply stated: 'Lollards, then, justified women's preaching by invoking the example of Mary Magdalen's public apostolate in Marseilles.'[4] Theresa Coletti likewise, after recalling Brut's use of Mary Magdalene as a defence for female preaching, has described Mary Magdalene as a 'touchstone for thinking about women's access to spiritual authority as preachers and teachers'. Safely building on this foundation, David Lavinsky recently has argued that the emphasis in Wycliffite sermons on Mary Magdalene's 'pryuylegie' granted by Christ lends support to female preaching within Lollardy.[5]

The sermon describing Mary Magdalene as preaching, however, is not a Lollard text.[6] It is from John Mirk's *Festial* – the most popular vernacular sermon collection in late medieval England. In other words, this text which so clearly describes a woman as 'preaching' is from an orthodox sermon, not a heretical one.[7] In contrast, the *English Wycliffite Sermons* – written

---

[2] Although John Wyclif did not die until 1384, Lollardy was established by the 1380s and 1390s. The starting place for scholarship on Lollardy is A. Hudson, *The Premature Reformation: Wycliffite Texts and Lollard History* (Oxford, 1988). See also *Lollards and their Influence in Late Medieval England*, ed. F. Somerset, J. Havens and D. Pitard (Woodbridge, 2003); R. Lutton, *Lollardy and Orthodox Religion in Pre-Reformation England: Reconstructing Piety* (Woodbridge, 2006); *English Wycliffite Sermons*, ed. A. Hudson and P. Gradon, 4 vols (Oxford, 1983–96). For women and Lollardy, see: M. Aston, 'Lollard Women Priests?', *Journal of Ecclesiastical History* 31 (1980), 441–61; C. Cross, '"Great Reasoners in Scripture": The Activities of Women Lollards, 1380–1530', *Studies in Church History, Subsidia* 1 (1978), 359–80; S. McSheffrey, *Gender and Heresy: Women and Men in Lollard Communities* (Philadelphia, 2011); F. Somerset, '*Eciam mulier*: Women in Lollardy and the Problem of Sources', in *Voices in Dialogue: Reading Women in the Middle Ages*, ed. L. Olson and K. Kerby-Fulton (Notre Dame, 2005), pp. 245–60; K. Kerby-Fulton, 'Eciam Lollardi', in *Voices in Dialogue*, ed. Olson and Kerby-Fulton, pp. 261–78. Following the established practice, I use the term *Lollard* to denote the English reform movement that originated with John Wyclif and the term *Wycliffite* mostly in regards to the sermon collection and other literature produced by the followers of Wyclif.
[3] Several of the previously listed scholars have discussed this. Alcuin Blamires includes portions of some of Brut's reputed claims in BL, MS Harley 31 as well as the trial transcript in *Woman Defamed and Woman Defended: An Anthology of Medieval Texts* (Oxford, 1992). A. Blamires and C. Marx, 'Women not to preach? A Disputation in British Library MS Harley 31', *The Journal of Medieval Latin* 3 (1993), 34–63. See also: A. Minnis, 'Respondet Walterus Bryth ...: Walter Brut in Debate on Women Priests', in *Text and Controversy from Wyclif to Bale: Essays in Honor of Anne Hudson*, ed. H. Barr and A. Hutchison (Turnhout, 2005), pp. 229–49.
[4] 'In theory at least, Lollards believed that both men and women were able to ascend the pulpit': K. Jansen, *The Making of the Magdalen: Preaching and Popular Devotion in the Later Middle Ages* (Princeton, 2001), p. 273.
[5] T. Coletti, *Mary Magdalene and the Drama of Saints: Theater, Gender, and Religion in Late Medieval England* (Philadelphia, 2004), p. 142. D. Lavinsky, '"Knowynge Cristes Speche": Gender and Interpretative Authority in the Wycliffite Sermon Cycle', *The Journal of Medieval Religious Cultures* 38 (2012), pp. 60–83, at pp. 66–70.
[6] A variation of the word 'preach' is used three times within the sermon to describe Mary Magdalene's actions. BL, MS Cotton Claudius A II, fols 91v–93v. For the printed edition, see John Mirk's *Festial*, Volumes I–II, ed. S. Powell, EETS OS 334–5 (Oxford, 2009).
[7] I use the term *orthodox* in the sense of conforming to established medieval Christianity – regulated

by followers of the Lollard movement – never depict Mary Magdalene as preaching. While she is described as 'a sterre of þe see to ȝyue lyȝt to men', Mary Magdalene's prowess as an evangelist is not discussed.[8]

A contradictory situation thus exists. On the one hand, scholarship continues to nurse the attractive idea that Lollardy afforded women special privileges.[9] Margery Kempe and Alice Rowley fit this assumed image of preaching Lollard women (although Margery herself was only accused of being a Lollard).[10] William Brut's words, as quoted in BL MS Harley 31, applaud women for preaching when men lacked the courage to do so: 'multe mulieres constanter predicaverunt verbum quando sacerdotes et alii non audebant verbum loqui et patet de Magdalena et Martha.'[11] It is in this same manuscript that Mary Magdalene is reputedly described by Lollards as an 'apostle of the apostles'.[12] On the other hand, when the *English Wycliffite Sermons* are compared with contemporary orthodox sermons like John Mirk's *Festial*, renderings of women in Lollard sermons appear less radical than has often been assumed. Female models within Wycliffite sermons fit comfortably with those found in orthodox sermons like *Festial*.[13] Moreover, when gendered differences do arise, it is often *Festial* which affords women greater privileges.

by the ecclesiastical hierarchy, headed by the archbishops of Canterbury and York in England and the papacy in Rome.

[8]   *English Wycliffite Sermons*, i, 430–1, lines 30–1.

[9]   For example, a recent textbook reader states, 'Lollards preached a reformed doctrine based on Wycliffe's writings. They promoted the popular reading of Holy Scripture in the vernacular and promoted equality of the sexes, including women preachers.' *Radical Christian Writings: A Reader*, ed. A. Bradstock and C. Rowland (Oxford, 2008), p. 56. Scholars such as Shannon McSheffrey and Fiona Somerset have cautioned that Lollardy may not have been as friendly towards women as has often been assumed. McSheffrey, *Gender and Heresy*; Somerset, 'Eciam Mulier'.

[10] See *The Book of Margery Kempe*, ed. H. Allen, EETS OS 212 (London, 1940), p. 28, lines 28–9, for an example of Margery Kempe accused of being a Lollard.

[11] BL, MS Harley 31, fol. 219r; as quoted by Aston, 'Lollard Women Priests?', 452 n. 14.

[12] BL, MS Harley 31, fol. 195r. 'Confirmatur, nam legitur de beata Maria Magdalena quod publice predicauit in Marcilia et in regione adiacente quam sua predicacione ad Christum conuertit. Quare vocatur apostolorum apostola gratia etc.' See Blamires and Marx, 'Women Not to Preach?', 55–6 nn. 81–91.

[13] My argument fits with a growing movement studying the continuity between Wycliffite sermons and orthodox sermons. Mary Raschko has argued that Lollard interpretations of biblical parables share similarities with their late medieval contemporaries. 'While Lollard authors differ from many of their contemporaries by addressing the whole text of the parable, their interpretations resemble more mainstream sermons insofar as they encourage contrition and virtuous living and promote an idealized social structure. More specifically, Lollard authors join other preachers in applying contemporary social theory to the biblical text so that it encourages particular types of physical and spiritual work.' M. Raschko, '"To þe Worschipe of God and Profite of His Peple": Lollard Sermons on the Parable of the Labourers in the Vineyard', in *Wycliffite Controversies*, ed. M. Bose and J. Hornbeck (Turnhout, 2011), pp. 175–92, at p. 176. In a similar fashion, Jennifer Illig, a doctoral student at Fordham University, recently delivered the paper 'Making Mary a Model: Teaching about Mary in *English Wycliffite Sermons*' at the 2013 International Congress on Medieval Studies at Western Michigan University, in which she highlighted significant parallels between the presentation of Mary in *English Wycliffite Sermons* and the Northern Homily Cycle.

In short, attitudes about women within Lollard sermons can be better understood from the vantage point of contemporary orthodox sermons. The last quarter of the fourteenth century witnessed the birth of the two most prolific and popular sermon compilations in late medieval England, John Mirk's *Festial* and the *English Wycliffite Sermons*. Both collections were written in the vernacular, survive in more than thirty manuscripts, and were intended at least in part for preaching to lay audiences. John Mirk, an Augustinian prior from Lilleshall Abbey in Shropshire, produced *Festial* – a practical compilation containing approximately seventy-four sermons which staunchly promote orthodoxy.[14] Produced most probably under the direction of a single scriptorium and written for the purpose of spreading heretical ideas (namely the teachings of John Wyclif), the English Wycliffite cycle contains 294 sermons which challenge many of the beliefs and rituals endorsed by *Festial*.

Regarding women, however, the *English Wycliffite Sermons* promote female models that often mirror *Festial*. Indeed, the Canaanite woman who called out to Jesus and Mary Magdalene who dared kiss Christ's feet were considered suitable exemplars for heretical and orthodox Christians alike. Yet, despite continuity in the biblical women they emphasize, the Wycliffite sermons often diverge from *Festial* in how they use these female exemplars. This difference can be connected to the pastoral programme flourishing in fourteenth-century England: namely, its acceptance by *Festial* and its rejection by the *English Wycliffite Sermons*. Initiated by the reforms of Fourth Lateran Council in 1215, outlined by Archbishop Pecham in 1281, and reinforced by both Archbishop Thoresby in 1357 and Archbishop Arundel in 1409, the pastoral programme developed from an initial focus on the basics of medieval Christianity into sweeping advice covering all aspects of pastoral care.[15] Orthodox sermons like *Festial* fulfil the pastoral programme by teaching parishioners how to meet the necessary requirements for salvation, often through using narrative models. Close examination of biblical women in the Wycliffite sermons as compared with *Festial* reveals that while the Wycliffite sermons adhere closely to the biblical text, their female exemplars mostly serve as passive models who – like Mary Magdalene's star – do little more than illuminate the general direction.[16] In contrast, female exemplars

---

[14] The most complete manuscript is BL, MS Cotton Claudius A II. For more information, see *John Mirk's Festial*, ed. Powell, pp. xix–cxxvii.

[15] Many scholars have discussed the pastoral care programme. See L. Boyle, 'The Fourth Lateran Council and Manuals of Popular Theology', in *The Popular Literature of Medieval England*, ed. T. Heffernan (Knoxville, 1985), pp. 30–43; J. Hughes, *Pastors and Visionaries: Religion and Secular Life in Late Medieval Yorkshire* (Woodbridge, 1988); L. Boyle, *Pastoral Care, Clerical Education, and Canon Law, 1200–1400* (London, 1981); W. Pantin, *The English Church in the Fourteenth Century*, repr. (Toronto, 1989); H. Spencer, *English Preaching in the Late Middle Ages* (Oxford, 1993); B. Barr, *The Pastoral Care of Women in Late Medieval England* (Woodbridge, 2008).

[16] I am indebted to Jennifer Illig for this metaphor of illumination. Although she used it in reference

in *Festial* represent active models who tread the path that male and female parishioners are encouraged to follow. Thus, without detracting from the significance of the Wycliffite sermons identifying women with special privileges and spiritual insight, the extraordinariness of these statements fades into the ordinary when they are compared with similar accounts in *Festial*.[17] Even the privilege granted 'vnto wommannys kynde' when the resurrected Christ first appeared to Mary Magdalene in the Wycliffite sermons is outshone by the Magdalene in *Festial*, as Christ 'aperud to hur bodyly furste of alle othyr, and suffred hur to touche hym an cussyn hys fette'.[18] While her presence is limited in the Wycliffite sermons to (mostly) the biblical accounts, Mary Magdalene in *Festial* is able to carry her message beyond the apostles and even have her public preaching blessed by Peter.

When the representations of women within the *English Wycliffite Sermons* are compared with orthodox sermons, striking similarities emerge. One obvious parallel stems from the Wycliffite use of the female exemplars found in orthodox sermons – even to the extent of including extra-biblical traditions.[19] Mary Magdalene, the most recognizable female saint in the late medieval world (next only to the Blessed Virgin Mary) provides a case in point.[20] She plays a similar role in both sermon cycles. The tradition conflating Mary Magdalene with Mary of Bethany and the sinful woman in Luke 7:36–50 began authoritatively with Gregory the Great's sermon in

---

to the Virgin Mary at Candlemas, it seems appropriate as well for the Magdalene reference as a 'star'.

[17] Coletti, *Mary Magdalene and the Drama of the Saints*, p. 145, highlights another oft-cited Wycliffite example that becomes much more ordinary when compared with *Festial*. She remarks how Mary Magdalene's unspoken confession supports Lollard rejection of auricular confession. Orthodox sermons accept the legitimacy of such private confessions, however, as numerous exempla attest (some of which pre-date Lollardy). See Barr, *Pastoral Care of Women*, pp. 114–20. The example of Mary Magdalene's tearful (and unspoken) confession while washing Christ's feet in *Festial* also demonstrates this.

[18] *English Wycliffite Sermons*, i, 430, lines 25–9; BL, MS Cotton Claudius A II, fol. 92r.

[19] Lollards often are assumed to reject extra-scriptural tradition, but this is not accurate. See M. Dove, *The First English Bible: The Text and Context of the Wycliffite Versions* (Cambridge, 2007), pp. 192–7. For more discussions of Wyclif and the Bible, see: K. Ghosh, *The Wycliffite Heresy: Authority and the Interpretation of Texts* (Cambridge, 2002). Ghosh remarks that 'Lollardy is therefore not just an anti-intellectual heresy advocating a fundamentalist return to the Bible', p. 2; see also ch. 4 for a specific discussion of the *English Wycliffite Sermons*; M. Dove, 'The Lollards' Threefold Biblical Agenda', in *Wycliffite Controversies*, ed. Bose and Hornbeck, pp. 211–26; Raschko, 'To þe worschipe of God and profite of his peple', pp. 175–92.

[20] Eve, the Blessed Virgin Mary and Mary Magdalene are by far the most frequently occurring female saints in late medieval English sermons, recorded as appearing in well over a hundred sermons each. In the seventy-four sermons of *Festial* alone, these women appear in at least twenty-six. Although my research is still ongoing in the *English Wycliffite Sermons*, these women appear in at least thirty-three of the 177 sermons in Volumes I and II (12, 24, 29, 32, 39, 46, 47, 177, 180, 184, 186, 187, 188, 189, 79, 100, 95, 75, 35, 89, 90, 93, 94, 96, 97, 99, 102, 113, 116, E1, E4, E10, E39). This is in stark contrast to the sixteenth-century *Certain Sermones or Homilies* in which Eve, Mary and Mary Magdalene seem to appear only a sparse fourteen times (eight of which are the Virgin Mary) in the much longer thirty-three homilies composed between 1547 and 1571. This research is part of my current book project.

591 and was continually reinforced, such as by the popular rendering of the Magdalene story in the late thirteenth-century *Golden Legend* (which, by this point, also combined aspects from the Mary of Egypt legend and an extra-biblical account of the Magdalene's apostolic work in Provence).[21] Hence, by the fourteenth century, the tradition of Mary Magdalene as a former-prostitute, former-demoniac, contemplative sister of Martha, tearful penitent who washed Christ's feet, and even itinerant preacher who lived in the wilderness, was a pillar of medieval English Christianity.[22] Both sermon cycles reflect the composite biblical image of Mary Magdalene, discussing her in the same presumed biblical context: as a demoniac (Luke 8), anointing Jesus (Matthew 26, Mark 14, Luke 7, John 12), attending the death and resurrection (Matthew 27–8, Mark 15–16, Luke 24, John 19–20), and accompanying her family Martha and Lazarus (Luke 10, John 11–12). An Ember Days sermon in the Wycliffite Ferial Gospels (Luke 7:36–50) names the sinful woman without hesitation as Mary Magdalene:

> Þis gospel telliþ hou Crist dide mercy to Mary Maudelen. Luk telliþ *hou o pharisee preyede Iesu to ete wiþ hym; and Crist entride [into] þe pharisees hous, and satt doun to þe mete. And lo, a synful womman þat was in þe citee, whanne she knew þat Iesu restide in þe pharisees hous, she brouȝte a box of oynement, and stood bihynde biside þe feet of þe lord Iesu, and bigan wiþ teeris to waysshe his feet and wipte hem wiþ þe heeris of her hed, and kisside his feet, and anoyntide hem wiþ þe oynement.*[23]

This parallels *Festial*: 'Þan/ answerid Magdaleyne and sayde þt scheo was a synful womman þt þe gospel spake/ of, þt whesse Crystes fette.'[24] Mary the mother of Jesus provides another clear case of Wycliffite sermons perpetuating established orthodox traditions. Since the time of the early church, theologians drew from scriptural interpretation (such as provided by Augustine, Jerome and Ambrose) and extra-scriptural sources, such as the *Protoevangelium of St James*, to argue that Mary remained a virgin until her death.[25] Religious tales, dramas and sermon stories, like the narrative of the doubting

---

21 Jacobus de Voragine, *The Golden Legend: Readings on the Saints*, trans. and ed. W. Granger, i (Princeton, 1993), p. 374; L. Tracy, *Women of the Gilte Legende: A Selection of Middle English Saints' Lives* (Cambridge, 2003), pp. 1–25 and 68–79.

22 Jansen, *The Making of the Magdalen*, pp. 33–46.

23 *English Wycliffite Sermons*, iii, 298, lines 1–7.

24 BL, MS Cotton Claudius A II, fols 93r–v. Although traditions were mixed about conflating the identity of Mary Magdalene with various other biblical Marys, tradition in England between the twelfth and fifteenth centuries mostly identified her with the sinful woman in Luke and the sister of Martha. It was not until the mid-sixteenth century in England that Mary Magdalene, at least in sermon literature, began to see some separation. The 1547 *Certain Sermones or Homilies*, for example, still identifies the woman in Luke 7 with Mary Magdalene. It treats Mary the sister of Martha and Lazarus, however, as a separate woman from Mary Magdalene. See also G. Constable, *Three Studies in Medieval Religious and Social Thought* (Cambridge, 1995), pp. 1–142.

25 J. Pelikan, *The Growth of Medieval Theology, 600–1300* (Chicago, 1978), pp. 72–7 and 160–74.

midwife whose shrivelled arm testified to the miraculous virginity of Mary, attest to the widespread acceptance of Mary's perpetual virginity by the thirteenth and fourteenth centuries. Wyclif, as we know, did not question this doctrine. Anne Hudson has claimed: 'No Lollard sermon contains any story material from outside the Bible – no classical anecdote, no pious saint's life story.'[26] Yet the authors of the *English Wycliffite Sermons* follow Wyclif's lead in not questioning the medieval tradition of Mary's perpetual virginity, despite general understanding about the extra-scriptural sources that helped formulate the doctrine. The Wycliffite Sermon for the Annunciation of the Virgin Mary (March 25, Luke 1) records that: '*And þis maydon was weddud to Iosep, þe whiche was of Dauiþus hows; and name of þe virgine was Maria,* and wel sche is clepud a virgyne soo ofte in þis gospel, for sche was virgyne whan sche was weddud, and virgyne aftur to hire deþ.'[27] *Festial* states in a similar, albeit more colourful, fashion:

> Þus oure Lady/ þat was as clene as any cristall at þe hotte love of þe Holy Goste oponeth hure/ herte and reseyvoth þe vertu of þe Holy Goste and at þe nyne moneth ende/ was delyuered of hyre Sone Ihesu Cryste and scheo aftur as clos a maydon as/ scheo was before.[28]

Of course, regarding the sacraments and ecclesiastical authority, Helen Spencer would have been correct in her observation that 'if Mirk and the compiler (or compilers) of the Wycliffite sermons could ever have been brought face to face, the resulting exchanges would have been exceedingly acrimonious'.[29] In respect of the biblical women who appear in the *English Wycliffite Sermons* and *Festial*, however, it seems that both owe much to the familiar – and often extra-scriptural – traditions of late medieval Christianity.

Wycliffite sermons also echo orthodox sermons in the ways they discuss biblical women: from emphasizing female weakness to ascribing female authority. A Wycliffite Easter Sunday Sermon (Mark 16:1–7) makes a tantalizing suggestion about Lollard attitudes towards women:

> Furst Crist aperude to þese hoolye wymmen [including *Mary Magdalene*] for to graunten a pryuylegie vnto wommannys kynde, for hit is seyd comunly þat Crist aperude ten tymes from howr of his rysyng to his stey3yng into heuene.[30]

Further investigation into the Wycliffite sermons dampens this sentiment when this 'pryuylegie' is clarified in a Ferial Sermon for Easter (John 20:11–18) as due to feminine weakness: 'Þis gospel telliþ hou Crist apperide to

---

26 Hudson, *Premature Reformation*, p. 270.
27 *English Wycliffite Sermons*, ii, 256, lines 21–4.
28 BL, MS Cotton Claudius A II, fol. 51r.
29 Spencer, *English Preaching*, p. 278.
30 *English Wycliffite Sermons*, i, 430, lines 25–9.

Mary Maudelen, for Crist wolde þat womman kynde hadde þis priuylegie bifore man þat he shewide hym aftir his deþ raþere to womman þan to man, for wymmen ben freele as water and taken sunnere prynte of bileue.'[31] In other words, Jesus's choice of a woman for his inaugural resurrection appearance was not an attempt to emphasize woman's worth or spiritual equality; it was simply because women – as the weaker sex – were more impressionable. *Speculum Sacerdotale*, an orthodox sermon compilation contemporary with the Wycliffite sermons and *Festial*, mirrors this backhanded compliment. It explains that the candle representing Jesus during the Easter service should be blessed of the deacon and not of higher ranking clergy because it honours the actions of Christ: 'Crist firste after his resurreccion schewyd hym vnto wymmen and denuncied and schewid his resurreccion to his disciples by the same wymmen, that were of febeler and lasse kynde.'[32] Both the Wycliffite sermon and *Speculum Sacerdotale* emphasize the 'pryuylegie' that Christ showed to women by appearing first to 'womankind' after his resurrection; both also temper the significance of this privilege by explaining it as due to female weakness.

Just as Wycliffite sermons and orthodox sermons mirror discussions of female weakness, they similarly mirror ideas about female authority. The Wycliffite Easter Sunday Sermon (Mark 16:1–7) points towards Mary Magdalene's pedagogical authority by describing her as a 'sterre of þe see to ȝyue lyȝt to men, and to putten hire fro dispeyr of hire furste synnes.'[33] Because of its open air arena and its intentional didactic modelling of the Magdalene, Lavinsky argues that this description 'legitimizes the public sphere as a scene of female preaching and instruction – in short, of female pedagogic authority'.[34] Yet this praising of Mary Magdalene as a public model whose story serves as a guide to other sinners is a sentiment also found in *Festial*, which opens the sermon dedicated to Mary Magdalene by emphasizing how she is a model for all sinners:

> For scheo/ was þe furste in tyme of grace þt dud penaunce for hyr synnes, and so/ recoured aȝeyne grace be doing of penaunce and repentyng þt scheo hadde/ loste be luste of þe flesse and so synnyng þe wyche is made a myrroure/ to alle synful to schewon how alle þt wollon levon hur synne and done pe/naunce for hur trespace þei schul recoure grace aȝeyn þt þei haue loste/ and ofte myche more, and so dude þis womman.[35]

In the same way that a mirror reflects our true image, Mary Magdalene

[31] *English Wycliffite Sermons*, iii, 199, lines 1–4.
[32] *Speculum Sacerdotale*, ed. E. Weatherly, EETS OS 200 (London, 1936), p. 115.
[33] *English Wycliffite Sermons*, i, 430, lines 30–1.
[34] Lavinsky, '"Knowynge Cristes Speche"', 69.
[35] BL, MS Cotton Claudius A II, fol. 91v.

reflects the actions of a sincere penitent who has confessed, performed penance, and dedicated himself or herself to the work of God. The Wycliffite Magdalene too serves at least as a distant mirror for 'how men schal come to serue Crist'.

> And hit is seid comunly þat, as þese hooly wymmen [Mary Magdalene and the women attending the tomb of Christ] hadden left þer formere synne and take þeir fresch deuocion, so men schulden come to þe chirche to take þis hooly sacrament, and þus come wiþ þese wymmen wiþ ly3t of þe sonne.[36]

Regardless of their orthodoxy, the sermons imbue Mary Magdalene with the pedagogical authority to instruct the hearers of the sermons to emulate her behaviour (her exact behaviour in *Festial* – sorrowing for sin, penance, and service to God, and her symbolic behaviour in the Wycliffite text – showing devotion by going to church). Late medieval Christianity, Lollard and orthodox alike, was a communal affair. Mary Magdalene represents in both sermons a true believer who motivates those around her to become involved in communal Christian devotion. From similar inclusion of extra-biblical traditions about Mary Magdalene and the Blessed Virgin Mary to parallel descriptions about female weakness and women's ability to serve as pedagogical models, *English Wycliffite Sermons* drew from the familiar Christianity of fourteenth-century England to produce images of women that – in many ways – looked much like their orthodox counterparts.

From the vantage point of contemporary orthodox sermons, extraordinary statements about women in Wycliffite sermons appear more ordinary. Even the seemingly provocative comments about women as having special spiritual insight – such as 'knowynge Cristes speche' – are similar to accounts of women in *Festial*.[37] The *Festial* sermon for Mary Magdalene describes her as given special 'grace' by Christ to 'knowyn hyr self'. 'Þan for it was often/ seyne þt Cryste of þe gresteyste synnerres, he made þe moste holy

---

[36] *English Wycliffite Sermons*, i, 430, lines 40–1, and 431, lines 62–6.

[37] *English Wycliffite Sermons*, i, 402, line 18. Lavinsky has emphasized this, arguing that Wycliffite sermons highlight women's spiritual insight which gives them interpretative agency. He focuses on biblical women in the Sunday Gospels (primarily sermons 41, 42, 46 and 47 in Volume I) who understand spiritual teachings in ways that others do not. Since Lollards were 'Bible men', as Pecock called them (R. Pecock, *The Repressor of Over Much Blaming of the Clergy* [1449], ed. C. Babington [London, 1860], pp. xxi, 36–7 and 85–7), it is not surprising to see biblical patterns like this. Women are often noted for their spiritual understanding in the Bible, such as their ability to recognize Christ when others do not. In John chapters 5–12, in which Jesus attempts to impress his identity as the Son of God on his followers, only a blind man and two women (Mary and Martha) recognize him. In words similar to Peter's declaration, Martha claims, 'I believe that thou art the Christ, the Son of God, which should come into the world' (John 11:27). Of course, this is also a pattern that we find in *Festial*, which contains many references to women especially attuned to Christ's words and spiritual teachings. For example, in addition to the references given, Mary Magdalene is described as having 'chosyn þe/ best parte' because she 'herde hys wordys þt comyn owte of Cristes mouthe'. BL, MS Cotton Claudius A II, fol. 100v.

aftyr,/ wherfor whan he seygh tyme he ʒaf þis wo*m*man grace to knowyn hyr self/ and repentaunce of hur mysdedus.'[38] Just as Mary Magdalene had the spiritual wisdom to recognize her own sin, the *Festial* sermon for St Thomas shows a female minstrel in India displaying the spiritual insight to recognize Thomas as an apostle of Christ. There was 'a woma*n* a mynstrel þt undurstod Thom*a*s wordes'. She fell down at his feet, and 'cryed þt alle men herdon, Ouþer þ*ou* art God or/ ellus Goddes dyscypul, ffor ryght as þu say dost hyt be fallen.'[39] She was the first in this pagan land to recognize an apostle of Christ. Women in *Festial* exhibit spiritual discernment just as their Wycliffite counterparts, and this spiritual discernment extends beyond biblical exemplars to even ordinary women like the minstrel listening to St Thomas.

Ironically, the ways that the Wycliffite sermons parallel *Festial* accentuates the gendered differences between the sermon cycles. Much has been made of Mary Magdalene as an inspiration for Lollard women preachers. Yet by contextualizing Wycliffite discussions of the Magdalene within orthodox sermons, two points become clear. First, the Wycliffite version of the Magdalene is less radical than what is found in orthodox sermons. Indeed, it is in *Festial* that the Magdalene's didactic authority as a model actually translates into the public authority of a preacher. Second, the influence of the pastoral programme in *Festial* makes it more inclined than the *English Wycliffite Sermons* to fashion women as active rather than passive models whose specific behaviour should be emulated. Mary Magdalene not only preaches in *Festial*, but she also serves as the first penitent – setting the pattern for future Christians.

Although Mary Magdalene appears often in the *English Wycliffite Sermons*, many of her appearances are lacklustre. The Ferial Sermon for the sixth week of Lent (John 12) relates the story of Mary Magdalene anointing Christ's feet. Aside from the biblical text, it mostly ignores her, focusing instead on the sin of covetousness and its (predictable) connection to medieval priests.

> *Iesu cam to Bethanye, where Lazar was deed, whom Iesu reiside. And þere þey maden hym a soper, and Martha seruyde hem, and Lazar was one of hem þat eetyn wiþ Crist. Mary Ma[u]delen tok a pounde of trewe oynement and precious, and anoyntid Iesues feet; and she wipte wiþ her heer his feet; and þe hous was fillid of smel of þe oynnement. And so one of Cristis disciplis seyde, Iudas Scariotis sone þat was for to traye Crist, 'Why is not þis oynnement soold for þre hundrid pens, and ʒouen to pore men?' But he seyde þis, not for he þouʒte of þe nedy men, but for he was a þef.*

The commentary follows the rendering of Judas' comment 'ʒouen to pore men', both in its mirroring of the masculine 'men' and its focus on covet-

---

[38] BL, MS Cotton Claudius A II, fol. 92r.
[39] Ibid., fol. 14r.

ousness. The sermon teaches that 'eche man' who treats God's property like Judas is a thief and that focusing on 'gostly almes' like the perfume is better than focusing on physical alms: 'And Crist tau3te his apostelis to chese þis betere and leeue þe w[o]rse. And þis ipocrisie is in prestis þat colouren þer coueytise by almes.'⁴⁰ The sermon never returns to Mary Magdalene. The sermon for the Assumption of the Virgin Mary (August 15, Luke 10:38–42) treats the account of Mary Magdalene and her sister Martha in a similar fashion: it centres less on the women and more on how their encounter with Christ has been misinterpreted by church teachings. The sermon states that Martha fed Christ's body while he fed Mary spiritually, and thus Jesus 'tawte þe chirche in þes wymmen'. Instead of emphasizing the importance of the contemplative life (Mary) over that of the active life (Martha), the sermon claims that there is a third better life: 'Þe þridde lif is þe beste, as Crist seiþ þat may not lye. And þis is somewhat here in erþe, but fully in þe blisse of heuene. And here dowten monye men wheþur of þes two lyues is betture. But men þat holdon byleue of Crist wyton þat þis þridde lyf is beste.'⁴¹ An encounter between Jesus and two women laid the foundation for this sermon, but women are mostly absent from it. The conclusion makes it clear that Mary and Martha and even Christians in general are not the main concern of the sermon; it is concerned with the problems in the medieval church stemming from the pope and priests choosing the wrong 'lif'. Although a Ferial Sermon for the third week after Easter (Luke 24:1–2) stays focused on the women who first saw the resurrected Christ, it does so to emphasize feminine weakness. It implies that, because the women were so afraid by what they saw at the tomb, their foolish (hysterical?) words caused the apostles to initially disbelieve the resurrection. '*And þes wordis weren semynge to þes men as þei weren fonned wordis,* for wymmen whanne þey ben afrayed speken ofte wordis out of witt. *And þes* disciplis *trowiden hem not.*' Even though Jesus appeared first to women, the sermon concludes with a statement endorsing masculine apostolic authority over the 'pryuylegie' granted to the women at the tomb: 'Petre and Ion passiden þes wymmen soone aftir in many poyntis.' It also reminds us that even as Mary Magdalene 'trowiden to þe aungelis þat Crist was risun and was alyue' before the apostles, Mary Magdalene still shared many of the faults of her peers: 'Mary Maudelen wiste not 3it alle þe treuþis of þis uprisyng, but hadde doute of many oþere, as it semeþ of Iones gospel.'⁴² In spite of the the attention given to Mary Magdalene for inspiring Lollard women preachers, her presence in these Wycliffite sermons is uninspiring.

It is actually the presentation of Mary Magdalene in *Festial* that seems more likely to have encouraged public female preaching. Instead of empha-

---

⁴⁰ *English Wycliffite Sermons*, iii, 164–5, lines 2–11 and 25–8.
⁴¹ *English Wycliffite Sermons*, ii, 289–92, lines 34–5, 60–4, and 84–93.
⁴² *English Wycliffite Sermons*, iii, pp. 209–10, lines 26–41. This is a reference to Mary Magdalene in John 20.

sizing her fear and weakness as in the Wycliffite sermons, the *Festial* sermon celebrates her bravery for going to the tomb. The Wycliffite Sabbath sermon for Easter week (John 20:1–9) contrasts the fear displayed by Mary Magdalene when she found the empty tomb with the fearlessness of the male apostles Peter and John: 'T[h]is gospel of Ion telliþ hou Mary Maudelen was afrayed in sekyng of Iesues body, and hou Petre and Ion diden.'[43] The *Festial* text has a different emphasis, stating that while:

> in hys passion þere as hys disciplus flowen away from hym for/ drede of þe deth scheo lafte hym neure tyl scheo wth othyr hadde layde/ hym in hys tombe. And whan no man durste go thyddur for þe armye/ knytus þt kep þe tombe, scheo spared for no drede of lyf, ne deth, bot/ in þe dark dawyng toke wt hur swete bawms and ȝod þider to haue baw/met Crystus body. Þus scheo louud Crste boþe leuyng and dede.[44]

The Wycliffite sermons note the authority of the masculine apostles surpassing that of Mary Magdalene. *Festial* does the opposite. It points out how Mary Magdalene's belief surpasses even that of an apostle and equates her authority with that of Peter. *Festial* records in the sermon for St Thomas the Apostle how St Gregory remarked that 'Me/che more Thomas of Ynde help me to þe feyth þt wold not byleue tyl/ he hadde hondeled and groput þe wondes of Cryst þen Mary Madele/yn þt byleued anon at þe forme syght.' When Peter in the *Festial* sermon is told of Mary Magdalene's preaching adventures, he sends his blessing to her and bids her friends to 'grete wel Mary Magdaleyne and alle hyre ferus'.[45] The *Festial* sermon presents Mary Magdalene as a missionary of Christ who is affirmed by Peter, preaches openly, performs miracles that parallel those of the apostles, converts a new land to the Christian faith, and shares a spiritual connection with Jesus that surpasses the spoken word.

Even when the Wycliffite sermons suggest the possibility of didactic authority for women, they refrain from showing women as exercising public authority. From her quiet study at Christ's feet to her silent and tearful confession, the traditional biblical accounts of Mary Magdalene emphasize her reticence and spiritual bond with Christ.[46] Only the accounts of her at the tomb show her speaking, and even then her words are verified by the apostles before they are believed. The Wycliffite sermons adhere closely to these biblical accounts. Mary Magdalene has a special connection with Christ, but

---

[43] *English Wycliffite Sermons*, iii, 204, lines 1–2.

[44] BL, MS Cotton Claudius A II, fol. 92r.

[45] Ibid., fols 13v and 93r.

[46] To be fair, *Festial* also emphasizes that women should be known by their reticence, in the sermon for the Assumption of the Virgin Mary. *Festial* does not rescue medieval women from their patriarchal and misogynist world. Yet, as the sermon for the Assumption of the Virgin Mary also highlights the Virgin as teaching the Apostles, it does seem to offer women at least limited ways that they can exercise religious authority. BL, MS Cotton Claudius A II, fols 100v–103r.

still mostly serves as a silent and passive model. Even the Easter Sunday sermon which praises her so highly ('Furst Crist aperude vnto Marie Maghdeleyn, and made hire sterre of þe see to ȝyue lyȝt to men, and to putten hire fro dispeyr of hire furste synnes') still spiritualizes her as a 'lessoun' for how men are to 'serue Crist' and be ready to partake in the sacrament: with 'fresch deuocion' and clothed in the 'vertewys' of 'byleue, hope and charite'.⁴⁷ In stark contrast, Mary Magdalene mirrors her description in *Festial* – stepping off the pedestal of a model and into the shoes of a penitent, preacher and apostle.

The Magdalene sermon in *Festial* suggests a reason for this different, yet still familiar, Magdalene:

> whan scheo herde þt Cryste was/ atte þe mete yn a manns houce, þt was kalled Symond þe pharasen, scheo/ toke a boyste wt oynement, such as men vsendon in þt cuntre for hete/ of þe sonne and ȝode þider, but for scheo durste note for schame gon befo/re Cryste scheo ȝode behynde hym and toke hys fette in hyr hands, and for/ sorow þt scheo hadde in hur herte, scheo wepte so tendurly þt therus of hur/ heyen woschon Cristes fette. Þan wt hyr fayre fax sche wypud hem aftur, *and*/ þan wt alle þe loue þt was in hyr herte scheo cussyd hys fette and so wt hyr/ box anoyntyd hem. Bot no worde spake scheo þt man myght here, bot sof/tely in hyr herte heghly scheo cred to Cryst of mercy and made a vow/ to hym þt scheo wolde neure trespace more. Þan hadde Criste compassion/ of hur an clensed her of vii fendes. þe whyche scheo had w*th*inne hur/ and forȝaf hur alle hur gylte of synne.⁴⁸

While the Wycliffite account of John 12 focuses on the crime of Judas, the *Festial* account of Luke 7 focuses on Mary Magdalene's contrition for her sin. Her story was meant to encourage sinful parishioners to express contrition and repent so that they could receive absolution. She thus serves as an active model: 'a myrroure to alle sinful to schewon how alle þt wollon leuon hur synne and done pe/naunce for hur trespase, þei schul recoure grace aȝeyn þt þei haue loste and ofte myche more'.⁴⁹ In other words, the Magdalene in *Festial* supports the pastoral programme. She provides an example of contrition, confession and penance for parishioners to emulate, as well as to bring to mind that they were all eligible, just the like sinful Magdala, to receive the grace of Christ. Like the Magdalene sermon, a primary goal of *Festial* was to teach parishioners the basic components of their faith and to encourage them to participate in the sacramental system.⁵⁰ Priests – as the only instruments

---

⁴⁷ *English Wycliffite Sermons*, i, 430–1, lines 29–31, 40–1 and 62–6.
⁴⁸ BL, MS Cotton Claudius A II, fol. 92r.
⁴⁹ Ibid., fol. 91v.
⁵⁰ *John Mirk's Festial*, ed. Powell, pp. xix–xliii. See also Barr, *Pastoral Care of Women*, and Spencer, *English Preaching*. Spencer demonstrates how the pastoral programme was translated

with the sacerdotal authority to teach about doctrinal issues and to administer the sacraments – had to pay attention to all parishioners, men and women. This responsibility was staunchly supported by the fourteenth-century church, in accordance with the decrees of Fourth Lateran Council of 1215: 'Omnis utriusque sexus fidelis, postquam ad annos discretionis pervenerit, omnia sua solus peccata confiteatur fideliter, saltem semel in anno proprio sacerdoti.'[51] This responsibility echoes in the accounts of the female exemplars in *Festial*, who, like Mary Magdalene, serve as reminders to priests and parishioners alike that women were just as much a part of the pastoral programme as their male counterparts.

The *English Wycliffite Sermons* reject priestly authority, and – consequently – reject this pastoral programme. The sermon for the Common of Many Confessors (Luke 12:35–40) states that if penitents 'axe we God mercy in oure þowȝt, and haue we sorwe for þis synne, and God is redy to forȝyu it, howeuere þat preestus faylon'. Further stressing that ecclesiastical authority is unnecessary for administering the sacraments, a Ferial sermon for the fourth week in Lent (John 11:1–45) states that 'it is an opyn blasfemye þat prestis forȝyuen þis synne in God, but ȝyue God forȝyue it first and seye to prestis þat [þei] shewen it'.[52] By rejecting the mediatory role of the priesthood, Lollards lessened the need for priests to perform sacerdotal roles while accentuating the role of the laity in salvation. It is no surprise that exhortations found in sermons like *Festial* for people to come to confession before they receive Eucharist, as well as the instructions and encouragement given to priests to make sure they properly fulfil their sacerdotal duties towards all parishioners, are absent from Lollard sermons. As it is at these moments that *Festial* sermons are most gender-attentive, perhaps it should not be surprising that *English Wycliffite Sermons* are much less so.[53] Even when specifically discussing biblical women like Mary Magdalene, the Wycliffite sermons still seem to firmly support Shannon McSheffrey's assessment of Lollardy: that it was made by and for men.[54] The Ferial sermon for the fourth week of Lent (John 11:1–45) shows this well. The text focuses on the grief of Mary Magdalene and Martha and their interactions with Jesus, culminating in the miraculous resurrection of their dead brother Lazarus. Aside from the scriptural references to the sisters, women are completely absent from the sermon. Indeed, the whole story is spiritualized into a lesson about how

---

from constitutions and instructional handbooks (mostly in the thirteenth and early fourteenth centuries) to sermons (later fourteenth and fifteenth centuries), pp. 196–227.

[51] *Conciliorum Oecumenicorum Decreta*, ed. J. Algerigo *et al.*, 3rd edn (Bologna, 1973), p. 245.

[52] *English Wycliffite Sermons*, ii, 158, lines 108–9; iii, 144, lines 99–101.

[53] *Festial* manuscripts consistently contain gender-inclusive language when preaching *pastoralia*. See Barr, *Pastoral Care of Women*, pp. 36–61. A cursory examination of the *English Wycliffite Sermons* immediately reveals that they rely mostly on masculine generic and androcentric nouns and pronouns.

[54] McSheffrey, *Gender and Heresy*, p. 149.

Christ – without clerical assistance – can 'reyse a soule fro synne to grace'. The nouns and pronouns used for the 'soul' are exclusively masculine. As the text reads: 'Þes boondis in whiche þis man cam forþ shewen þe myracle of Crist, hou he mouyd þis body þat was deed to come forþ þus al boundyn; and it bitokeneþ also þat men þat ben vnbounden of prestis ben bifore quykened of God.' Far from the grief of Mary and Martha, the sermon concludes by denouncing priests who dare to forgive sin in 'men' as blaspheming against God.[55] When the androcentric perspective of Wycliffite sermons is compared with the orthodox sermons of *Festial*, the rejection of the pastoral programme by Lollardy takes on a gendered significance. The resurrection of Lazarus is used in a similar way in *Festial*, but with a gendered difference clearly connected to the pastoral programme. The *Festial* sermon for Palm Sunday opens with a call for 'Gode Cryston Me*n and* Wo*m*men' to hear how Lazarus, the brother of Mary Magdalene and Martha, was raised from death to life. As in the Wycliffite sermon, *Festial* compares parishioners to Lazarus: 'for yere bene many of ȝow raysyd frome dethe to lyue./ þt hath lyne dede fowre dayes, þt bene synful thoutus, synful speches,/ synful werkys, in synful customes.' Unlike the Wycliffite sermon, *Festial* specifically references these parishioners as both men and women and attributes their resurrection to their success in following the pastoral programme: 'Where fore iche C*r*isten man *and* wom/man schal þis day beron palmes in p*r*ocess*i*on schewing þt he haþe fogh/ton wt þe fend, *and* haþe þe vuctery of hym be clene schryuing of/ mowþe, repentaunce of herte, *and* mekely done his penaunce, *and*/ in þis wyse ouercomyn is oure enmye.' Wycliffite sermons were not concerned with motivating individual souls to participate in the sacraments. Hence they lacked the reason provided by the pastoral programme to reach out specifically to 'iche C*r*isten man *and* womman'.[56]

John Mirk's *Festial* and the *English Wycliffite Sermons* have much in common, including the religious and patriarchal traditions of fourteenth-century England which informed them both. Despite theological differences, the two sermon collections incorporate many of the same female exemplars, the same traditions about biblical women, and the same strengths and weaknesses about women. In fact, statements about women in the Wycliffite sermons which might otherwise seem extraordinary appear less so when compared with contemporary sermons. A noticeable gendered difference, however, exists. *Festial*, committed to reinscribing orthodoxy, actively uses its female exemplars to help teach the pastoral programme to both male and female parishioners. *The English Wycliffite Sermons*, which rejects the pastoral programme, renders its female exemplars (including Mary Magdalene) more passively – calling into question, yet again, the persistent idea that Lollardy was hospitable towards female religious authority.

---

[55] *English Wycliffite Sermons*, iii, 140–4, lines 78–9, 96–9 and 102.
[56] BL, MS Cotton Claudius A II, fols 54r–v.

A final comparison encapsulates the gendered significance made by the pastoral programme. The sermon for the Second Sunday in Lent in both *Festial* and the Wycliffite Sunday Gospels includes the Woman of Canaan's encounter with Christ from Matthew 15. In this familiar story, Jesus responds to the woman's plea for a miraculous healing of her daughter by telling her, *'Hit is not good to take [þe] breed þat falluþ to children and ȝyuen hit to howndes to ete* fro þese children.' When the womman responds that even dogs are allowed to eat table crumbs, Jesus proclaims, *'O womman! greet is þi feiþ.'* The Wycliffite text explains the woman as 'knowynge Cristes speche' – she understands the spiritual import of Jesus's words that even pagans (the dogs) may become God's children. Yet for a sermon which revolves around this scripture passage, it is striking how absent the woman is from the message. The text spiritualizes the woman as 'þe substaunce of mannys sowle' that is miraculously transformed from pagan into Christian and emphasizes the ecclesiastical establishment which is 'werren vpon' Christian 'men'.[57] Thus, although recognizing the Woman of Canaan's spiritual insight, the sermon does little else to address women.

The *Festial* sermon uses the Woman of Canaan differently. It contextualizes the story within a larger discussion of the pastoral programme: how 'Gode Men and Wommen' need to cleanse their souls during Lent through confession and penance. It too sees the Woman of Canaan as a representative, albeit in this instance, of a successful penitent. Instead of leaving her in the spiritual realm as a disembodied and genderless soul, as in the Wycliffite sermon, *Festial* channels this biblical woman into the medieval parish through telling the story of an ordinary woman. This female exemplum character was too ashamed to confess her sin until she met Christ. He put his hand into the wound in his side and asked her: 'Whatte felys yu and scheo/ quakyd for fer and sayde Lorde I fele yure herte. Þan sayde Cryste, Be yu no more aschamyd to schew me yure herte þan I am to suffyr ye to felon myn herte.' The woman confessed her sin to a priest and the sermon concludes that she was then forgiven.[58] The Woman of Canaan becomes in *Festial* a successful penitent who actively models participation in the sacraments. In contrast, the Woman of Canaan in the Wycliffite sermon is passive. Her story is a backdrop to show how the conversion of a soul is based on Christ's grace and not the tyranny of priests.

Each sermon, of course, is teaching a lesson. The *Festial* sermon is encouraging parishioners to participate in the sacraments and the Wycliffite sermon is emphasizing the role of the individual over ecclesiastical authority. These different emphases have gendered implications. The Woman of Canaan in both sermons signifies something larger than herself, but it is only in *Festial* that she directly connects to ordinary medieval women through her trans-

---

[57] *English Wycliffite Sermons*, i, 401–6, lines 11–24, 65 and 84–91.
[58] BL, MS Cotton Claudius A II, fols 46r–47v.

formation into a female parishioner. In this way, the spiritual insight of the Woman of Canaan – that she too can share in Christ's grace – becomes accessible to female parishioners who also, through contrition and confession, can know Christ's heart. This portrayal of the Woman of Canaan in both *Festial* and the Wycliffite sermon parallels how each portrays Mary Magdalene. In the *English Wycliffite Sermons*, the women are passive guides: the Woman of Canaan illustrates the process of salvation and Mary Magdalene illuminates the path to the resurrected Christ. In *Festial*, the women are active models: the Woman of Canaan mirrors the actions of a female penitent while Mary Magdalene becomes the first penitent by washing Christ's feet with her tears. Indeed, it seems that while Mary Magdalene may have shone brightly for Lollards as a familiar and even spiritually insightful exemplar, it is the reflection of the Magdalene in *Festial* that provided medieval women with a practical role model that they were called to follow as well as to admire.

INDEX

Wessington, John, prior of Durham
   43, 49, 56
White, Sir John   125
Wigmore, lordship of   103
Wilde, Elias   67
Wilton Diptych   93
William I, king of England   62
Winchester, bishops of, *see* Lusignan;
   Raleigh; Sandale; Stratford
Winforton (Hereford)   108
Wingfield, Sir William   130, 134
Wolde, William de   4–5
Wolvesey Castle   44
Worcester
   bishops of, *see* Bransford; Clifford;
   Gainsborough; Reynolds;
   Wakefield
   cathedral   45–6, 50, 52–5
Wrey, John   73, 80
Wright, Nicholas de   15 n. 69

Writs
   Darrein presentment   65
   Ne admittas   65
   Quare impedit   65, 69, 71
   Quare incumbravit   65
   Quare non admisit   65, 69–71, 80
   Venire facias   101
Wyke
   John de, prior of Worcester   43
   William   67–8

Ydfen, Thomas   105
York
   archbishops of, *see* Arundel,
   Melton; Neville; Thoresby;
   Zouche
   Ordinances of (1318)   10

Zouche, William de la, archbishop of
   York   44 n. 5

FOURTEENTH CENTURY ENGLAND
ISSN 1471–3020

VOLUME I

VOLUME II

VOLUME III